Design Your Business

This actionable and lively guide helps aspiring entrepreneurs to acquire a designer's mindset to transform ideas into successful products, and designers and technologists to identify entrepreneurial opportunities through a unique mix of product and business development toolkits.

Unlike other books focusing either downstream on the launch of a new venture or upstream on ideation and the acquisition of an entrepreneurial mindset, *Design Your Business* helps innovators to cross the chasm between attractive ideas and actual products, a crucial test in any entrepreneurial endeavor and one which most innovative ideas do not pass. Throughout the book, readers will learn about methods, steps, and resources to unleash their creativity, understand users' needs, build and test prototypes, and design beautiful products. At the end of this design journey, readers will find an essential business toolkit including business model design, intellectual property protection, funding, and development of effective communication skills that will help them to lay the foundation of a successful venture built around a successful product.

This book will become an essential and thought-provoking resource for aspiring entrepreneurs, makers, students of entrepreneurship and new venture creation, and professionals seeking to adopt a design mindset and agile project management in their projects and organizations.

Luca Iandoli is Dean of the Collins College of Professional Studies at St. John's University. Luca was a Fulbright Visiting Scholar at the MIT Center for Collective Intelligence and served as associate professor at the University of Naples Federico II, Italy, and as visiting professor at Stevens Institute of Technology, USA. His research focuses on collective intelligence, interaction design, and design-driven entrepreneurship.

Kevin T. James is Director of Finance and Business Operations in the Office of Student Success and Enrollment Management at St. John's University. Previously, he served as an Assistant Dean and Director of Fiscal and Administrative Affairs in the Collins College of Professional Studies at St. John's University. He is currently a doctoral student at Johns Hopkins University, focusing on entrepreneurial leadership in education.

Slides and teaching materials based on this book are curated from the authors and available for free at this link https://elegantdesignthinking.com/category/learning-resources/

Design Your Business

A Creative Pathway to Transforming
Ideas into Successful Products

Luca Iandoli and Kevin T. James

Routledge
Taylor & Francis Group

NEW YORK AND LONDON

Designed cover image: © Max Hergenrother

First published 2024
by Routledge
605 Third Avenue, New York, NY 10158

and by Routledge
4 Park Square, Milton Park, Abingdon, Oxon, OX14 4RN

Routledge is an imprint of the Taylor & Francis Group, an informa business

© 2024 Luca Iandoli and Kevin T. James

Library of Congress Cataloging-in-Publication Data
Names: Iandoli, Luca, 1972– author. | James, Kevin (Doctoral student at
  Johns Hopkins University) author.
Title: Design your business : a creative pathway to transforming ideas into
  successful products / Luca Iandoli and Kevin James.
Description: New York, NY : Routledge, 2024. | Includes bibliographical references
  and index.
Identifiers: LCCN 2023048208 (print) | LCCN 2023048209 (ebook) |
  ISBN 9781032387284 (hardback) | ISBN 9781032387260 (paperback) |
  ISBN 9781003346463 (ebook)
Subjects: LCSH: Creative ability in business. | Product design. | Business planning. |
  Entrepreneurship.
Classification: LCC HD53 .I226 2024 (print) | LCC HD53 (ebook) |
  DDC 650.1—dc23/eng/20240116
LC record available at https://lccn.loc.gov/2023048208
LC ebook record available at https://lccn.loc.gov/2023048209

ISBN: 978-1-032-38728-4 (hbk)
ISBN: 978-1-032-38726-0 (pbk)
ISBN: 978-1-003-34646-3 (ebk)

DOI: 10.4324/9781003346463

Typeset in Sabon
by Apex CoVantage, LLC

To Miriam,

Thank you for your unwavering support and for being my constant muse and partner on this incredible journey.

Luca

To Martha, Thank you for your constant support on this journey. Your belief in me has truly been a guiding force, pushing me forward.

Kevin

Contents

Acknowledgments

This book is the result of several years of work during which we received support, encouragement, ideas, suggestions, and constructive criticism from many colleagues, students, and friends:

Minna Aslamowitz, Martha Ayewah, Steve Farella, Neil Feinstein, Almerinda Forte, Carmine Gibaldi, Max Hergenrother, Basilio Monteiro, Katia Passerini, Martin Puris, and Giuseppe Zollo.

A special thanks go to the students in our courses at St. John's University "Creativity, Innovation, and Entrepreneurship" and "Principles of Management," with whom we have experimented and discussed many of the materials contained in this book.

We also had the opportunity to share our ideas with the participants in several initiatives and programs organized by the Design Factory Global Network (DFGN), such as the Design Factory Bootcamp and the International Design Factory Weeks. These events and the great colleagues who are part of the network offered us excellent opportunities to reflect on ways to combine design and entrepreneurship. The Design Factory's unique learning philosophy proved to be an invaluable intellectual space and source of creative energy. These colleagues include Tua Björklund, Kalevi Eetu Ekman, Felipe Garate, Peter Joore, Paivi Oinonen, Sara Santos Figueroa, Urakan Semkan, and representatives from the many design factories scattered around the world, including Assaf Krebs, Anita Kocsis, and Matteo Vignoli.

Thanks to our editor, Meredith Norwich, for believing in this project and for her support, guidance, and patience.

Finally, much gratitude is due to our families for their love and support.

Introduction

Have you ever wanted to design the next big product, the next smartphone, the next board game, or even the next TV show? Taking concepts from the back of our mind and attempting to make them come to life is very challenging: most of us who read this book may wonder about these things, but only a few of us actually take the plunge to make these items real. We think of entrepreneurship as a journey of discovery, one that is not necessarily pinned on just the final product but the journey to get to the product. We emphasize the importance of adopting a design mindset to navigate the complexities of product development. Throughout this book, we dive into this mindset and offer ways to position yourself to be prepared to solve problems that your customers are struggling with.

In Chapter 1, we highlight the design-driven mindset, influenced by the IDEO framework on Human-Centered Design, we highlight the critical cognitive approaches that are essential for successful ventures. As we venture into Chapter 2, we spend a significant time examining the impact creativity has on entrepreneurial pursuits, within this chapter and through a significant portion of the book we challenge the notion that creativity is limited to individualized action and explore creativity in the world of collective actions. Chapter 3 is where we first introduce the central character in the design-driven process to the customers. The customer remains the central character on our journey but it's their journey that really matters, the one that begins when they struggle with something and to seek additional support to improve their lives. This is the start of the process to validate our ideas as potential products.

Starting in Chapter 4, we begin the creative process by crafting pitches of our potential solutions. We look at the concept of the pitch as a critical tool to validate a problem and offer a potential solution. We focus our intentions on ensuring we have the "right" problem before we start developing a prototype. The iterative and prototyping process begins in Chapter 5, where we develop the first iterations of our solutions. Chapter 5 builds upon Chapters 1–4 and applies it in a concrete way. We believe this chapter is fun. Chapters 6, 7, and 8 encourage entrepreneurs to approach prototyping as a way to balance between simplicity and complexity in product design, so products are not designed to be boring but offer a unique experience for the user without being overwhelming and unnecessarily complicated.

The final chapters explore entrepreneurship as a journey that pushes an innovator to conquer many challenges, witness success, and even manage failures. We posit that the entrepreneur journey is valuable, even when failure occurs, because failure can be a vehicle for growth and transformation (Chapter 9). We provide aspiring entrepreneurs with an essential business toolbox to move the first steps in the process of building an entrepreneurial project around the product. We present a framework for implementing a business venture with

DOI: 10.4324/9781003346463-1

your product, based on value proposition and business model design (Chapter 10). Another chapter is dedicated to methods and tricks to improve the communication and presentation of business ideas (Chapter 12). Chapters 11 and 13 help the reader to understand the fundamentals of intellectual property and funding.

Our book offers a comprehensive, design-driven approach to entrepreneurship, blending design thinking, creativity, and business strategies. Our goal is not just to equip you, the aspiring entrepreneur, with the knowledge and skills needed to navigate the complexities of business and product development but also to encourage you to embrace failure, iterate, and always—continually!—innovate. We invite you to start the journey with us with Chapter 1.

Chapter 1

A design mindset to entrepreneurship

Houston, we have had a problem.
—Jack Swigert, radio message to the control tower during the Apollo 13 mission, 1970

In the fields of observation chance favors only the prepared mind.
—Louis Pasteur, lecture at University of Lille, December 7, 1854

1.1 Product-centered entrepreneurship

Google Nest is a leading company in the growing market of home automation. Nest is an excellent example of a successful venture built around a new product. In an interview released to Guy Raz for the NPR podcast *How I Built This*,[1] Tony Fadell, a former Apple executive and founder of Nest, reports that he had the idea to design an intelligent thermostat while he was working on the project of building an energy-efficient home (Raz, 2016). This challenge was not only a good problem to solve but also led to Fadell's insight that the whole home energy system hinges on a minor device: the thermostat.

Traditional thermostats are typically so hard to operate that most people use their heating system less efficiently, wasting money and energy. In trying to solve his problem of finding a better technology to make his home more comfortable and environmentally friendly, Fadell understood a vital lesson that can be applied to many products: for a technology to be successful, it must function as an extension of human capabilities and support spontaneous behavior, as opposed to being a barrier that stands in the way between us and what we want to accomplish.

So, he came up with a new design: a simple and stylish knob (Figure 1.1, top left) reporting only essential information, equipped with a digital chip interfacing the thermostat with a smartphone app to control the system remotely and provide energy analytics and additional functionalities.

Nest was founded around this product idea in 2010. Four years later, the company was bought by Google for $3.2 billion. Innovation at Nest continued with the same approach: to create user-friendly technology for connected and smart homes. New products were built around the Nest platform, such as security cameras, alarm systems, smart doorbells, smoke and carbon monoxide detectors, voice-operated speakers, and the like (Figure 1.1a–c). All Nest products can talk to each other and can be controlled through a smartphone to create a connected home network through devices that are easy to install and configure.

DOI: 10.4324/9781003346463-2

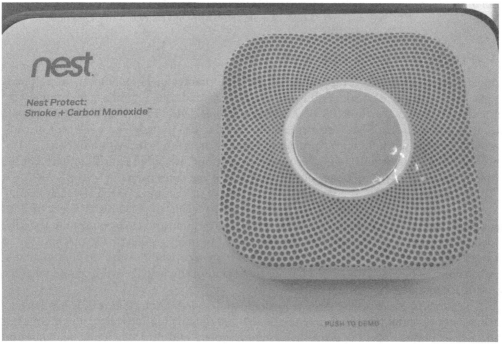

Figures 1.1a, 1.1b, 1.1c **Some products from the Google Nest Smart Home platform**. a) Nest thermostat, b) smoke detector, and c) voice-operated speakers with a tablet.

Which entrepreneurial lessons can we extract from this designer's story? Let's look at a few of them.

First, most successful ventures start around a brilliant new product or service. Second, a great product is based on a great design that puts users at the center, something we refer to with the expression "Human-Centered Design" (more on this in a bit). Third, good design always stems from a worthy-to-solve problem, a problem that someone is struggling with

Figures 1.1a, 1.1b, 1.1c Continued

and trying to address actively. Fourth, in the age of the Internet of Things and ubiquitous 24/7 connectivity, products are often designed as platforms around which entrepreneurs can find many occasions to create additional revenue channels and, more importantly, innovation opportunities (think, for instance, of the possibility of controlling this ecosystem through our voice via digital speech recognition apps such as Siri and Alexa).

* * *

This book argues that a design-driven and platform-focused approach will increase the chances of entrepreneurial success. Of course, launching a successful new business requires many other essential skills beyond the ability to design a product. We could easily create a list of companies that failed because they were too product-centered and neglected critical aspects such as financial viability, business development, talent, and team management. Nevertheless, developing a product is a necessary condition for success.

Unfortunately, most entrepreneurship manuals neglect the critical step of transforming an idea into a product and take for granted that a well-designed product is somehow available. Or it is assumed that good design results from well-executed market research and well-articulated value proposition.

The relationship between market intelligence, strategic wisdom, and product design is a little more interesting. It is a chicken-and-egg problem in which good design leads to better market and business insights, which, in turn, helps improve your design. It's an iterative, two-way process in which we must start somewhere. In this book, we argue that we should start with the product. By adopting Human-Centered Design in entrepreneurship, we show that the design journey from an initial idea to a viable prototype will provide entrepreneurs with invaluable user knowledge they can leverage to create a new venture.

The other benefit that such an approach offers is the acquisition of a maker mindset and the awareness that good design and a deep understanding of user needs are not linked in a simple cause-effect relationship but that they are both achieved via an iterative process that alternates making with experimentation through a process of discovery. This book provides its readers with a toolbox and methods to master this learning process, systematically increase their creative skills, and pursue innovation with an entrepreneurial mentality. Welcome to entrepreneurship by design!

1.2   Entrepreneur is as entrepreneur does: design-driven entrepreneurial mindsets

In a famous paper titled " 'Who is an entrepreneur?' is the wrong question," scholar David Gartner (1988) revolutionized entrepreneurship research by stating that what sets entrepreneurs aside from non-entrepreneurs is not specific personality traits and attitudes but the fact that entrepreneurs are pretty good at creating organizations. What matters is what an entrepreneur does, not who an entrepreneur is. Following Gartner's insight, we claim that what sets entrepreneurs apart is how they act and think. The good news is that entrepreneurs are not born but made by learning and honing practical and mental skills.

For this reason, before introducing the readers to our method starting from Chapter 3, in this and the following chapters, we provide a more analytical description of which skills are needed at the individual and team levels to support a design-driven entrepreneurial approach. The IDEO framework for Human-Centered Design (IDEO, 2016) is an excellent starting point for identifying a critical this unique set of skills (Figure 1.2):

- Optimism: the ability to see and build the future in favorable terms
- Creative confidence: the ability to develop innovative solutions and be bold enough to bring them to the public

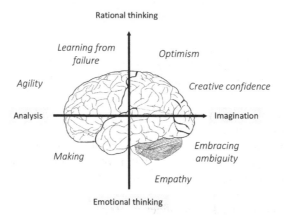

Figure 1.2 **The IDEO mindsets behind Human-Centered Design and design-driven entrepreneurship**. The picture emphasizes how the skills that form the IDEO framework for Human-Centered Design work across our left and right brain (imagination versus analysis) and our top and bottom brain (rational versus emotional).

- Embracing ambiguity: seeing and feeling opportunities in uncertainty
- Empathy: the ability to deeply understand other people's problems and needs at the emotional level
- Making: the ability to build, tinker, and give form and body to ideas.
- Agility: the ability to scale ideas and projects through iterative and adaptive project management.
- Learning from failure: the ability to "fail smart" through an experimental mindset to maximize learning and minimize loss

As shown in Figure 1.2, we use a visual relying on the traditional distinctions between the right brain and left brain (imagination versus analysis) and the higher and lower brain (rationality versus emotions) to suggest that this skill set integrates rational and emotional thinking, imagination and analysis.[2]

1.3   Empathic entrepreneurship: eliciting users' insights through participation, observation, and discovery

Successful entrepreneurship is, first and foremost, about finding a problem worth solving. Increasingly, entrepreneurship originated in the DIY world by makers motivated to solve a specific problem they are facing. This type of motivation is called *intrinsic*. Studies show that intrinsic motivation is far more powerful in mobilizing us than extrinsic motivation, driven by rewards and incentives such as economic profit.[3] In other cases, entrepreneurs find significant problems to solve through careful research and observation. This path is a bit more complicated because it requires us to focus on other people's issues and needs by adopting their points of view. It entails suspending our ego, observing without prejudice, and even participating in the struggles of the people we want to help. This ability to put ourselves in someone else's shoes and deeply understand and care about other people is empathy. It often stems from the genuine will to make ourselves useful to others and society. Let's look at a few examples.

Magdèlene Barjolo and Alexandria Duruji, two students in our entrepreneurship program at St. John's University, wanted to find an entrepreneurial way to support women's emancipation in less privileged communities. Through a design thinking approach, they identified a significant cause of disruption in young girls' educational and personal lives leading to school abandonment and social stigma: lack of access to menstrual health products. They then started a company called Sending Her Essentials, which provides virtual and physical help to young women who do not have the means to manage their menstrual health effectively.

An excellent example of emphatic entrepreneurship in the for-profit world is the well-known coffee shop chain Starbucks. In an interview,[4] the Starbucks founder, Howard Schultz, reports that the critical idea behind Starbucks came to him while observing casual coffee-drinking behavior in Milan, Italy. While he was there, he observed "the theater, the romance, and the nectar of the gods, which is espresso. . . . All the elegance, the style." But what struck him was "the sense of community" (Raz, 2017). This observation was behind Schultz's intuition that a new form of coffee business could be created around the drink itself, based on the ideas of having coffee as a social practice and of a coffee shop as a "third place" where people can hang out in addition to the other two main places of their life (home and work). This idea was not entirely new; after all, coffeehouses have been around since the 18th century. Schultz, however, had the business genius of building an innovative and scalable business model around relevant social practices and needs. This ability is at the core of Human-Centered-Design.

We explore empathy in Chapter 3 as the critical entrepreneurial skill for customer discovery.

1.4   Creative entrepreneurship: entrepreneurship by oxymorons

There are many paths to creativity, and we discuss this topic more in-depth in Chapter 2. Often, truly novel ideas are received with skepticism and criticism. Think about some of the best inventions ever made. Sometimes they are so simple that one thinks: how has nobody thought about that before? Reversing this logic, we may kill a good idea just because it seems too good to be true or because of our fear of being judged and ridiculed by others. Our focus here is not on the creative process but on the boldness and courage it takes to put our new ideas out in the world for others to judge them. The ability to stand and even profit from public judgment is what IDEO defines as creative confidence.

Nowhere is this boldness more evident than in oxymorons. An oxymoron is a rhetorical device that combines opposite and even contradictory elements, such as "affordable luxury." The best oxymorons capture a subject's complex and nuanced character and transform a logical contradiction into a meaningful and powerful statement. Some great entrepreneurial ideas are based on oxymorons. Still, since an oxymoron defies logic and common sense, the expression of such beliefs is often accompanied by skepticism, sarcasm, or even ridicule.

The idea of a computer on every desk (or in every pocket) seems obvious today. But for generations of creatives and tinkerers that pursued this in the 1960s and the 1970s,[5] well before the personal computer became the commercial product we know today, "a computer on every desk" was a technical and economic contradiction. However, these young minds were so sure and stubborn about their final success that, in most cases, their enthusiastic followers did not care that the actual machines were complicated, unreliable, and in some cases, did not work at all. In one instance, the "final" product was announced in *Popular Electronics* magazine when it was just an untested prototype. It was the Altair 8800 created by MITS (Figure 1.3). The company shipped an exemplar to the magazine for a product

Figure 1.3 **Altair 8800 interface panel**. The Altair 8800 computer did not have a screen and a keyboard like modern computers, but the user interface was a set of switches for programming and LED lights to read the elaboration results.

review, but the device never arrived due to a strike, and the magazine ended up printing a picture of an empty case on the cover, trusting MITS' assurance that the computer worked as described.

As you can see in Figure 1.3, the Altair 8800 did not look like modern computers, notably because of the absence of a screen, an expensive accessory back then. The input/output interface was just a series of LED lights and switches showing the computer answers as a lights-on/lights-off sequence and bleeps. It is hard to imagine something more primitive and less user-friendly than this. Nevertheless, the Altair had its glorious days among early computer enthusiasts. It made a fundamental contribution to the history of the personal computer and the technological revolution that led to the creation of more viable commercial products, such as the ones created later by Apple and Microsoft.

Of course, the mainstream computer industry was skeptical that a personal computer was a viable idea from a business point of view. Ken Olsen, founder of DEC and one of the most successful and visionary computer entrepreneurs, infamously declared: "There is no reason for any individual to have a computer in his home."[6] DEC was number 2 in the computer makers' market in the 1980s, and this opinion was largely shared in the industry. Imagine Bill Gates looking at the software you are developing and telling you that that is not a great idea. It would be quite a blow to your confidence! Nevertheless, mainstream criticism did not deter these digital pioneers from exploring a crazy notion that eventually revolutionized our economy and daily life.

We could compile a long list of creative oxymorons behind successful entrepreneurial endeavors. Think of IKEA's attempt to democratize design in the furniture industry through its "plan for everybody" campaign. Another example is the Italian nonprofit Slow Food Foundation, created as a grassroots organization in 1989 "to prevent the disappearance of local food cultures and traditions, counteract the rise of fast life and combat people's dwindling interest in the food they eat, where it comes from, and how our food choices affect the world around us."[7]

Slow Food started a movement in the food industry based on enjoying food at your own pace, excellence in sourcing ingredients, respect, protection, and marketing of local specialties and traditions instead of standardization, low quality, and environmentally unsustainable global supply chains.

We explore ways to boost your creative confidence in Chapters 2, 4, and 5.

1.5 Makers' entrepreneurship: build it and they will test it

Entrepreneurs are makers and builders before becoming businesspeople. They want to get things done and prove they have a point. Many entrepreneurs are tinkerers who play with existing ideas and repurpose them to serve specific users better. While entrepreneurship requires much more than the ability to design good products, many early-stage entrepreneurs are primarily occupied with building instances of their products to shout out, as an ecstatic Gene Wilder impersonating Dr. Frederick von Frankenstein in the cult movie *Young Frankenstein*, "It—could—work."

Silicon Valley became famous, among other things, for its "garage entrepreneurship." Hewlett and Packard started HP in a garage, just as Jobs, Wozniak, and others started companies in their own garages. Why garages? They are conducive to tinkering, craftsmanship, experimentation, and testing. The personal computing movement we referred to in the Altair anecdote was brought to fruition by enthusiasts who were makers and users simultaneously. It is the same geek-ish energy and excitement present in any DIY or hobbyist community. The internet and open-source hardware and software advances have made the makers' movement connected and global.

If you are an aspiring entrepreneur and are not really into making things and experimenting, you should reconsider. Many advantages originate from this approach to entrepreneurship. While we make those explicit in the rest of the book, we can provide some anticipations here:

a) *Making is empowering*: building something that works and embodying your idea in a demonstrable device or service will give you a fantastic morale boost and make you much more confident.
b) *Making is learning*: making will help nurture your problem-solving ability, grow technical competencies and empirical mindset, and improve your understanding of technical and economic trade-offs. Effective learning always comes as a mix of the cognitive and the experiential, the mental and the manual, the abstract and the concrete.
c) *Making helps you understand your users*: once you build even a simple and initial version of what you have in mind, you can test it with real users and get invaluable feedback from them that you cannot get through even the most sophisticated and in-depth market research.
d) *Making helps you connect with communities of people* who are open to sharing what they learn with their peers.

We help you build a maker mindset and skills portfolio in Chapter 5 by introducing you to the joy and importance of prototyping and the many techniques and tools to build your prototype.

1.6   Scientific entrepreneurship: test for failure

We all know we can learn from failure. Entrepreneurship literature and mantras are all about the importance of learning through mistakes. Failure has become something we want to celebrate. There is some truth behind even some forms of exaggerated exaltations of failure. However, proponents of learning through failure sometimes minimize or omit to say that, often, failing equates to hurting yourself morally, economically, and even socially, since many cultures are not so tolerant and forgiving of those who fail.

How do we approach risks while still being able to learn from our failures? We can learn from mistakes in two ways: the hard way and the scientist's way. Scientists won't ask people to crash their cars against a wall to perform a safety test. Instead, they have a method to maximize what they can learn from a small, safe, and rigorous test while minimizing human and economic losses.

Here we can turn to science, not business or economic science, but Science with a capital *S*. We refer to the scientific method, the invention behind any modern human discovery. The scientific method applies to any human endeavor in which we want to prove a point. Entrepreneurs are no different from scientists: they need some rigorous process to validate their hypotheses and increase their chances of success before sinking significant effort and money into their idea.

What does failure have to do with science? Everything. The scientific method proves, not truth, but that a hypothesis holds until it fails. Thomas Edison is said to have remarked, "I have not failed; I have only found 10,000 ways in which my idea won't work."[8] Scientists and engineers set themselves up for failure in running a test. They design controlled experiments on a smaller scale to understand what could go wrong and why it did not work the way it was supposed to. We describe the application of the scientific method to entrepreneurship in Chapter 6. Here is a summary of how it works:

1. *Make your assumptions explicit.* Typically, these assumptions refer to who the customers are, what benefits they expect from the product, which product features they see as associated with these benefits, and so on.
2. *Design tests aimed at showing whether your assumptions are wrong*: this translates into the creation of carefully designed experiments under controllable and measurable conditions.
3. If the test succeeds, go back and revise your assumption. If it doesn't, you *might* be right.

Number 3 tells us that, unfortunately, the method will not guarantee certainty. It will just rule out possible sources of likely failures and will force you to revise the assumptions that could cause these future failures. Think of a crash test, in which the many simulated, lab-based, controlled crashes result in knowledge that can help prevent damage and save human lives, but it won't prevent all crushes form happening for additional reasons.

The history of the many **Lego** failures and successes can be a helpful example of the difference between aspirational innovation grounded on wrong assumptions and systematically iterating for success through a user-centered approach (Robertson, 2014). After the tremendous growth the company experienced in the 1980s, thanks to the success of its famous brick games (Figure 1.4), sales stagnated during the 1990s. **Lego** reacted by launching new product lines, but they all were failures that brought the Danish company to the verge of bankruptcy in the early 2000s. These failures had something in common: the mistaken assumption that the new generations of kids were profoundly different from earlier ones and would prefer video games to traditional games. Following this faulty assumption, **Lego** ambitiously set out to reinvent the future of play as its mission.

However, the sales figures of new products like Galidor, a GI Joe–like action figure with an associated TV show, and Jack Stone, a collection of brick sets with fewer pieces that were easier and faster to assemble than other sets, were largely disappointing. It took these and other expensive failures to understand that **Lego** core customers bought the bricks exactly because they liked them. Customers did not want radical innovation but liked that **Lego** could innovate "around" the existing product.

Learning from its mistakes, **Lego** started experimenting with revamping its product lines, finding synergies between the traditional building sets and the digital gaming experience through successful innovations such as the Bionicles series. These new products were more contemporary and updated variants of **Lego** classic building-block games and introduced a carefully tested storytelling element. Some of these ideas resulted from learning from kids what they liked or disliked. Kids were shown pictures of characters and scenes and were asked to comment and build stories around those suggestions. This is the approach behind creating the **Lego** popular Ninjago series (the fact that the villains were evil skeletons was one of the ideas offered by the young testers). More recently, **Lego** adopted this experimentation approach through co-creation, a methodology that leverages customers' creativity in new product design. It works as a competition, with Lego enthusiasts proposing new game ideas to the company (check the LEGO idea contest on this site: https://ideas.lego.com). The best ideas are implemented in small sample series that are then tested with real users to see which ones meet the taste of the Lego fan base.

Figure 1.4 **Lego at NASA**. Students used **Lego** bricks to "Build the Future" at NASA's Kennedy Space Center, in Cape Canaveral, Florida, on November 3, 2010. The "Build the Future" event was part of prelaunch activities for the STS-133 mission.

We describe how scientific entrepreneurship works and can be applied to your project in chapter 6.

1.7 Agile entrepreneurship: iterate, iterate, iterate

We have outlined the product development process as building a prototype, testing it with real users, and adopting a systematic experimental approach to validate your assumptions. This method leads to the most crucial advantage of the entrepreneurship-by-design system: agility. In everyday life, as in business, being supple and rapidly changing your assumptions, plans, and execution is a critical skill. Agility became popular in software development after it became clear that a serial (or "waterfall") approach to software design led to failure because developers would find out too late that the customer requirements were wrong. When you commit significant resources in the wrong direction for a long time, it is challenging from both the economic and psychological points of view to rethink and remake what you have already built.

The entrepreneurship-by-design approach is all about iteration and scalability. The motto here is "Fail fast, fail small, fail cheap"—and then try again with revised assumptions and an updated design.

The well-known design thinking cycle is based on multiple iterations with five main steps. After each iteration, two outcomes are possible: you could take a step toward refining your idea on a path converging towards an ultimate solution or find evidence that your initial assumptions were wrong and you now need to pivot towards a different problem and solution. This approach is scalable because it helps you channel and commit resources and investments as you make progress and validate your thoughts. In this way, changing requirements and specs won't be too costly if you catch mistakes early enough. This is extremely valuable, especially in the early stages of product development. Slack was founded to pursue the design of a massively multiplayer online game, not the collaboration platform for which it is known today. That platform was an internal tool Slack's developers created to collaborate internally while developing the game. Later, they realized they had stumbled into a much better problem to solve: how to help people collaborate better digitally. The gaming spirit of the origins survived in the developers' ability to build Slack: a platform that made everyday professional digital interaction and collaboration more fun and engaging.

This story offers a few lessons. For starters, had the gaming platform been in a more advanced state of development and not in the light beta version it was at the time of pivoting, it would have been difficult for Slack to let it go. Second, iterative experimentation can serendipitously lead you to discover a better problem to solve when you are looking for something else. Third, if the Slack developers had never created the platform to support their game prototyping activities, they would not have had the eureka moment to divert their effort toward designing an entirely different product.

1.8 Positive entrepreneurship: embracing ambiguity and positive thinking

Entrepreneurs work under high uncertainty, especially in the early stages of new venture creation. Is this product something customers want? Are we going to be able to differentiate our product from the competition? Is there a viable business or financial model for it? Where can we find help, support, and funding? These are just some of the most stressful

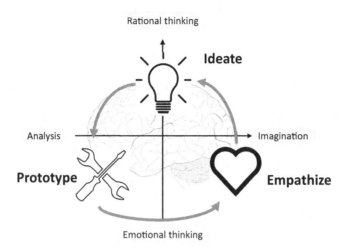

Figure 1.5 **The Design Thinking Cycle**. The cycle comprises three steps executed iteratively: ideation, empathizing, and prototyping. The process can start anywhere. For instance, an idea should be assessed considering the needs and feelings of the people the idea has been created for. The revised idea should then be embodied in a prototype for actual testing. The test results help revise the idea and start a new assessment cycle.

Source: IDEO, 2015

questions we might be unable to answer at the beginning of our journey. Rushing to solve uncertainty can lead to wrong assumptions and mistakes, which will have an impact on morale as well as on the budget.

There are ways through which entrepreneurs can escape this depressing trap. The entrepreneurship-by-design approach is a method to maximize the chances of discovery while minimizing the costs of failure. From a psychological point of view, the technique helps early-stage entrepreneurs to achieve small wins and learning, which will act as an intrinsic reward compensating for the frustration associated with inevitable failures. In other words, design-driven entrepreneurs will enjoy the discovery process and be better equipped to transfer the result of their learning to other applications and endeavors.

Rewording the famous Forrest Gump's quote, we claim that an optimist is as an optimist does. Optimism is not an attitude, a personality trait, or an aspiration but an outcome of human-centered, design-driven entrepreneurship. After all, we know from experience that optimism is essentially the product of positive reinforcement and our ability to make the most of negative feedback, two powers our proposed approach dramatically enhances.

Ahmed Bouzid is the founder of WitLingo, a digital speech recognition company. This artificial intelligence–powered technology is embedded in the famous Alexa, Cortana, and Siri applications. Many analysts say digital speech recognition will soon become the dominant way we interact with computers and intelligent products. Doing business in an industry driven by the growth of emerging technology always comes with high uncertainty. Surprisingly, the primary source of such delay is not the difficulty of predicting advances in technological development but the fact that nobody knows what users will do with this tech and what the "killer app" will be.

In an interview with Bouzid (Iandoli, 2022), his positive thinking emerged from a user-centered, design-driven mindset. Product development is strongly driven by customer discovery and collaboration with early adopters. His optimism regarding the prospect of growth in the industry and for his company was equally moved by the rapid pace of technological advancement and the company's ability to get early adopters excited and willing to experiment and learn what speech recognition might do for them. In the interview, he repeated a few times that, in such a context, entrepreneurs do not have to worry about the competition, that they are competing against themselves, their prejudice, bias, and mental models to escape the risk of misrepresenting what the customer problem is.

1.9 Conclusions

In this chapter, we make a case for product-centered entrepreneurship. Starting a venture requires much more than just having a product. To undertake the next steps of the process, the entrepreneur must have the ability to build something that makes sense for the prospective users and solve problems they are struggling with. We show how design thinking and, more broadly, a designer mindset can help entrepreneurs to become makers and bring their ideas to life through some tangible or testable artifact that can be used to test the market, validate assumptions, and get to know the technical constraints better and in an experiential way. As well, we have outlined the characteristics of the ideal design-driven entrepreneur. These characteristics should be seen as skills that can be acquired and nurtured instead of personality traits or individual talents we might be born with.

The next chapter explores how these attributes can scale to the team level. A creative team is needed and is usually present when a new venture is started. Chapter 2 shows how creativity and innovation result from the team's collective intelligence.

Key takeaways for this chapter

Lesson learned	Implications for your entrepreneurial project
There is no such a thing as a great company without a great product.	• Ideas are cheap. Anybody can come up with a good idea, but success is measured in how the idea is implemented, packaged, and delivered. • Do not jump from ideas to a business plan. There is so much more you must learn about the critical step of transforming your idea into a testable product or service. Many aspiring entrepreneurs fail at this point. • Building a prototype is one of the best ways to learn about your prospective customers, markets, and technology.
Good entrepreneurs do not manage uncertainty—they hedge risk while maximizing learning.	• The design-thinking cycle is an effective way to "fail smart." If you fail early, fast, and small, you can maximize learning while containing your loss. • Ego is your number-one enemy, not competitors. You must be humble in recognizing what does not work in your idea and admitting which assumptions are wrong. Being passionate about what you do must get along with not feeling attached to your creations. You are on a mission to save the world and help others, not to tell them how good and right you are.

(Continued)

Lesson learned	Implications for your entrepreneurial project
Cognitive flexibility is crucial.	• Talented entrepreneurs are hard to classify psychologically because their cognitive skill set is highly flexible and morphs to adapt to evolving situations. It is OK if your brain has a preference and is particularly good at something, but you must learn how to develop the think skills that you do not use much. This is difficult and sometimes frustrating. Imaginative people hate to get tangled in the weeds of feasibility, and rational people do not want emotions to get in their way. The reality is that you need all the complexity of an adaptable and flexible mind to support discovery, learning, great planning, and sound execution.

Notes

1 This podcast series contains a great list of design lessons available in interviews with entrepreneurs and innovators.
2 The validity of this concept has been questioned as an oversimplified representation of how our brain works. We use it here mainly as a visual and easily understood device to illustrate the need for integration of different skills and the flexibility and adaptability of entrepreneurial thinking.
3 Daniel Pink makes a convincing case about how extrinsic rewards are ineffective when we want to promote creative behavior. See his book *Drive: The Surprising Truth About What Motivates Us* (2011) and his popular TED Talks.
4 The interview transcript and audio are available at www.npr.org/2017/09/28/551874532/live-episode-starbucks-howard-schultz.
5 For a history of the personal computer, see Swaine and Freiberg's *Fire in the Valley* (2014).
6 Olsen later justified this remark he originally made in 1977 by saying that his words were taken out of context. His statement is sometimes unjustly offered as an example of business myopia. The reality is that nobody could really predict at that time the computing revolution that eventually brought "a computer on every desk and in every home." (This became the mission of a small startup in 1980, Microsoft.) DEC and other giant computer companies of the time mainly served the rich market of corporate and government computer applications, so they were not interested in a consumer market.
7 See the Slow Food Foundation's mission on the organization's website at www.slowfood.com/about-us/.
8 As quoted in: [J. L.] Elkhorne. "Edison: The Fabulous Drone," in 73 Vol. XLVI, No. 3 (March 1967), p. 52. Thomas Edison made a similar statement in 1890 in an interview published in *Harper's Magazine* (Larson Lathrop, 1890).

References

Gartner, W. B. (1988). "Who is an entrepreneur?" is the wrong question. *American Journal of Small Business*, 12(4), 11–32.

Iandoli, L. (2022). When solutions are in search of problems: New venture creation in the booming market of digital speech recognition. *SAGE Business Cases*. https://sk.sagepub.com/cases/new-venture-creation-booming-market-digital-speech-recognition

IDEO. (2016). *IDEO guide to human-centered design*. www.ideo.com/post/design-kit

Larson Lathrop, G. (1890). Talks with Edison. *Harper's Magazine*. https://harpers.org/archive/1890/02/talks-with-edison

Pink, D. H. (2011). *Drive: The surprising truth about what motivates us.* Penguin.

Raz, G. (2016). How can we design for a better experience? *NPR TED Radio Hour.* www.npr.org/transcripts/478560438, last accessed August 2023.

Raz, G. (2017). Interview with Howard Schultz. *How I built this, NPR Radio.* www.npr.org/2017/09/28/551874532/live-episode-starbucks-howard-schultz, last accessed August 2023.

Robertson, D. C., & Breen, B. (2014). *Brick by brick: How LEGO rewrote the rules of innovation and conquered the global toy industry.* Currency.

Swaine, M., & Freiberg, P. (2014). *Fire in the valley: The making of the personal computer* (Third edition). Pragmatic Bookshelf.

Chapter 2

A creative mindset for entrepreneurship

One is company, two's a crowd, and three is a party.

—Attributed to Andy Warhol

2.1 Four persistent misconceptions about creativity and entrepreneurship

Listening to our favorite music on the go is today something most of us take for granted. However, it took the genius of a group of managers, inventors, and visionaries at Sony at the end of the 1970s to make this concept mainstream. The invention of the Sony Walkman reveals how creativity matters and how it works in developing a new product (Nayak & Ketteringham, 1986).

The critical insight came from Sony's former president and honorary chairman Masaru Ibuka, who proposed combining two different inventions into one product. Two other Sony labs had independently designed a portable stereo player and a lightweight headset. Both products were considered technical or market failures. The player had been created to develop a portable stereo recorder. Still, Sony's engineers could not embed stereo and recording technologies in a little device with the technology available then, notwithstanding Sony's technological leadership in small electronics.

While Ibuka had a critical insight, all he had was just . . . an idea! It took Sony a long time to transform that idea into a market breakthrough. During the two years it took to complete this process, Sony had to solve three key market and operational dilemmas. The first dilemma was that there was no market for portable music. The second was pricing: the Walkman was quite an expensive gadget. The third was operations: how to ramp up production and distribution to make and sell hundreds of thousands of devices that Sony had never made before and for which there were no safe market prospects.

Read the full story in the excellent case study by Nayak and Ketteringham (1986). You will find out how the development of the Walkman was the outcome of perfect teamwork and several iterations in which Ibuka's idea was only the ignition. Sony's CEO Akio Morita embraced and sponsored the portable music narrative, Mitsuro Ida and his team were the key technology gatekeepers and designers in the development of the prototypes, and Yasuo Kuroki and Kozo Oshone were the brilliant managers in the Consumer Product division who solved the considerable engineering challenges of scaling the production to Sony's mass-market level.

The team had to fight internal skepticism and resistance, despite the endorsement of the top management. The process was not immune from failures. The most significant mistakes

DOI: 10.4324/9781003346463-3

were trying to sell the Walkman to the wrong market segment (teenagers), and the underestimation of sale volume, which led the Sony manufacturing division to produce fewer units than the market was demanding. Sony learned from its mistakes and adapted successfully to these and other pitfalls.

The Walkman story contains some lessons about creativity and how it can serve entrepreneurs. We will use these lessons to question the following four common misconceptions about creativity and how it works, and we will discuss and debunk each of these myths in the following sections.

1. *Creativity and innovation are not the same*: creativity is about generating novelty, and innovation is about executing and adopting novelty. The Sony case shows that successful entrepreneurial creativity happens when invention *and* execution are both mastered.
2. *Creativity is not about unleashing your imagination*: it took Sony much tinkering and some critical failures to find out what problem the Walkman was solving and who the users were. By trial and error, Sony discovered a new and emerging market niche that acted as an early adopter. Marketing experts labeled these people Yuppies (young urban professionals), individuals who valued technology as a status symbol and were affluent enough to pay for the expensive gadget. They also became role models for the larger markets of teenagers, the initial target for Sony.
3. *You are not born creative*: creativity is as much the result of circumstances as individual effort and qualities. Novelty is more likely to be produced by recombining existing resources and various skills through observation and discovery than by inventing something from scratch. Sony did not develop portable music through a strategic plan. Creating the Walkman was an iterative process in which even the initial insight was determined by what was already available *there and then*. The company learned from its mistakes. The internal dialectic helped to question assumptions. Some improvisation occurred. Trials and failures have the critical benefit of generating inputs for us to rethink and adjust. *Creativity is not about who we are but about what we do.*
4. *Creativity is not the prerogative of a handful of individual geniuses*: it takes many minds to achieve brilliant results. Entrepreneurs should not act as individual problem-solvers isolated in their labs or workshops and prisoners of their biases. They should engage with the physical and social reality of their endeavor. This engagement requires finding complementary skills and expertise, reaching out to the relevant communities of practice, getting out of the building, and talking with users and customers. Creativity and problem-solving have a collective and socially distributed character. Sony achieved this by relying on a diverse team in which diversity of skills was complemented by team cohesion, shared values, and respect for others. We will show in sections 2.6 and 2.7 how the alchemy of a good team can be dissected and understood and how we can translate the same recipe to increase teams' creativity.

2.2   Creativity is not innovation; innovation is not creativity

Dartmouth College professors Vijay Govindarajan and Chris Trimble asked hundreds of managers to define innovation (Govindarajan & Trimble, 2010). They discovered that managers overwhelmingly equated innovation with creativity, and we suspect many entrepreneurs would do the same. We agree with our Dartmouth colleagues that innovation and creativity are separate concepts. Creativity happens when we develop novel ideas, while innovation involves adopting and executing a novel idea.

A simple example is digital photography. When Kodak engineers invented digital photography (yes, you read it right, Kodak was one the first companies to invest significantly in digital pictures), they imagined that a photo could be stored in a computer as a set of digital pixels. In this example, innovation would be creating a new business based on digital photography. Kodak, however, decided to stick with its core business of printing pictures (Barabba, 2022).

Figure 2.1 shows that creativity and execution can partially overlap. When novelty and execution happen together, we have the most exciting results. Think of the ability to execute as the force that elevates the potential of your invention, as in the following success equation:

$$\text{Success} = (\text{Invention})^{\wedge \text{Execution}}$$

Understanding that creativity and innovation happen only in sequence is vital. Resolving nontrivial problems usually requires iterating between invention and execution in cycles, following the scalable approach suggested in chapter 1, inspired by Design Thinking (see Figure 2.2).

Rare is the case in which our invention is immediately and flawlessly executable. More important, the feedback we obtain from early execution will help us devise better ways to

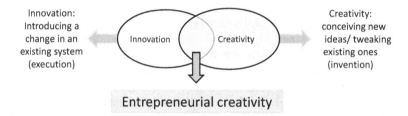

Figure 2.1 **The difference between creativity and innovation**. Creativity and innovation are two different processes: creativity is about finding novel ideas and applications, and innovation is about changing a system—for instance, by adopting and implementing new technology.

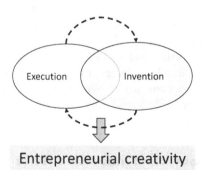

Figure 2.2 **The relationship between execution and invention**. Execution and invention are mutually dependent and happen in a sequence. A novel idea is subject to testing and validation through some form of initial implementation. The results can be leveraged to improve the initial idea. The cycle typically requires many iterations.

solve a problem and thus improve our invention. This observation quickly leads us to beat the next creativity myth: creativity is about unleashing your imagination.

2.3   The imagination fallacy versus creativity as tinkering

The romantic narrative of artists and scientists as solitary and melancholic geniuses who achieve great results despite being marginalized and misunderstood by society is a cliché. This misfit's narrative often extends to any grand human accomplishment, including entrepreneurial success. However, let's critically examine this stereotype by looking at artists.

While there is much individual variability in terms of personality traits, material circumstances, cultural influences, and the many more factors that have an impact on artistic creation, most great artists share two characteristics: 1) they are highly socially connected to a dense network of colleagues, friends, patrons, adversaries, masters, disciples, and so on; 2) they spend most of their time experimenting with alternative renditions of the same idea.

A great example is Ernest Hemingway. Some of his novels, such as *A Moveable Feast* and *The Sun Also Rises*, contain many autobiographical references. These readings show that the great writer would spend most of his time talking with friends and colleagues at cafés and restaurants or visiting their homes while being a proactive socialite and highly connected participant in artistic and social communities. Try googling Hemingway's manuscripts. In that case, you will find pictures with countless corrections and revisions through which he achieved the crystalline, minimalistic, and highly polished writing style for which he is well known.

The quest for perfection, a frequent characteristic of great artists, illustrates well the interplay between the invention of novel ways of expression and the execution of an idea, helping find unique and outstanding ways to package a message.

You can extend this analogy to entrepreneurship:

1. The idea is the message, your statement to the world, your answer to what your customers expect and demand;
2. Your product is the medium, your work of art, through which this message is effectively packaged and delivered.

Again, a parallel between art, design, and entrepreneurship can be made. According to Malcolm Gladwell (2011), Steve Jobs' attitude toward innovation was "more editorial than inventive." Confronted with what he viewed as uninspired work, Jobs demanded more. Of quality innovation, he said, "I'll know it when I see it." MP3 players, smartphones, and tablets were around before the iPod, the iPhone, and the iPad. Jobs did not invent anything; instead, he borrowed existing ideas, and his genius consisted in finding out what was wrong. He was not a developer or a designer but had a unique talent for recognizing good design when he saw it. Think of this as reverse creativity: instead of finding new solutions, identify severe flaws in existing solutions and improve on them.[1]

Experimentation, tinkering, and tweaking are valuable because they exonerate us from articulating what we do not know (yet). We know when we see it. Even better, we know when we break in, play, manipulate, and test things.

A practical implication of this perspective is that entrepreneurial creativity is 10% thinking and 90% doing. Do not overthink; do not speculate. Unleash action, not your imagination, and be open to surprise and fortuitous discovery.

A problem with this dual view of creativity is that it requires an adaptable mindset that can switch seamlessly between the contemplative and the practical. As we will see in the next section, this duality is not a problem. It's an essential trait of creative thinking.

2.4   The dual brain

Arguably, invention and execution require different cognitive skills. Inventions rely more on intuition, holistic perception, emotional and nonverbal thinking, and expressions of ideas through creative imagery, whereas execution is powered by analytical thinking, ordering, planning, and logic.[2] This dualism is reflected in opposite problem-solving approaches (executive, i.e., using reasoning and planning, versus creative, i.e., relying on emotions and metaphors) and differences in the psychological profiles of the decision-makers (creative and visionary versus concrete and practical). These differences are sometimes a source of frustration in teams when opposite personalities clash regarding how to approach a problem and whether concrete, immediate results should be valued more than creative, long-term ones.

However, the fact that individuals have different preferences in their thinking modes does not imply that one stable set of psychological traits is associated with a creative personality.

First, whether we prefer invention or execution, we should not ignore the other dimension. Inventive people should train and grow their executive sides, and vice versa. A second option is to create teams comprising individuals with different skills; however, creatives and executives need to listen to each other, and teamwork can generate conflict (more on this in the next section).

Second, psychological research shows that while thinking preferences exist, the most creative people exhibit opposite traits on either side. In his book *Creativity: The Psychology of Discovery*, Mihaly Csíkszentmihalyi (2013) reports empirical findings from hundreds of interviews with high-profile creative individuals such as artists, scientists, and entrepreneurs. The data show no stable correlation between creativity and possessing certain psychological traits. Instead, the data show that a high level of creativity is typically exhibited by complex personalities in which presumptively mutually exclusive features coexist. We summarize the list of these opposites identified by Csíkszentmihalyi in Table 2.1.

Following Berghman and Hekkert (2017), Iandoli and Zollo (2022) classify these traits into two categories: those that can facilitate focus, convergence, and simplification (search for unity), and those that are more likely to favor divergence, exploration, and complexification (search for novelty). We resort to this approach to identify strategies to optimize the design of your product in Chapters 7 and 8. Following this perspective, creativity results when we can modulate the amount of disorder (entropy) in our thinking and making. Sometimes we need to reduce entropy in our plans or designs when these are unclear, chaotic, and confusing; sometimes, we must increase entropy because our creations are too simple compared to the complexity of the task at hand.

2.5   Beyond you: creativity as an interpersonal process

The next die-hard myth is that creativity is a subjective process. While individual cognitive abilities must be activated to allow individuals to achieve creative results, we tend to discount the importance of the input we receive from others, such as our immediate coworkers, prospective users, customers, or even random bystanders.

Table 2.1 Creativity is generated by the coexistence of opposite psychological traits in the same individual. (Iandoli & Zollo, 2022, adapted from *Cs.kszentmihalyi (2013)* courtesy of Bloomsbury Publishing).

Execute (Converge)	Invent (Diverge)	Creative individuals . . .
Rest	Physical activity	alternate intense physical activity with rest and idleness
Convergent thinking	Divergent thinking	balance their effort between exploring new possibilities with the development of a deep knowledge of their interests
Discipline	Playfulness	stick to a strict working routine while having fun and even enjoying the hard work
Realism	Imagination	unleash their imagination without losing contact with reality and feasibility
Introversion	Extroversion	enjoy introspection and solitude as well as social life
Humble	Proud	are humble enough to acknowledge their limits but proud about what they know and learn
Masculine	Feminine	exhibit both masculine and feminine traits (achievement versus relationship-oriented personality)
Tradition	Rebellion	possess deep and sophisticated knowledge of a domain but can escape disciplinary boundaries and dogmas
Objective	Passionate	use data and facts to prove their theories but are driven by genuine passion and love for their work and objects of interest
Enjoyment	Pain	Go through time of enjoyment and satisfaction as well as through anxiety, disorientation, and pain

We should look at creativity as the result of interpersonal processes for many reasons, and all of them have significant implications and practical suggestions for becoming more creative as a collective.

For one, information is distributed across many individuals and sources. Other people may have the experience or the complementary knowledge we are missing. In a research project on which one of the authors was working, we stumbled on technical coding issues and got stuck for a few days without being able to fix the problem. So, we decided to post a question on an online open-source community board and received an answer with the fix in 10 minutes. The internet has enormously amplified our ability to reuse information created by others, ensuring substantial productivity gains, like three days versus 10 minutes. The caveat is that you must know where you can search. A way to do this is to establish membership in online communities where savvy peers can be found.

The second reason creativity is a collective process is that human interaction can be leveraged both to retrieve existing information and generate new knowledge. A simple and powerful social mechanism to create new insights is conversations.

By studying conversations occurring between the members of teams of problem solvers in a professional context, Hargadon and Bechky (2006) model this generative process as a sort of collective dance based on three "movements" (Figure 2.3): help-seeking, help-giving, and reframing.

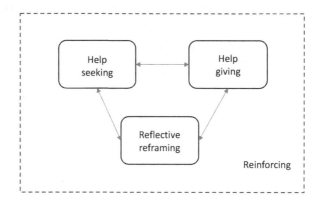

Figure 2.3 **Creativity as a collective process**. A group creates new and better ideas through conversational interaction in a three-step process: someone asks for help from the other members, who are available to help and provide it. The search for an answer often helps the team reframe the problem into a different one or in a way that is clearer or easier to solve.

Typically, the process starts with stating a problem or question and requesting help from the other team members. In a well-functioning team, members will address the request and do their best to help solve the problem. In the attempt to solve the problem as a team, individual contributions may add up until a "precipitating moment" is reached and the problem is reframed—that is, restated in a different format in which its resolution becomes more effortless. As Hargadon and Bechky state: "Moments of collective creativity involve considering not only the original question but also whether there is a better question to be asked" (2006, p. 492).

We can apply the model to the Walkman case. The request for help came from the team that developed the failed stereo recorder. Although other departments provided support, Sony did not yet have the technology to integrate stereo and recording functionality in the same device. Chairman Ibuka's insight helped reframe the question: what if we try to build an excellent portable music player *instead*? The cycle started again, and the result was identifying another device that could be coupled with the player: portable headphones. This equated to reframing the question from "portable recording" into "creating personal portable entertainment." Eventually, this was the novel value proposition: customers were willing to pay a premium price to create a personal entertainment sphere that could ensure privacy without isolating themselves and by connecting their favorite music to a specific experience or situation.

The model in Figure 2.3 can also identify other factors that lead to team creative failure.

The flaw can be in the help-seeking process. Hubris or fear of appearing incompetent may induce individuals to withhold their requests. Help-giving may be hindered by a lack of trust, internal competition, or a cutthroat working culture. A lack of diversity of skills, backgrounds, and alternative points of view can thwart reframing.

All three steps require the presence of virtuous team dynamics. Unfortunately, while teams can be significant generators of creative insights under the right conditions, they can also work as a formidable machine to kill creativity. Let's look at dysfunctions and variables that can transform a team from a lively group of creative problem-solvers into an assembly of disconnected individuals who kill invention and simultaneously delay execution.

2.6   A liquid model of team creativity

2.6.1   How to (not) kill creativity in your team

The reframing model illustrated in Figure 2.3 captures key processes of how a well-functioning team can generate new ideas. It also shows that popular techniques to support team creativity, such as brainstorming, will be useless if certain preconditions are not met: 1) the team members must be available to ask for and receive help; 2) the team has the resources (time, skills diversity, etc.) to support effective reframing. What's the point of generating ideas that do not address a request for help?

In the real world, however, it is not unlikely that such conditions are not met and that teams can become very dysfunctional and kill the same creativity they are supposed to generate. The study of groups is a massive field in organizational psychology. This extensive literature provides theories and tools to increase team effectiveness.

We rely on teams when single individuals do not possess complete information and skills to deal with or resolve a complex task autonomously. You can think of a team as a collective computational system that, like a computer, aggregates and recombines different inputs from different sources into new representations of the knowledge needed to solve a problem. Teams fail for two opposite reasons: 1) team members settle prematurely on a suboptimal solution; or 2) they diverge too much and do not achieve any consensus or shared output. Using a metaphor from physics, we refer to the first problem as "knowledge freezing" and to the second as "knowledge evaporation" (see Figure 2.4). When knowledge freezes, it may freeze in the wrong shape. More importantly, once knowledge is frozen, it becomes hard to change. When a team does not converge quickly enough, collective knowledge evaporates and gets lost. A well-functioning team keeps knowledge liquid as long as possible, iterates between freezing and liquefying to explore different solutions, and minimizes knowledge evaporation. On such a team, the members keep feeding their knowledge to a shared bucket to ensure the team has enough liquidity to work.

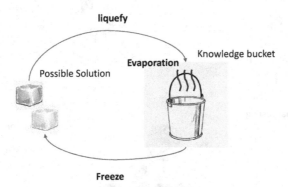

Figure 2.4 **A physics metaphor to describe team creativity**. Teams help improve collective knowledge by facilitating a cycle in which knowledge is created and questioned (liquefied) through multiple points of view and contributions. The metaphor highlights ways in which a team can become dysfunctional. This happens when group thinking prevents the members from questioning existing solutions, which leads to "freezing" the group knowledge and preferring the status quo, or when conflict stands in the way of converging toward shared solutions ("evaporation").

Let's use this metaphor to describe group common pitfalls:

1. *Group thinking*: Team members conform too quickly to a dominant opinion. In our metaphor, the knowledge is frozen prematurely and not questioned.
2. *Common knowledge*: Team members withhold individual information and focus on what they think they have in common with other members. In our model, this equates to not feeding enough water to the shared bucket.
3. *Diversity-based infighting*: Diversity of ideas creates fractures in the teams. Team members feed their knowledge to separate and smaller knowledge buckets or refuse to contribute to the shared bucket. Conflict acts as a flame under the buckets and accelerates evaporation.

This metaphor shows that the leading causes of team malfunctioning can eventually be reduced to two related factors: 1) the team errs on either side of the mix between convergence and divergence; 2) the team is unbalanced in terms of its composition and level of participation. This first mistake can be fixed by designing meetings so that convergence and divergence modes are alternated by design. For instance, in the notes on the wall method (see Figure 2.5), team members are asked to brainstorm silently by attaching sticky notes with brief descriptions of their ideas on a wall. In the second step, participants sort the notes, still keeping interaction to a minimum. For instance, they can move the sticky notes around to identify similar ideas or clusters of related ideas. Only in the third step do the team members deliberate to develop a joint outcome. The three steps can then be repeated in one or more iterations to see if the first output can improve.

Other techniques try to eliminate interaction as much as possible or completely, such as the Delphi method, in which team members make individual estimates whose average is fed back to the same participants, who can then reconsider their initial guess based on the group estimate.

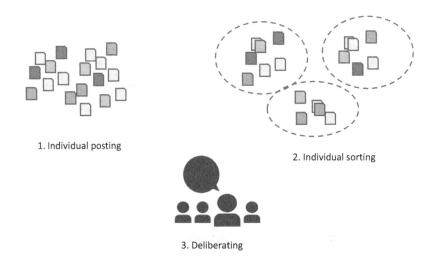

1. Individual posting

2. Individual sorting

3. Deliberating

Figure 2.5 **A notes-on-the-wall method for group brainstorming.** The technique supports alternating divergence and convergence in group discussions by forcing members to work independently in steps 1 and 2 and letting them interact only in step 3.

The second factor is the one that deserves the most attention because it is determined by deep causes that undermine the team equilibrium and eventually generate premature freezing or knowledge evaporation. Let's look at some of the most critical factors.

2.6.2 Tips for creating and managing creative entrepreneurial teams

Let's try to distill the lessons that the science of groups teaches us into a list of actionable interventions to reduce the risk of team failures. Here is a list of variables to consider:

- Team size
- Team composition
- Engagement
- Psychological safety.

Large teams are ineffective because they have too much liquidity and magnify all factors leading to team failure. Research shows that performance peaks when the number of team members is 5–9 (Hitt et al., 2017).

Diverse teams perform better than homogeneous ones. Regarding our liquid metaphor, think of each team member contributing different ingredients to the liquid mixture that accumulates in the shared bucket. If more elements of the right type are mixed, a chemical reaction producing a desirable outcome is more likely to happen. However, if we combine the wrong ingredients, we risk creating a useless or even dangerous blob.

Diversity is a double-edged sword: the proper diversity makes our team more intelligent, the wrong one dumber. Scott Page (2008) provides a helpful criterion to distinguish the two: diversity in values is undesirable because people are not likely to compromise on what they feel is right or wrong. Diversity in means is instead a resource: the standards include different skills, wide-ranging knowledge, varied ethnic or cultural backgrounds, and multiple perspectives. Diversity of means indicates that a team potentially has a more extensive toolbox. Research on team intelligence also shows that a balanced mix in terms of gender should be pursued. In particular, adding women to teams is beneficial because it generally helps increase the level of empathy in a group (Wooley & Malone, 2011).

Engagement refers to the team's ability to promote active participation by all the members. In his book *Social Physics*, Alex Pentland (2014) describes engagement as follows:

> Average performers think teamwork means doing their part on the team. Star performers see things differently. They push everyone on the team toward joint ownership of goal setting, group commitments, work activities, schedules, and team accomplishments. That is, star performers promote synchronized, uniform idea flow within the team by making everyone feel part of it, and try to reach a sufficient consensus so that everyone [will] willingly go along with new ideas
>
> (p. 62).

The continuous, abundant, and, more importantly, uniform idea flow is the output of a team whose members are equally engaged and motivated and where dominant voices are absent. A good proxy metric for engagement is a relatively balanced distribution of conversational turns by the various members during a meeting. This balance can be enforced by embracing and reinforcing a social norm that pushes members to express themselves and listen to others simultaneously.

Psychological safety is the one key factor in the alchemy of a well-oiled and highly functioning team. Psychological safety is a shared belief that the team is safe for interpersonal risk-taking because "members can show and employ themselves without fear of negative consequences of self-image, status or career" (Kahn, 1990). A research project conducted at Google[3] on what makes a team effective identified psychological safety as the common denominator behind excellent team performance. Consider the list of common team pitfalls in the previous section. The lack of psychological safety can explain why people withhold information, do not question dominant voices or points of view, and refrain from asking or providing help. In our experience, the more telling indicator of team malfunctioning is silence, perhaps interrupted by one loud, dominant voice. Even teams characterized by brutal conflict are preferable to those in which everybody is afraid to express opinions.

2.7 Conclusions

In this chapter, we have debunked some common misconceptions about creativity.

Creativity is not the same thing as innovation. The two concepts partially overlap, and it is this overlap, in which invention and execution coexist, that originates entrepreneurial creativity.

Creativity is not a special gift but a skill that can be honed and trained. There is no such thing as a creative personality; creativity increases when opposite personality traits are activated.

Key takeaways for this chapter

Lesson learned	Implications for your entrepreneurial project
Creativity and innovation are different things	• Balance invention and execution in your project • Alternate invention and execution to learn from mistakes and revise the initial design. • Tinker and experiment to generate continuous improvement
Flexible creativity	• Practice opposite behaviors as suggested by research on creativity. If you are lazy, do intense workouts. If you are very organized with your time, practice scrambling your agenda. If you are an introvert, practice extroversion. Creativity is originated by complex behavior and paradoxes.
Collective creativity	• Individual creativity is overrated. We always owe it to others. Be open to feedback and engage with others, be humble, ask questions, spark conversations, observe, explore, and engage. • Teams may be creative machines if set up properly. Balance convergence and divergence in discussions, do not bring too many people around the table, and make sure you have diverse backgrounds and skills. More importantly, make sure people feel psychologically safe to express themselves and are engaged. Be wary of egocentric participants and dominant voices. Make sure everyone is willing and will speak up and promote fair distribution of conversational turns in a meeting.

Creative output is seldom obtained by working in isolation; the feedback we receive from others is fundamental to checking assumptions and identifying the information we miss.

Since creativity is more likely to be generated through social interaction and creation with other individuals, teamwork can increase the likelihood of finding creative insights. For this reason, in the second part of the chapter, we proposed a model of effective teamwork distilled from the vast literature on team science, along with suggestions we can apply to create effective teams. These include team ideal size, internal diversity, engagement, and psychological safety advice.

In the next chapter, we apply this co-creation approach to understanding of our potential customers to identify their needs and pain points our solution should address.

Notes

1. A great example is the iPhone presentation at Macworld 2007, during which Jobs did an amazing breakdown on why the current models of smartphone were not working for the average consumer. See www.youtube.com/watch?v=x7qPAY9JqE4.
2. The popular belief that creative functions are localized in the right hemisphere of the brain and the executive ones in the left hemisphere has been questioned and was eventually debunked by research in neuroscience. However, the dualism surfaces at the cognitive level in terms of individual preferences to think and work predominantly with either sets of skills (see Bunderson, 1989).
3. A Google People Analytics team studied extensively what factors affect team effectiveness in a project named Project Aristotle—a tribute to Aristotle's quote "The whole is greater than the sum of its parts." The goal was to answer the question "What makes a team effective at Google?". More details can be found at the following link and in Duhigg (2016). https://rework.withgoogle.com/print/guides/5721312655835136/.

References

Barabba, V. P. (2022). To illustrate how a decision process should work, let's examine how an inquiry center with a learning and adaptation approach might have helped Kodak take advantage of a missed opportunity and avoid its eventual fall into bankruptcy. In *A systems thinking decision-making process* (pp. 135–139). Springer.

Berghman, M., & Hekkert, P. (2017). Towards a unified model of aesthetic pleasure in design. *New Ideas in Psychology*, 47, 136–144.

Bunderson, C. V. (1989). The validity of the Herrmann Brain Dominance instrument. *The Creative Brain*, 1(1981), 337–379.

Csíkszentmihalyi, M. (2013). *Creativity: Flow and the psychology of discovery and invention*. Harper Perennial.

Duhigg, C. (2016). *Smarter, faster, better: The secrets of being productive*. Random House.

Gladwell, M. (2011). The real genius of Steve Jobs. *The New Yorker*, November 6. https://www.newyorker.com/magazine/2011/11/14/the-tweaker

Govindarajan, V., & Trimble, C. (2010). *The other side of innovation: Solving the execution challenge*. Harvard Business Press.

Hargadon, A. B., & Bechky, B. A. (2006). When collections of creatives become creative collectives: A field study of problem solving at work. *Organization Science*, 17(4), 484–500.

Hitt, M. A., Miller, C. C., Colella, A., & Triana, M. (2017). *Organizational behavior*. John Wiley & Sons.

Iandoli, L., & Zollo, G. (2022). *Elegant design: A designer's guide to harnessing aesthetics*. Bloomsbury Publishing.

Kahn, W. A. (1990). Psychological conditions of personal engagement and disengagement at work. *Academy of Management Journal*, 33(4), 692–724.

Nayak, P. R., & Ketteringham, J. M. (1986). *Breakthroughs!* Rawson Associates.

Page, S. (2008). *The difference: How the power of diversity creates better groups, firms, schools, and societies-new edition.* Princeton University Press.

Pentland, A. (2014). *Social physics: How social network can make us smarter.* Penguin.

Wooley, A., & Malone, T. (2011). Defend your research: What makes a team smarter? More women. *Harvard Business Review*, June. https://hbr.org/2011/06/defend-your-research-what-makes-a-team-smarter-more-women

Chapter 3

Empathy

The art and practice of customer discovery

3.1 Introduction: let's plan a trip

During the summer of 2022, one of the authors (Kevin) and his partner needed to take a trip to Washington, DC, to visit some of their close friends. Like most people, they started a planning process with the most critical question: how will they get there? At the time, they were living in New York City, so they had a few options: renting a car, taking the bus, taking the train, and even flying to DC. In seconds, they identified each alternative's constraints, as well as pros, and cons:

- The trip was less than a week away, but they didn't want to spend much on transportation.
- They wanted a comfortable trip experience, less stress the better.
- They wanted to get to Washington, DC, the fastest way possible.

Both of them searched each transportation option's website against these constraints and considerations. The search became daunting as they quickly searched each site and, in the back of their minds, they started to map out the best decision. For context, see Table 3.1.

Kevin's partner looked at him and jokingly asked: "Are you all right? You look intense!" Kevin smiled and said, "I am just trying to decide." Kevin started to become stressed out over the decision. There was a factor of emotion in his decision-making process. He recalled past experiences (both good and bad) and realized that there were transportation options that he wanted to avoid. Eventually, they decided to take the train. The train met two of their three criteria, and their prior experiences with the train were excellent.

Drawing parallels between deciding how to travel to a destination and the realm of product design reveals insightful connections. Much like selecting a mode of transportation, choosing a product involves an interplay of practical and emotional considerations. Practical factors, easily observable and tangible, play a pivotal role in this decision-making process. Observation happens when we engage with the world with our five senses: sight, touch, hearing, taste, and smell. When we observe, we learn about the products around us. Once we obtain some knowledge, we apply our own filters to the observations and perceptions, and apply our own existing mental models that can influence our thoughts about a product. This process can provide insight and guide us in deciding whether a choice is the best for us. Other times, adopting such a rigid framework or being carried away by emotional attachment to specific options can push customers into a rabbit hole and make them blind to different formulations of a problem.

DOI: 10.4324/9781003346463-4

Table 3.1 Considering our travel options against our considerations and constraints.

Options	Rent a Car	Bus	Train	Airplane
Variables and Preferences				
Price (cheapest)	$340 (including $125 for gas)	$80	$250	$333
Comfort (most comfort)	Mildly comfortable	Small seats, not comfortable	Larger seats, more legroom	Tighter seats, less comfortable
Fast (fastest way possible)	4–5 hours driving (each way); could be more with traffic	4–5 hours traveling (each way) could be more with traffic	Guaranteed to arrive in 3.5 hours	1-hour flight
Pros	Control over when we leave and return	Cheapest way to get to DC	Comfortable, consistent, and quick.	The fastest way to get to DC
Cons	Rising gas prices/traffic	The most uncomfortable	Cost	Most expensive, have to deal with security, and need to find a way to the airport

Sometimes decision-makers end up obsessing with the means, or they taken for granted "why" they wanted to go on the trip to begin with. If the reason to go to DC is to spend time with friends we seldom see, we should prioritize minimization of travel time. If, instead, we want to transform the opportunity to see these friends into an occasion to leisurely explore and find some time to bond and reconnect with our partner, maybe speed is not the top concern.

The saying "the customer is always right" is both true and false. It is true in the sense that customers have the final words on what really matters to them; it is also false because they sometimes they do not know what they want or have difficulty articulating it unambiguously.

In this chapter, we help you navigate the complexity of understanding what the customers want and how we can support them to find out what they want and need. This approach is based on a combination of methods to help entrepreneurs collect observations and insights. We also propose a method based on co-creation, in which we assume that customers are not just passive providers of existing information but active subjects with whom we must engage to make sense of and discover things jointly.

3.2 The difference between observation and insight

Before we present methods and tools to perform customer discovery, let's clarify the difference between observation and insight. Understanding this difference is crucial to adopting the right mindset and applying the methodology correctly.

Observation is "an act of recognizing and noting a fact or occurrence often involving measurement with instruments" (Merriam-Webster, 2022). Observations are often based on collecting raw data and extrapolating through what we see, hear, or research. An insight is "the capacity to gain an accurate and deep intuitive understanding of a person or thing" (Martec, 2021). Insight means looking at our observable data and drawing a conclusion based on it. Let's take the same example from earlier. This insight gains depth as it encompasses more than a mere fact; it involves the infusion of our emotions and sentiments. By acknowledging the value of privacy and the opportunity for meaningful conversations during a road trip, we imbue the observation with a richer, more nuanced significance. In essence, the transition from observation to insight involves the creation of a deeper meaning, anchored in our personal experiences and emotions.

Here's another example to illustrate the difference between observations and insights and why they are complementary forms of knowledge to advance our understanding of the problem. Suppose you are a product manager overseeing the development of healthy dog food, and you are observing your customers' behavior in terms of what they do and what their preferences and habits are when it comes to feeding their furry friends. You may collect data regarding when the pets eat and record that they are fed daily at 8 a.m. and 6 p.m. That is an observation. However, you also collect the fact that pets tend to eat at the same time as their human owners. You begin to draw a possible conclusion that pet owners considered their pets as family members since they eat when the rest of the family does. This is an insight, because we take the observable data and draw conclusions (Feinstein, 2022).

It is important to note that observations and insights are equally important. Observations with no insights are considered unprocessed data. Insights without proper observations are assumptions based on our knowledge and not warranted by objective evidence based on the customer's experience.

Understanding our customers is measured by our ability to get satisfying answers to these questions:

- What influences our target customers to buy our product? What is the critical deciding factor?
- How can our product solve their need? Does it solve their need?
- How can we help them to make sense of what they want? How can they help us to suggest possible solutions to their problems?

Seeking the answers to these questions is our way of empathizing with our customers. Customer empathy is one of the most critical aspects behind the design of successful products. This chapter illustrates methods, tools, and tips to build customer empathy by increasing our ability to observe our customers' experiences and derive valuable insights from the observation process.

3.3   A Human-Centered Design approach to customer empathy

Customer empathy "is understanding the underlying needs and feelings of customers. It goes beyond recognizing and addressing their tactical requirements and puts things into further context by viewing things from their perspective." (Product Plan, 2022). For the most part, almost every product is designed from the perspective that a customer will eventually get to use it. The challenge is perfecting our ability to empathize with our customer base and build products that meet their needs.

3.3.1 The customer interview

As mentioned in Chapter 1, Human-Centered Design focuses on building deep empathy with the people we are designing for. According to IDEO.org, Human-Centered Design is "a process that starts with the people you're designing for and ends with new solutions that are tailor-made to suit their needs" (IDEO, 2015).

The human design process starts with finding inspiration during the ideate/empathize steps (see Figure 1.5). The empathize phase focuses on learning on the fly. There are several ways this process can be done.

The first way is to interview them. A customer interview can help illuminate the primary problems and the pain points our prospective customers are experiencing. The interview should be open-ended, whereby almost any question can be asked. However, there is an expectation that you, as the interviewer, should come into the interview with, at the minimum, a game plan. The Difference Incubator (2022), an Australian-based consulting firm, developed an excellent framework for building your customer interview game plan.

Your game plan refers to your own goals for understanding your customer. In this phase, you should develop a few topics or questions to be answered or clarified during the interview. A sampling of these questions can be found in Table 3.2.

Questions should be open-ended, leaving all the space your customers need to explain the problems and how they have been trying to solve them. In this phase, they must remain as descriptive as possible. Yes/no questions and questions that limit the type of responses your customers can give are not helpful and can produce misleading findings. At least in this phase, you should refrain from showing any instance of a possible solution to your interviewees. If you do that, you will tunnel their attention prematurely towards possible alternatives at a time when you should instead focus on getting insights into the problems they are facing.

In addition, an interview is not limited to individual customers; depending on the scope of the problem, you may consider doing an individual, group, or even an expert interview. A group interview is an interview with multiple people where you ask the group questions about the problem. An expert interview is an interview with someone knowledgeable—an expert—in the field. You do not have to interview the most authoritative and hard-to-reach experts in your domain. An expert may be someone with wide professional knowledge of

Table 3.2 Sample questions for a customer interview. Adapted from (Product Plan, 2022) & (Future Founders, 2020). Interview questions should be open ended and aimed at collecting information objectively. It is crucial for interviewers to not prompt or bias customers' answers with the interviewer's expectations.

Tell me a bit about . . .
Describe the last time you . . .
What was it like when . . .
Can you tell me a story about a time you struggled with [issue related to your problem?
Why was that [hard, frustrating, etc.]?
What was the hardest part about this problem you faced?
Why was this the hardest part?
How did you solve this problem at the time?
How did you find that solution? What frustrates you about this solution?
Are you actively searching for/trying other solutions?

an activity or a topic. For instance, if you are developing an app to improve food donations from restaurants to shelters, experts could include any of the following: shelter managers, restaurant owners and managers, charity managers, volunteers, and so on.

There are pros and cons for each of these types of interviews: The individual interview allows you to focus on one person at a time and discover in-depth knowledge about their lifestyle and aspirations in terms of your product/problem. However, you must conduct several individual interviews before you have enough concrete data to model a prototype.

> **Tip:** For the individual interview, start with open or general questions as a way of ensuring they open up to you. Once they do, then go deep with the questions to understand their feelings about a product. (IDEO, 2015)

The group interview allows you to get a quick understanding of a community's life, dynamics, and needs, but because these interviews are typically done with a group of 7–10 people, getting in-depth can be a challenge. Finally, the expert interview allows you to question an expert to get their insights; they can help you get a systems view of your project/problem area. However, the challenge would be getting in contact with an expert during this phase.

> **Tip:** For the group interview, use a neutral space and be sure to think about ways to engage quieter members of your group. (IDEO, 2015)

The IDEO field guide to Human-Centered Design provides a very rich assortment of interview techniques, examples, and templates (IDEO, 2015).

3.3.2   The customer journey

Another way you can shape your customer interview is to shape your questions around exploring the customer journey. The customer journey is "the set of interactions that a customer has with a brand in buying a service or product. Put plainly, it considers the complete interaction road map—from brand discovery to purchasing and beyond" (QuestionPro, 2022).

This approach can be helpful when customers have already had experiences with existing products they are currently using to solve the problem we are investigating. The customer journey is broken up into five significant parts: awareness, consideration, conversion, retention, and advocacy. The customer journey is a typical journey that most customers take when interacting with a product/brand.

Looking at the steps of the journey, an approach you can take in developing questions for the interview is to examine the thought process a customer may take during each step. Here is an example of some questions you can ask based on this model.

Table 3.3 Framing questions in the context of the customer journey.

Phase of the customer journey	Questions you can ask related to that phase
Awareness	What first prompted/triggered you to look for [this product category]? Note: we're not asking about your business or other businesses just yet, we just want to understand why they're looking for X in the first place.
Consideration	What options were you considering? Why? Note: This helps us understand what features are important to the m—this may be different from what we think they think is important.
Conversion	What did you end up choosing? Why? How long did it take to decide?
Retention	How are you finding your experience with it? Will you continue to buy from them? Why?
Advocacy	Would you recommend this brand/product to others? Why?

Source: (The Difference Incubator, 2020)

> **Tip: Dear Diary/Journal:** Each phase of the Human-Centered Design process can be daunting because you will receive much information. Therefore, we recommend finding a way to record all your feedback. You can buy a physical journal for this process, or as an alternative, you can consider using a digital note-taking system. We have found some success using tools like Evernote. Digital notes have multiple advantages. They can be stored, organized, and imported into other documents, and they are harder to lose. Whatever you choose, be sure you have a way to search your notes later. At some point, you may be asked to justify why certain decisions were made with your solution. A journal will save you time later. Keep good notes!

3.3.3 During and after the customer interview

As you begin the interview, you should first introduce yourself, explain the purpose of the interview, and then begin by asking your opening questions.

> **Tip:** During this phase, it's essential to remain objective and neutral. Try to avoid questions that may confirm your own biases about the problem; instead, allow your customer to direct their thoughts and ask questions from the point of clarification, not simply confirmation.

Once the interview has been completed, document the answers you receive and then prepare for your next one. During this phase, we are often expected to interview many people, so expect to conduct this interview a few times.

Tip: In our Creativity and Innovation courses, many of our students ask, "When do we know we have enough data from interviews to stop doing interviews and move on to the next ideation phase?" It's an excellent question. Our suggestion is to rely on the law of decreasing returns. At some point, after conducting more interviews, you will start to notice that the value of the information you are getting is less and less. Another sign is to see when the new data confirms what you already know about the problem instead of generating new knowledge. Then you might be ready to move on to the next phase.

While customer interviews offer us the ability to go extremely deep with understanding our customers' primary concerns, sometimes we would like to validate our customer assessment by asking a more extensive set of customers even beyond the group interviews. In these instances, we may conduct surveys where we ask general questions to get a sense of validating our customer concerns shared through the interviews. However, we must remember that surveys may provide only surface-level data and can't replicate the deep data we receive from one-on-one interviews.

3.3.4 *Find inspiration by alternating convergent and divergent thinking*

At this point, you conducted your interviews about your customer's problem; now you are ready to generate as many ideas (and prototypes) as possible to solve their problem. This process is called ideation.

Ideation is a process wherein you make sense of what you learned, identify design opportunities, and prototype possible solutions. We believe this is where we can have the most "fun" with the Human-Centered Design process. To properly frame and provide context on the ideation process, we want to step back and discuss how our thinking during this phase could go.

After you complete your interviews, you may have many thoughts, ideas, and even plans. If you work with a team of other people, they may also feel the same and may have abundant thoughts, ideas, and plans, but keep in mind that their interpretations of the findings may be different. Diversity of thought is valuable. This is *a moment of divergent thinking*. Divergent thinking is a reasoning modality to generate multiple unique ideas or solutions for a problem through spontaneous, free-flowing thinking (airfocus, 2022). Eventually, you (and/or your team) will need to find a way to boil down all these ideas into something that can be presented to your customers. This process of narrowing your ideas is called *convergent thinking*. Convergent thinking is a reasoning modality that encourages individuals to aggregate disparate information to solve a particular problem (Caughron et al., 2011).

While we would love to believe that the process is straightforward and only happens once, the process can happen several times over, especially as we, as product developers, start to build, test, and refine the prototype. (We discuss more about prototyping in Chapter 5). This process of conducting divergent and then convergent thinking is known as the double-diamond process (see Figure 3.1) (British Design Council (2016), Humble (2022).

The double diamond process is integral to the Human-Centered Design process because it pushes designers to learn how to narrow their focus, directing their effort on the essential

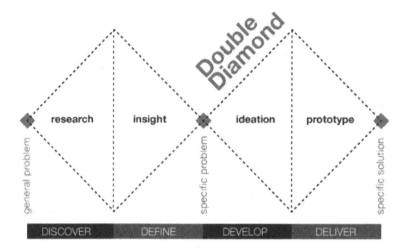

Figure 3.1 **The Double Diamond Process of Design**. The diagram illustrates the iterative process of convergent and divergent thinking. The first diamond concludes upon identifying and understanding the general problem (designing the right thing). The second diamond involves alternating divergence and convergence to design the solution effectively (designing things right).

things to our customers and ultimately finding a solution to meet their needs. You can compare this model with the knowledge-freezing model described in chapter 2 to model how teams should continuously revise and question frozen knowledge to improve their understanding of the problem or the design of the solution.

After you design an initial solution ("prototype"; see chapter 5), you must test it with the people you created it for. Reaching out to these people with a simple prototype is known as getting rapid feedback. Rapid feedback lets you know if your prototype is on the right track to solving its problems and if your solution needs to be tweaked. Testing your prototype provides you with additional opportunities to build customer empathy.

> **Tip: Keep good notes!** During the ideation phase, each time you make a change to your prototype, be sure to mark the change down in your journal. It will help you to track these details, especially when you need to understand why a change was necessary. This sounds tedious, but in product development, it can save you from making a costly error by helping you avoid things that were already done before.

3.4   Problem-driven learning: five characteristics of a good problem

As we have mentioned, the human-centered design process is firmly centered around people because our ultimate objective is to ensure we find a "good" problem. When thinking about tackling a good problem, we need to understand what the characteristics of a good problem are. Now, we realize that "good" is highly subjective. However, we offer a framework in this section that can help you narrow down this subjectivity and increase your chances of identifying a good problem. Our framework is based on a medical metaphor.

Medical professionals, like doctors and physicians' assistants, often use deductive reasoning to diagnose their patients. They are spending time to ask questions, understand the patient's lifestyle, and determine how the patients are attempting to solve their ailment. If this sounds like our search for a good problem, that is because the metaphor is spot on.

When product developers attempt to solve their customers' problems, they should ask the same questions and follow the same process doctors apply when diagnosing a patient. Customers are in "pain" and have "symptoms" through which their lack of ease is manifested. They can tell us about their symptoms, but they may lack an understanding of the cause of the pain. It is the designer's task to understand what causes that pain and work back from the symptoms to the real cause of the disease. The pain or discomfort should be intense enough for the user to care. If the user/patient cares, they are actively trying to fix the problem through some "self-medication"; however, nothing seems to work.

Thus, to get a better glimpse of this metaphor, we interviewed a surgeon, Dr. Martha Ayewah, about how she approaches diagnosing a patient. We realized there are some exciting parallels we can draw from her experiences.

Dr. Ayewah is a surgeon in New York City. She mentioned that whenever she starts a diagnosis, she asks her patient: "What is your main concern?" This simple question begins the process of understanding what pains them. In the same way, when we ask similar questions, we are also trying to understand what is causing our customers' pain. What seems to be the problem? An additional question is: What are the main reasons for your concerns? Notice that this moment is all about the patients and how they feel. It is not about the treatment or the doctor's skills. Another reason the doctor/patient metaphor is a good example is that sometimes patients do not know how to describe their problem or do not even know they have one. A good doctor will listen first and identify issues that may go unnoticed by the patients themselves.

Dr. Ayewah's next question is: What is your family history? To better determine a remedy or solution, understanding a person's history, including their family history, is essential, as it can give us a road map for things to avoid. In the same way, understanding a customer's experience is vital to understanding their past practices and behaviors.

When Dr. Ayewah examines a patient, she might notice a common symptom that many other patients are experiencing.

In the same way, when product developers interview many people, they start to develop a sense of the larger group of customers the problem is affecting. This means they are beginning to create a strategic target market to focus on. Once we know who would fit this target, we can research how many people would be affected by our solution. Is the target market small? Is the target market large?

Dr. Ayewah often recognizes that many medications on the market help ease symptoms of illnesses. At the same time, new medications are continuously being developed to cure many diseases and some remedies or medications are the right ones for a given patient while others may not be. Every patient is different, and reactions to medications are also different. In the same way, product designers must evaluate all possible solutions to the problem in the market today, those that work well and those that don't. Regrettably, in some instances, the problem is too unique and hard to solve. In other cases, existing remedies work just fine. While this could be good news for the doctor and the patient, it is not for an entrepreneur, who must find evidence of a gap in the market and that his solution is unique and novel, that could fill that gap.

Dr. Ayewah also recognizes that patients would often attempt to remedy their illness. She would ask: Are you currently taking any medications? It seems like a simple question, but it can guide the doctor in determining the best remedies a patient should take. In the same way, as product developers, we often ask our customers: What have you done previously to solve this problem? The answers we receive from customers to this question can help us to define their old solutions and perfect better solutions.

Putting this process together, we can summarize the elements of a good problem in the following table. In addition, if we layer these elements on a Likert scale, we can rate any problem and determine if this is a problem we should attempt to solve or defer. As a broad guideline, if your score is lower than 15, you should discard the problem and keep searching for a good one.

3.5 Conclusions

Looking back at the beginning of this chapter, we started this discussion of customer empathy by examining the decision-making process of someone taking a trip to Washington, DC. The problem appeared simple: How am I going to get there? Throughout the chapter, we learned that perhaps that is the most challenging question to answer. To create a solution for a customer, we must understand that customer. We must understand their problem, how they attempt to solve it, and develop our solutions for their problem. Using the Human-Centered Design process (inspiration, ideation, and implementation), we can deeply invest time in learning about our customers' needs and achieve customer empathy. In the next chapter, we keep investigating building customer empathy by focusing on a critical step: articulating our value proposition.

Table 3.5 Rating sheet for a good problem.

A Good Problem . . .	Low	Likert Scale	High
. . . is easily **identifiable**	Not identifiable	1 2 3 4 5	Easy to identify
. . . contains enough **historical data**	Very little historical data	1 2 3 4 5	A lot of historical data
. . . has an identifiable and sizable **target market**	Small target market	1 2 3 4 5	Sizable target market
. . . has an **attempted solution on the market** (even if the solution doesn't work)	Has many solutions	1 2 3 4 5	Has few solutions
. . . has customers who are currently attempting to use a solution	Customers not active in finding a solution	1 2 3 4 5	Customers active in finding a solution

Key takeaways for this chapter

Lesson learned	Implications for your entrepreneurial project
Observation *and* insight	• Collect a lot of data and spend enough time observing your prospective customers' behavior. Data is what they do; insight is why they do it. • Delay insight until you have enough data. Premature insight can be based more on your prejudice or previous knowledge than on facts. Make sure you have enough evidence to back up your insight. • Practice counterfactual thinking. Identify multiple explanations of the same behavior and chose the one that has more empirical support.

Lesson learned	Implications for your entrepreneurial project
Customer empathy	• Your ego is your enemy. Open your mind to input from your prospective customers; do not judge reality with your eyes and mental model. Make an honest effort to feel how they feel. Do not act as an external observer when you want to understand the emotions your customers feel. Emotions can be felt only when you immerse yourself in the same experience. • Experiment with different tools and ways to empathize with your customers. Interviews, observation, journaling, simulation, etc., will all contribute precious data that you won't obtain with only one approach. Be respectful of how your customers prefer to interact. Do not force them into an interview if they do not want to or cannot talk about something. • Practice convergent and divergent thinking. Do not stop once you find something interesting; keep going until you hit decreasing marginal returns on the information you collect. Delay convergence as much as you can. Look for other people's inputs starting from your customers to screen information and converge towards sound conclusions.
Good problems	• The problem is key; the solution is a consequence. Once you understand and represent the problem in the right way, the solution will be much easier to find. • Good problems for entrepreneurs have precise characteristics. They can be described and are relevant to a sufficiently high number of people. People care about them and are trying to act on them. Some solutions are around but do not perform well. • Rethink the definition of a problem, find more problems, and use early prototypes of a solution to test whether they address the problem (even if they are not yet fully developed and fully functioning—more on this in Chapter 5)

References

airfocus. (2022). Divergent thinking. *airfocus.com*. https://airfocus.com/glossary/what-is-divergent-thinking/, last accessed November 2023.

British Design Council. (2016). *Eleven lessons. A study of the design process.* www.designcouncil.org.uk

Caughron, J. J., Peterson, D. R., & Mumford, M. D. (2011). *Encyclopedia of creativity* (Second edition). Academic Press.

Feinstein, N. (2022). Personal conversation at St John's University, Summer 2022.

Future Founders. (2020). *Future founders customer discovery worksheet*, August 8. FutureFounders.com

Humble, J. (2022). What is the double diamond design process? *The Fountain Institute*, May 7. www.thefountaininstitute.com/blog/what-is-the-double-diamond-design-process

IDEO. (2015). *The filed guide to human-centered design.* www.designkit.org, last accessed August 2023.

Martec. (2021). What makes insights actionable? *Martec Group*. https://martecgroup.com/what-makes-insights-actionable/#:~:text=An%20insight%20is%20defined%20as,insights%20put%20data%20into%20motion

Merriam-Webster. (2022). Observation definition and meaning—Merriam-webster. *Merriam-Webster*. www.merriam-webster.com/dictionary/observation

Product Plan. (2022). What is customer empathy—Definition and overview. *ProductPlan.com*. www.productplan.com/glossary/customer-empathy/

QuestionPro. (2022). Customer journey—What is it, How to use it and examples. *QuestionPro.com*. www.questionpro.com/blog/customer-journey-map/

The Difference Incubator. (2020). Customer empathy interviewing—TDI. *The Difference Incubator*. https://tdi.org.au/customer-empathy-interviewing/

Chapter 4

Creative confidence, part 1

Say it! Articulate your value proposition

The first [umpire] says, "I calls 'em like they is!"; the second, "I calls 'em like I sees 'em!"; and the third, "There ain't nothing there until I calls 'em!

—(Karl Weick)

4.1 Now entering the tank

In 2009, the American business reality show *Shark Tank* premiered on American television. It is described as follows:

> Hopeful entrepreneurs come to the Shark Tank seeking an investment to start, grow or save their businesses. If the Sharks [investors] hear a great idea, they're ready to invest using their own money. . . . But first, the entrepreneur must convince a shark to invest the amount they are asking for
>
> (CNBC, 2022)

When *Shark Tank* premiered in the US, it was entering a saturated reality TV market. We believe what pulled people into this show was the exciting storytelling created by real people as entrepreneurs to persuade the "sharks."

Shark Tank glamorizes entrepreneurship and the art of the pitch. However, we must be mindful that the form of the pitch we see on *Shark Tank* is also built around entertainment. If you watch *Shark Tank*, there is dramatic music and exciting camera shots, and the intention is to entice us to watch. A pitch in the real world may be less exciting. However, they are still critical storytelling and emotional exercises that help entrepreneurs position their offerings and get resources to run their businesses or build their products.

A pitch is a form of words used to persuade someone to buy or accept something (Rossette-Crake, 2019). The form of pitching that is done on *Shark Tank* is what many would refer to as an "investor pitch," a format of the pitch where "entrepreneurs present their business plan to convince investors to finance the project" (Rossette-Crake, 2019). While the investor pitch is an essential form of the pitch, we argue that there are different pitching formats one should be able to perform to be successful.

This chapter focuses on a particular and trendy format known as an elevator pitch. The elevator pitch is a "concise, carefully planned, and well-practiced description of your product or service to convince others about your offer's viability, uniqueness, and value (Pagliarini, 2006). The idea is that the pitch should be well crafted and concise enough for anyone to understand in the time it would take to ride up in an elevator.

DOI: 10.4324/9781003346463-5

We firmly believe that there is an art and science to crafting a pitch. When you can combine presentation techniques and tricks with the ability to create a good story that is emotionally salient for our listeners, you've done it.

4.2   The fundamental objectives of a pitch

The fundamental goal of any pitch is to persuade someone that what you can offer them is addressing their problem in ways that are better than the status quo. Over the years, researchers have argued that the action of the pitch (also known as the "ask") is an essential mechanism for purposeful practice in entrepreneurship (Dew, 2018), and the ability to pitch or to ask has been known to be one of the deciding factors contributing to the success of an entrepreneurial venture. Let us look at a few great examples of entrepreneurs who asked for help.

- Oculus Virtual Reality Headset: This famous VR headset was, at one point, a side project of Palmer Luckey, who started building headset prototypes at the age of 15. He continued the project while working as an engineer at the University of Southern California's Mixed Reality Lab. Eventually, he decided that he needed a significant investment to take the project further and, in 2012, launched a $250,000 Kickstarter campaign, which succeeded in raising $2.4 million. He eventually sold this project to Facebook for more than $2 billion (Robinson, 2017).
- Virgin Group and Richard Branson: Richard Branson "borrowed money from his mother in 1971 to keep his fledging London record shop afloat" (Kabbage American Express, 2022). Richard would eventually expand the Virgin brand into multiple businesses in various industries.
- Amazon and Jeff Bezos: Amazon "launched in 1994 with a $300,000 investment from his parents and loans from his bank account. Beyond that, Bezos scrambled to raise $1 million from 20 local investors—a major accomplishment since Bezos knew few people in Seattle and the Internet was still unknown to most" (Leibovich, 2000).

You may have noticed a few patterns in these examples.

- Every entrepreneur had a well-fleshed-out business idea.
- Each entrepreneur built their strategy for asking for money from various sources (e.g., asking parents, friends, investors, banks, and crowdfunding platforms; see more on funding mechanisms and strategies in Chapter 13).
- Each entrepreneur convinced others to give to their project, although their ideas might have seemed too ambitious for the time.

While there are many examples of successful entrepreneurs who went out and asked for the resources they needed to grow their business, there are also thousands of young entrepreneurs who never reached this point, because their concept needed additional testing, the entrepreneur was asking or pitching to the wrong people—or even worse, they did not ask for the support they needed. Research has indicated that the path to being an entrepreneur is not special but rooted in deliberate practices and actions (Mitchell, 2007). This means that it takes deliberate actions to become an entrepreneur, and in the case of this chapter, the ask/pitch is a critical and intentional action that all entrepreneurs must be prepared to do.

4.3   The fundamental model of the pitch

Robert Pagliarini, president of Pacifica Wealth Advisors, argues that all pitches should be designed to answer six questions (Pagliarini, 2006):

1. What is your product or service?
2. Who is your market?
3. What is your revenue model?
4. Who is behind the company?
5. Who is your competition?
6. What is your competitive advantage?

In this chapter, we focus on the critical ingredients of a pitch. You will find more advice on effectively communicating your idea in Chapter 12.

These six questions should provide an overview of your business, product, or service to prospective investors and customers. An effective pitch is a pitch that can function to answer these six questions concisely, typically in three minutes. This rigid time constraint makes the pitching practice exciting and valuable for entrepreneurs for several reasons.

First, if you cannot summarize in three minutes the value of what you are offering, it may mean you have an underdeveloped idea or that it is hard to make an argument to show that your offer is innovative and superior to what is already available. Second, by working hard to find a better way to say what you say, you pump your communication muscle to identify the killer tagline and wording that will make a breach in the head and heart of your listeners. Third, the harsh time limit is a reminder that investors use pitching as a screening methodology. The objective of your pitch is not to describe what you do but to get your listeners to want to know more. The ultimate success metric of a pitch is obtaining a follow-up meeting, during which you will be given more time to go into the details.

We will review each of these questions in the following sections and offer tips for maximizing the value of your pitch.

1. *What is your product or service?*

In this section, you must tell your prospective customer or investor what you are selling. Is it a product? Is it a service? Both? Within three minutes, you should go into only some details. The content of this question should be limited to enough detail that the person hearing the pitch can imagine what you are selling them. Follow-up conversations can be used to discuss further functionality or additional particulars of the product/service. Stay simple: What are you selling? When describing what you offer, use a solution/problem format. Your product helps [whom] to address [issues] when trying to solve [problem]. It is not about you and what you do but why you do it (Sinek, 2009) and whom you are helping.

2. *Who is your market?*

Who are you selling this product or service to? What is the size of the potential market? Investors like to understand the market as it allows them to begin to imagine your potential revenue stream(s). Describing your potential customers is essential; who are they? Are they unhappy with existing solutions? Once potential users have been described, how many of these "potential users" are in the market. (See Chapter 10 for methods to describe your users and estimate your market size.)

3. What is your revenue model?

This question is quite simple: how do you plan to make money?

- How much money are you projecting to make? If you are selling a product? How do you plan to sell your product? Do you plan to sell in traditional stores, online, or both?
- If you are selling a service? How do you plan to sell the service? Is it a subscription service, or is it a pay-per-use service?

This question is often a make-or-break for a pitch. The pitched revenue model should provide some sense of what future revenue would look like.

4. Who is behind the company?

Who oversees the company? Who are the masterminds behind the product or service? What are the skills of your team members, and do you have all the skills you need? This is a great time to discuss what makes you and your team the right people to market the product or service. Showcasing expertise or experience is essential!

5–6. Who is your competition? What is your competitive advantage?

Does your product or service have some form of competition? In other words, are there individuals who are already working on some form of your product or service? We often encourage entrepreneurs never to assume they do not have competition. In some rare cases, you may not have a clear competitor, but customers are already finding ways to solve the problem without your product.

What makes your company, product, or service different from your competition? What makes your company, product, or service better than the status quo? Discuss the advantages that make your offering superior to what is already in the market.

Beyond answering these questions, your pitch should contain a few additional items:

A Hook:

- A good pitch should contain a moment that can grab an investor's attention, a statement, or a question that piques their interest, making them want to hear more (Pagliarini, 2006).

Passion:

- A great pitch should showcase an entrepreneur's enthusiasm for their product or service. You must be passionate and confident about what you are doing to persuade others.

A request:

- Be sure to ask for something at the end of your pitch. What you can ask depends on where you are in your business/product development. Do you need money to build or improve your prototype? Do you need a capital infusion to support R&D efforts? Do you need money to penetrate a new market? Having an ask shows that you know what you need and know the next steps.

4.4 Articulating your value proposition

In the courses we teach, we often encourage our students to frame their pitch by focusing on what their product's value proposition should be. The value proposition of a product or service can be defined as follows: it is a product or service that helps customers to do more "affordably, conveniently, or effectively a "job" they have been already trying to do, with given resources and constraints" (Christensen et al., 2009).

The concept of value using this definition can be framed in four different contexts:

1. Affordability—Financial Value

- A product or service should allow customers to accomplish a task at a more affordable rate, creating financial value for the consumer.

2. Convenience—Time Value

- A product or service should allow a customer to accomplish a task faster than without it. Faster includes easier to use and learn, portable, 24/7 service, and so forth.

3. Effectiveness—Performance Value

- A product or service should allow customers to accomplish tasks more effectively.

4. Volitional Value

- A product or service should help customers solve a problem they were trying to solve without it.

When crafting a pitch, it is crucial to identify what aspect of your value proposition should be emphasized. While everything may seem essential, you can only excel at some things. In which respect is your solution making a difference compared to existing ones? Think of any product you know and ask yourself which of these dimensions the product design is focused on. For instance, IKEA, with its stylish but inexpensive furniture, and low-cost air travel companies are all about making affordable something that previously was out of reach for many people. Bang & Olufsen and Bose are all about designing sound devices that deliver the finest sound quality at home or on the go.

Notice also the job metaphor used in Christensen et al.'s definition. Customers "hire" your product to perform a "job" that they are already trying to do. *What is the 'job' the target community members are trying to do?* How are your customers actively trying to solve the problem? What is their goal, what resources do they have, and what are the constraints within their community? Will your solution make their lives easier (convenience), make it better (effectiveness), or make it cheaper (affordability)? When asking these questions, we often frame the solutions in the voice of the consumer. Framing the voice of the consumer can also strengthen the pitch.

Table 4.1 The four different pitches based on different types of ask. Adapted from Dew (2018).

Basic pitch
  The pitch focuses on entrepreneurs pinpointing stakeholders whom they wish to target and asking them to provide what they need.
  The keywords: "Please provide me with X."
  Example: *I am looking for $20,000 to start my business.*
Transitional ask or pitch:
  This pitch focuses on an entrepreneur targeting stakeholders but often includes a negotiation, especially a quid pro quo: each person gives something to get something. It is often seen on *Shark Tank*, where the goal is to raise financial capital in exchange for equity in a business.
  The keywords: "You give me X and I'll give you Y."
  Example: "*I am looking for $20,000 for 15% equity in my company.*"
Tentative ask/pitch:
  This pitch occurs when an asker and askee try to understand how committed each might be to supporting the other.
  The keywords: "Might you be willing to support me with the following . . .?"
  Example: "*Would you be interested in contributing to this product?*"
The co-creative or effectual ask/pitch:
  This pitch is strategically aligned with providing an open-ended framework, allowing for the potential stakeholders (askees) to set their own terms. It allows potential stakeholders to help shape the venture in return for their commitment to become involved in some way. What makes this ask very different is that stakeholders have a hand in co-creating the firm or otherwise involve themselves in the product you are creating.
  The keywords: "What would it take for you to commit to this project?" and "This is what I need to commit."
  Example: "*We are in the early stages of developing a cutting-edge product that aims to revolutionize task management. Instead of presenting a fixed plan, we invite potential stakeholders like yourself to co-create this venture with us.*"

In Chapter 3, we discussed the concept of divergent versus convergent thinking, especially in refining an idea. When you pitch your idea, you will often receive feedback on your idea. This feedback should be used to refine your product or your pitch. Feedback may cause you to begin with divergent thinking.

4.5   The different forms of pitches

Research in entrepreneurship has indicated that entrepreneurs engage in four diverse types of asks/pitches. Each ask has a specific framework based on the following: An asker knows precisely what they want, and the goal is to induce the akee to invest. (Dew, 2018).

It is believed that entrepreneurs use some version of each pitch. While there are multiple versions of a pitch, the most important thing we must consider is that a pitch is fundamentally about creating a relationship with someone: understanding their need, connecting to their emotions, and convincing them that your solution is right.

4.6   Tips for pitching on the internet

While it is assumed that most business pitches are happening in person, but online pitching is becoming a more common approach. For instance, many organizations, including our university, conducted pitch competitions through the Zoom platform during the COVID-19 pandemic. Even companies like ContainIQ, a company with a data monitoring and tracing platform for Kubernetes (Kubernetes "are open-source system for automating the deployment, scaling, and management of containerized applications" (Kubernetes.io, 2023)), raised $2.5 million by pitching to more than 93 investors on various online platforms like Zoom (Fintech Inshorts, 2021). In this section, we want to spend a little time providing some tips to make the process of pitching via an online platform as easy as possible (Fintech Inshorts, 2021; Phipps-Morgan, 2022).

Step 1: Pick the right platform

Over the past several years, several video platforms have come to the forefront of online communication. Zoom, Microsoft Teams, and Google Hangout have each taken a portion of the world market share. Therefore, ensuring your team chooses the best platform for an online pitch is vital. Sometimes, the decision may be taken out of your hands, as the potential investor may have a preferred platform to use. We (as the authors) suggest you become familiar with all common platforms and choose one that appears to be the most accessible for you and has a secondary option if the other platform has any issues. Whichever platform you use, ensure you know how to use it, especially when it comes to common troubleshooting tasks such as camera and audio settings.

Step 2: Secure your location

Before you even get to the day of your pitch, identify a location that will allow you to present your product in the best light. It should be a location where, if you need to demo a prototype, you can do so with ease. During the pandemic, many individuals worked from home, so it is not surprising that for some entrepreneurs, many elements and steps of the product development process took place in someone's home. If you plan to pitch your product at home or another personal location, ensure your location is presentable. Remember, the goal of the presentation is to highlight the product and you; you do not want anything to distract your investors. Be mindful that clear and professional audio is more important than video performance. Invest some money to purchase a good microphone and a videoconference lamp. Using a virtual background is perfectly fine. You could consider creating one as a branding opportunity.

Step 3: Check your Wi-Fi/internet and your equipment prior to your pitch

Technology is flawed, and there is always a chance for some form of failure during a presentation. Before your presentation, test your Wi-Fi connection, ensuring that the connection is stable; if the connection proves unstable, try connecting to an ethernet port if one is available. Ensure you have a fast internet connection, especially if you have many participants and plan to share visually rich content or stream videos (this is easy to check through a free online speed test; anything less than 60 Mb/sec is at risk of failure). In addition, check the computer or mobile device you plan to use for the pitch to ensure the web camera and microphone are operational. In the event of a failure, we recommend you have ready a backup webcam (with microphone) and an alternate laptop or other mobile device.

Step 4: Practice, Practice, Practice

If you plan to pitch as a team, practice as a team to develop a pitch centered on sharing the spotlight. Know each other's strengths in talking about the product and plan around that. Conversely, if you plan to pitch as an individual, practice your pitch as an individual. Ensure your pitch answers the six questions that every pitch should have. Be sure to practice your pitch to as many individuals as possible. Feedback at this point is critical before you run your pitch with potential investors. Record and rewatch yourself and find out what can be improved.

Step 5: Engage with your investors

One of the challenges that video calling platforms have created is a phenomenon known as "Zoom fatigue." Zoom fatigue is the exhaustion you feel after a video call or conference (White, 2021). The phenomenon of social distancing during the early phases of the COVID-19 pandemic, with the resulting increase in videoconferencing and calls, has resulted in society in general feeling "Zoomed out." There is sometimes an unwillingness to remain connected on long or repetitive Zoom calls. As a result, you must find ways to engage your investors to ensure your product and your pitch stand out. When pitching to more than 93 investors, ContainIQ adopted a strategy of asking questions throughout the presentation. Some of the sample questions that were asked were:

- Before the call, did you get a chance to look at our deck, website, etc.?
- Could I give you some background on myself and my cofounder?
- Have you invested in any companies in similar or tangential spaces?
- Are any of your portfolio companies using [insert related technology/software/product here]?
- How much do you know about the total addressable market?

This strategy keeps investors engaged during the pitch and even encourages open conversations. Can this approach eat up time from the pitch? It can, but it can also create a favorable experience for your investors. We recommend attempting this sparingly.

4.7   Conclusion

Crafting an effective business pitch is both an art and a science. It's not just about meeting specific criteria but about presenting a compelling story that convinces others to believe in your vision and your product. The ability to pitch effectively is crucial for securing funding and support to bring your products to life. In this chapter, we delved into the intricacies of pitching, exploring various models and techniques to master this skill. We focused mainly on the underlying principles and theories of good pitching. Once you understand the fundamentals, you will be in the ideal position to effectively use the many online and offline tutorials and tools.

We began by acknowledging the allure of shows like *Shark Tank*, which glamorizes entrepreneurship and pitching. TV pitches teach us that a pitch must be entertaining and have a storytelling component centered on emotional factors and the speaker's personality. A pitch is about not just what you do but how you present your business and yourself and how much your story resonates with the listeners.

The fundamental pitch model involves answering six key questions that provide an overview of your business or product to potential investors or customers. Remember that these are just the essential ingredients, not the recipe. The recipe is packaging and delivering these elements in a cogent and short narrative.

Additionally, we emphasized the importance of value proposition, as it encapsulates how your product helps customers do more affordably, conveniently, or effectively what they already try to do. Understanding the context of value creation regarding affordability, convenience, effectiveness, and customers' motivation and urgency to solve *their* problem allows for a deeper understanding of and connection with your target audience. At the same time, articulating your value proposition following the job metaphor approach will help you and your team achieve a deeper level of analysis and insight into customers' problems and how you will help them. Such an exercise provides another opportunity for you to rethink your offering creatively.

Furthermore, we discussed the different forms of pitches entrepreneurs engage in, ranging from direct requests to co-creative endeavors. Each pitch type serves a specific purpose and requires understanding the dynamics of building relationships with potential stakeholders. Additionally, as virtual presentations become more prevalent, we offered tips to ensure a successful online pitch, from choosing the right platform to engaging with investors effectively to combating Zoom fatigue.

Finally, a good pitch results from the same design thinking cycle described in Chapter 1. By following the empathize-ideate-prototype path, through a few iterations if needed, you can frame your pitch in the customer's language using the value proposition framework, test your pitch by getting early feedback from friendly but honest listeners, and finally prototype your pitch, using technology to help if needed. As in baseball, you will pitch a lot but strike less than you pitch, so keep failure into account and learn as you go through it. You will never pitch twice the same way!

Key takeaways for this chapter

Lesson learned	Implications for your entrepreneurial project
People don't buy what you do, people buy why you do it	• A pitch is a story, a way to connect emotionally and rationally with your listeners. Given the limited amount of available time, you cannot go over technical pros and cons and other details. Your objectives are to provide a clear and concise picture of what you are doing and get your listeners interested to know more about it.
Building blocks and tricks	• Use a checklist to make sure you are not forgetting about any of the fundamental ingredients of a pitch. Make sure you have a clear and consequential ask aligned with your progress. • Use the job metaphor to address the problem and the solution from your customers' point of view. Ask yourself why someone should "hire your product." Take this opportunity to reflect on your proposal and revisit it in creative ways. • Focus on your product's distinctive value driver, why it is better than other solutions, and why you are uniquely qualified to make it.
Experiment and practice	• You won't get it right the first time, and probably not even the second or third time. Like anything else in this book, a good craft requires iteration and experimentation across the empathize-ideate-prototype cycle. The prototype this time is the pitch itself. • Learn from failure and collect feedback, then go back and revise. • Practice a lot, until you can do it on autopilot. At that point, your words will come out naturally and you will be able to focus on how to engage with your listeners, as opposed to "performing" the presentation.

In conclusion, pitching effectively is an essential skill for entrepreneurs seeking success. It involves combining artistry with scientific precision, understanding the needs of your audience, and presenting your product or service in a way that resonates deeply. By mastering the various elements and forms of pitching, entrepreneurs can navigate the competitive landscape and secure the resources necessary to bring their visions to fruition.

References

CBInsights. (2021). ContainIQ. *CBInsights*. www.cbinsights.com/company/containiq

Christensen, C. M., Grossman, J. H., & Hwang, J. (2009). *The innovator's prescription*. McGraw-Hill.

CNBC. (2022). Shark tank about. *CNBC.com*. www.cnbc.com/shark-tank-about/

Dew, N., Ramesh, A., Read, S., & Sarasvathy, S. (2018). Toward deliberate practice in the development of entrepreneurial expertise: The anatomy of the effectual ask. In K. Ericsson, R. Hoffman, A. Kozbelt, & A. Williams (Eds.), *The Cambridge handbook of expertise and expert performance* (*Cambridge handbooks in psychology*) (pp. 389–412). Cambridge University Press.

FINTECH INSHORTS (2021). CONTAINIQ: Raises $2.5M in seed funding. https://www.fintechinshorts.com/containiq-raises-2-5m-in-seed-funding/

The Investopedia Team. (2023). *Target market: Definition, purpose, examples, market segments*. https://www.investopedia.com/terms/t/target-market.asp#:~:text=A%20target%20market%20is%20a,age%2C%20income%2C%20and%20lifestyle

Kabbage American Express. (2022). The top 10 borrowed sums success stories. *Kabbage.com*. www.kabbage.com/resource-center/finance/best-borrowed-sums-business/

Kubernetes. (2023). https://kubernetes.io

Leibovich, M. (2000). Child prodigy, online pioneer. *The Washington Post*. www.washingtonpost.com/archive/politics/2000/09/03/child-prodigy-online-pioneer/2ab207dc-d13a-4204-8949-493686e43415/

Mitchell, R. K. (2007). The central question in entrepreneurial cognition research. *Entrepreneurship Theory and Practice*, 1–27.

Pagliarini, R. (2006). What is an elevator pitch? *American Venture*, 31.

Phipps-Morgan, A. (2022). The art of online pitching: How to nail your next virtual presentation. *Pitch.com*. https://pitch.com/blog/art-of-online-pitching

Robinson, R. (2017). 5 crowdfunded side projects that became million-dollar companies. *Forbes.com*. www.forbes.com/sites/ryanrobinson/2017/09/18/crowdfunded-side-projects-that-became-million-dollar-companies/?sh=459a837b3f1d

Rossette-Crake, F. (2019). *Public speaking and the new oratory: A guide for non-native speakers*. Palgrave Macmillan Cham.

Sinek, S. (2009). How great sleaders inspire action. *TED Talk*. www.ted.com/talks/simon_sinek_how_great_leaders_inspire_action?language=en, last accessed August 2023.

White, T. (2021). 'Zoom Fatigue' is real – Here's how to cope (and make it through your next meeting). Healthline.com. https://www.healthline.com/health/zoom-fatigue, last accessed 2023.

Chapter 5

Creative confidence, part 2

Make it! The importance of prototyping

If you build it, they will come.
—Kevin Costner playing Ray Kinsella in the movie *Field of Dreams* (1989)

5.1 There is a maker superhero in each of us

In 2008, Marvel Studios produced the first film in its Marvel Cinematic Universe, *Iron Man* (Marvel Studios, 2021). *Iron Man* tells the story of Tony Stark, a billionaire industrialist and genius inventor who is kidnapped, held in a cave, and forced to build a devastating weapon. Instead, using his intelligence and ingenuity, Tony makes a high-tech suit of armor and escapes captivity. An hour and 40 minutes into the film, there is a scene where Tony rapidly develops a suit of armor to escape his captives. Known as the Mark I, it is crude and limited, built using the limited tools and resources he had at the time, such as simple tools and metal scraps (Fandom.com, 2020). The Mark I, in a way, was the prototype of the final Iron Man suit (see Figure 5.1). The story of the Iron Man Mark I prototype reflects the spirit of early prototyping, in which you develop a "blueprint" and use whatever you can find to make it real as soon as possible, even with limited resources and investment. The Iron Man armor evolved in subsequent films, creating new iterations like the Mark II and Mark III.

We can also approach Tony Stark's experience in building the Mark I prototype as a metaphor for the experience many entrepreneurs have during the prototyping process. Parallel to Tony's experience, entrepreneurs may feel pressure from many factors that could hinder them in developing their prototypes. Those factors include a lack of time, limited resources, and even a lack of technical and practical knowledge to accomplish the task. In Tony's case, captors threatened his life and available resources in the cave were less than ideal for what he wanted to build. On top of that, he needed more time to mockup and test the rapidly developed Mark 1 armor. While these factors could hinder the successful execution of prototypes, we have also found that prototype development can be successful in these moments of compression and that rushing your idea into something, even when you do not feel ready, has more benefits than costs.

Tony's imprisonment in a cave when developing the Mark 1 Armor presents another metaphor; sometimes, we might be in the dark when developing prototypes for the first time. We sometimes start in a place where the factors that could make the prototype work are not apparent. In a way, each of us begins in a metaphorical cave. Prototypes become easier to develop, refine, and reproduce through prototype iteration. This process of prototype iteration can eventually provide us with the metaphorical light needed to escape our "cave."

DOI: 10.4324/9781003346463-6

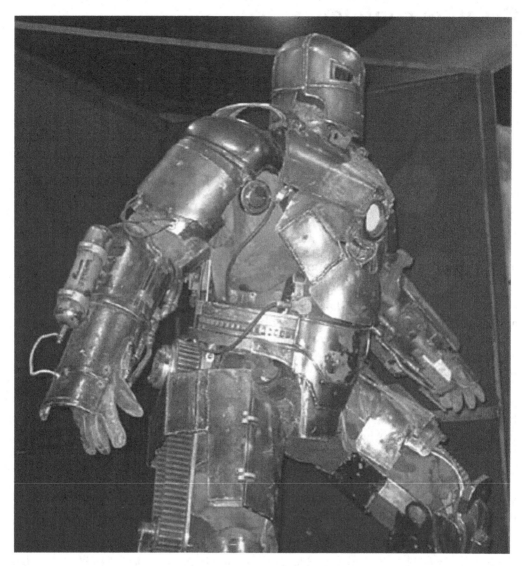

Figure 5.1 Iron Man Mark I Concept: the "prototype."

Source: Wikimedia Commons

To a certain extent, as innovators and entrepreneurs, we are all on a path to creating our version of a Mark I prototype with our ideas. Although we may not be a genius or a billionaire like Tony Stark (let alone being held captive by a villain), we all can build prototypes. The questions are: What type of prototype can we develop? What are the benefits of early and iterative prototyping? How do we do it?

This chapter answers these questions to transform you into an avid maker.

5.2 Prototyping as emotional design

Before we dive into the different types of prototyping, we need to understand how emotions may play a role in the design process. During fall 2020, early in the COVID-19 pandemic, one of the authors taught an undergraduate course in creativity and innovation at St. John's University. Social distancing meant everyone was forced to take classes online synchronously. After the students split up into teams and developed their initial ideas for products or businesses, they reached the week where it was time to "make it real" with a rapid prototype. Almost everyone in the class froze; the reason for this was interesting. Many students were not design or engineering majors, so they asked, "How do we prototype?" Teaching this was a new challenge for us. Another critical aspect was being forced to interact with the instructors and other team members solely online and without physical access to the university labs and makers' spaces. It was a moment of pure anxiety.

We decided it would be sufficient to encourage students by telling them that prototyping is a big word that reflects humans' spontaneous and natural abilities and behaviors. Each student brings a set of skills and experiences that make them ready to create a simple prototype. For example, as toddlers, many of us are exposed to toys and drawing instruments, like Legos and crayons. During our formative years, we built or drew things and created stories for the things we created, using only our imaginations. This process allowed us to develop value around the things we made.

Some nurture those skills into design or engineering careers or hobbies as we grow up, but many people neglect their personality's playful and creative side. Regardless, the history of human evolution and anthropological studies clearly show that the ability to make and use tools has shaped human nature and society (Ingold, 2013; Leroi-Gourhan, 1964). This ability is also clearly reflected in our development as individuals, especially at a very young age, when we build from ideas, create complex artifacts, and, more important, tell stories about the things we make. We refer to this with the expression building a prototype for our purposes.

Storytelling and prototyping go together and are critical in the Human-Centered Design process. For example, look around the room right now and notice the various products around you. Pick one of those items and quickly define its purpose, then think back to your experience with the item. Recall stories you can attach to it and stories about what you might do with it. Was the experience positive or negative? What feelings/emotions come to mind? What memories do you associate with this object? Almost everyone can connect emotionally to some product. There is meaning/purpose in its very existence (Norman, 2004).

Emotional design applies to technological devices as well. Let us pick the Amazon Alexa device many of us have in our living rooms. Growing up, we thought it would be cool to say, "Computer, what is the weather like today?" Fast forward to now, when we can ask that question and many more. The Alexa device responds with a human-sounding voice and answers: "In New York City, it is 80 degrees Fahrenheit. It will be partly cloudy tonight. Expect a low of 63 degrees." While we know Alexa is just an algorithm, we interact with it as if it had a personality and an identity. Alexa developers have done their best to humanize their design by programming it to tell jokes and adding the possibility of some funny ways to answer questions. Even one of the most advanced technologies available today has an "emotional design" side that many people respond to with joy.

5.3   Why do we prototype?

There are other reasons why we prototype that complement what was previously discussed. The process of developing prototypes requires time, patience, and effort. Entrepreneurs often spend significant time creating, testing, and retesting iterations of a single prototype. The process will seem repetitive at times, and it should be. It is improbable (if not impossible) to get the "right" prototype on your first try.

Prototypes are developed with the strategic intent to support entrepreneurs within the product development process in a few ways (Björklund et al., 2017). First, they provide us with a concrete way to easily communicate our ideas physically and digitally. Second, the action of prototyping often leads to experimentation. Experimentation is done to fine-tune a design iteration by alternating rapid tests of our prototypes with users and developing new versions as improvements are identified. This level of experimentation aims to produce small wins for entrepreneurs. Small wins are "a series of controllable opportunities of modest size that produce visible results" (Weick, 1984) discovered in the prototypes we create. Successful execution of prototypes produces small wins. Small wins lead to individualized self-efficacy, which can provide a framework for eventual success.

It is equally important to be mindful that emotion plays a massive role during the prototyping process, this time from the user's point of view. As mentioned in Chapter 1, in the Human-Centered Design process, we develop products that support people's needs. Therefore, we must understand their emotions and motivations for wanting the product and find a way to keep the product design centered on them.

Amanda O'Grady, a design strategist at Intuit and contributor at UX Magazine, in her article "Designing with Emotion Means Being Brave," takes it one step further and argues the following: "Emotional connections are two-way streets. Evoking real and meaningful emotion from our customers requires that we, as designers, bring real and meaningful emotion to the table, too." (O'Grady, 2015). O'Grady makes a case that when we design a prototype, we must keep three things in mind (see Figure 5.2).

Figure 5.2 The Three Acts of Bravery to Increase Emotion for Customers

Source: Adapted from (O'Grady, 2015)

When we design a prototype for our customers, we must engage their emotional needs to connect with them. We often witness our customers' attitudes and feelings about a product during our discovery process, so we must keep their feelings, attitudes, and beliefs in mind. According to O'Grady, we must protect our design from being lost by designing for all stakeholders (customers and shareholders), creating our prototype with boldness, and developing our prototype around our customers, not the product. Now that we have learned what prototyping is, let us explore a few ways to prototype.

Prototypes are essential for designers' teams since they support cognitive, collaborative, and emotional visualizations (Passera, 2017). By visualizing and interacting with an artifact, we can better understand how the prototype works and are more likely to have insights on what to improve (cognitive level). Physical and empirical interactions with the material give us a better emotional assessment of our creation (emotional level). Prototyping with others, such as users, customers, or our fellow designers, helps us to get better feedback because we talk *through* something, as opposed to the information we could get by talking *about* something in the abstract.

5.4 Low-fidelity prototyping

In this next section, we go over several ways of prototyping. Many of these are geared to early and rapid prototyping. Depending on your skill level, you may push the boundaries of what you wish to design. As with customer interviews, when building a prototype, you must remember your customers' problems and what they are looking for in the solution. During the next phase, be prepared to test the prototype with customers again (and again). Most research into prototyping indicates that we should start with low-fidelity prototypes. While high-fidelity prototypes are built to ensure a solution works, low-fidelity prototypes are artifacts created to test how well we understand a problem.

Low-fidelity prototypes are early and minimalistic versions of our products and exhibit minimum functionalities. However, they must still be built by defining a set of minimal specifications regarding visual design, content, and interactivity. In Figure 5.3, the example is the development of a smartwatch. We could create a version of the watch with some simple and inexpensive materials just for the sake of testing its look and feel (visual design), some basic form of interaction such as ways to wear the watch, and perhaps simulating the smartwatch applications through content displayed via some other medium, such as a storyboard or other visualization. At a very early stage, we might need more time and money to develop software that works on the watch. Our objective in these early stages could be more focused on figuring out alternative ways to wear and use the watch compared to the ones that are already existing.

In Chapters 6 through 9, we provide plenty of suggestions on how to identify and scale up this minimal set, depending on what we want to test and learn and the level of complexity of the final product.

Low-fidelity prototypes have many advantages (Babich, 2017) (Pernice, 2016):

1. Low-cost: These prototypes are often made on paper, with simple and inexpensive materials, or through more expensive but still inexpensive digital rendition via PowerPoint and website builders like Wix.com and Adobe Dreamweaver.
2. Fast: Making a low-fidelity prototype can be done with little effort. Many of our students made new prototypes in a few hours.

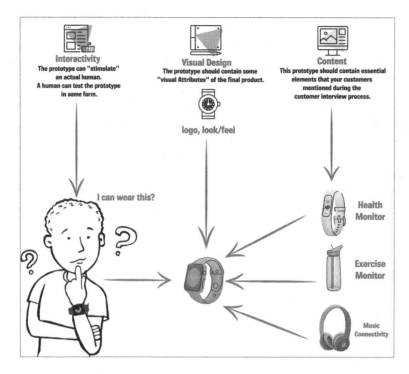

Figure 5.3 Low-Fidelity Prototyping Example

Source: Adapted from (Babich, 2017), (JUSTINMIND, 2021)

3. Collaborative: Low-fidelity prototyping is a great way to work together in the design process and use clarify the design and the prototype.
4. Scalability: Low-fidelity prototyping allows designers to test hypotheses before significant investment is made to build a high-fidelity prototype of the final product.

Low-fidelity prototypes are used in the first part of the double-diamond design process (see Figure 3.1) when the objective is to build the right thing (as opposed to creating something right, which is the objective of the second step).

Unfortunately, low-fidelity prototyping has some limitations. The main one is that it may take more work for the customer to fully understand the product and what it is supposed to do. It may take a deeper level of explanation and a little more imagination from the user. Remember, low-fidelity prototypes typically have limited functionality, so we, as designers, must be aware of our and our users' expectations during early testing.

Let us now look at some techniques to build low-fidelity prototypes.

5.4.1 Paper prototyping

Paper prototyping uses paper (either physical or virtual) to develop low-fidelity prototypes. Typically, you can use paper to prototype in three ways.

- Drawing consists of sketching a visualization of the product you want to design.
- Wireframing consists of taking individual drawings you have created and establishing a structure and narrative of how a product works.
- Physical prototyping consists of using actual paper to develop a prototype.

If you are thinking of paper prototyping, we recommend exploring UIstencils.com, which has several tools that will assist you in the drawing phase of your prototype.

Depending on what product or solution you are trying to develop, drawing can be a great way to initiate the process. For example, if you are working on a mobile app, you could draw a phone with an example of what the app may look like on screen. If you are building a physical product, then you would be expected to draw a mockup of that product. Drawing a prototype requires the least amount of technical skill; however, it can be decisive when you take your intangible thoughts and visualize them in a way that allows others to begin the critiquing process.

At this phase of development, drawing your prototype allows you the chance to put your imagination into your work. Feel free to explore every possibility at this phase without worrying too much about practical limitations in your final design.

Wireframing is a technique you can use on paper or in digital prototyping tools like web or app design platforms. Wireframing asks that you build a narrative about your user experience with your product. Let us take the example of building a mobile app. While showing an example of the app's main page is helpful (Figure 5.4), creating multiple images that show a user experience is even more beneficial to selling your prototype.

Finally, if you build a physical product, you can also consider developing a physical prototype with paper and cardboard. Creating a physical prototype is more adventurous. It allows you to theorize what the final physical product might look like. A great example would be the development of the Nintendo Wii U. The Nintendo Wii U was a gaming console centered on creating the user's ability to play games on a TV or directly on the gamepad controller.

During the Wii U's development, to get a sense of how the gamepad controller would feel in someone's hands, the lead designer, Kazuyuki Motoyama, developed a rapid product prototype to showcase to the president of Nintendo, Satoru Iwata (Figure 5.4). Iwata chuckled at the prototype, mainly because it was made of cardboard. According to Motoyama: "We would not know how it felt unless we could actually hold it, but since we did not have one,

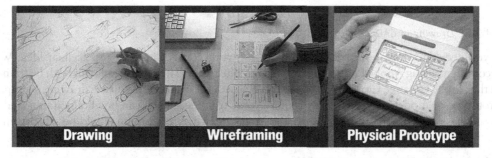

Figure 5.4 Three versions of paper prototyping. From left to right: drawing, wireframing, and physical prototype.

Sources: iStockphoto and (Nintendo, 2012).

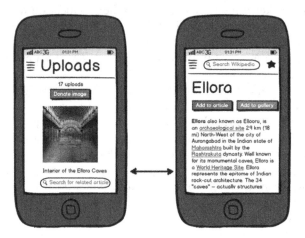

Figure 5.5 A Sample Wireframe

the only thing to do was make one. In the middle of the night, I cut pieces of cardboard and glued them together" (Nintendo, 2012). Holding this cardboard prototype gave the president a sense of what the product would feel like. Iwata recalled, "It holds differently than a tablet, and the screen size is not like that of an iPad or smartphone" (Nintendo, 2012). Although the Wii U received mixed reviews, the console was praised for its innovative design and approach (Langley, 2014). Eventually, the Wii U design provided a framework for the Wii U successor, the Nintendo Switch, released in 2017.

5.4.2   Computer-aided design

Computer-aided design or CAD—digital modeling—is the use of computers to aid in creating, modifying, analyzing, or optimizing a design (Narayan, 2008). CAD is another way to develop a prototype at any stage when used effectively. Suppose you are starting with your prototype. CAD is a great way to experiment with taking a paper prototype into a more three-dimensional model. This section reviews a few online programs and approaches you can use to explore CAD.

5.4.2.1   Drawing in CAD

If you decide to draw your prototype, digitizing your concept may be an excellent idea. We recommend using Adobe Photoshop and Adobe Illustrator. These programs can both be found in the Adobe Creative Cloud Suite. They can be used, for instance, if you are drawing a simple prototype or modeling a logo. They require some training, which can be obtained in a traditional class or through other mediums like YouTube, whereby training would be self-driven.

5.4.2.2   Mobile app development in CAD

What if you are designing a mobile app? There are plenty of tools that are already out there that support young designers in their quest to create an app. Many of these tools do not require any coding experience. How can you build an app without coding? This is a question that our students ask us all the time. Honestly, it is a valid question and a point of contention. In the app development world, there is a notion that people who know how to code are the only ones building apps. This statement is not exactly true; it takes a team of individuals full of people with coding and noncoding experience build some of the world's best apps. Before an app is coded, its concept must be designed, wireframed, and reviewed. This is where good design and understanding of the user experience are essential.

App prototyping tools make app design more straightforward and more accessible for the noncoder because they focus on the app's look, "feel," and user navigation. Once you have your app's interface and workflow right, you can move to code so that the app can actually work. New "no-code" software like Marvel, JUSTINMIND, and Figma makes it easier for anyone to prototype an app. In addition, the Adobe Creative Suite has Adobe XD, which is excellent for digital wireframing and user experiences, especially in mobile apps. An app cannot work without code behind it, but these tools allow you to visualize and even test with users the appearance and navigation features of an app. For instance, you can install one of these "fake apps" on an actual phone and ask users to navigate the various screens and functionalities to measure how much they like it and find it easy to use.

The concept of no-code programming is not new. One of the best-known no-code tools is Microsoft Excel, launched in 1985 (Formstack, 2021). However, the use of no-code programs and software has risen over the past few years. In fact, it has been reported that "71% of individuals choose to use no-code tools" because of their speed and ease of use (Formstack, 2021). According to Formstack (2021), no-code software development allows anyone to create digital applications without writing a single line of code. It involves using tools with an intuitive, drag-and-drop interface to create a unique solution to a problem. The resulting solution can take many forms—from building mobile, voice, or e-commerce apps and websites to automating tasks or processes. What has further accelerated this trend was the COVID-19 pandemic in 2020. The pandemic changed how many of us work, forcing many to work remotely, and eliminating traditional paper processes. The world scrambled to adjust and become more digital.

5.4.3 3D printing

Another way to do physical prototyping is 3D printing. The 3D Printing Industry website defines 3D printing as making a physical object from a three-dimensional digital model, typically by laying down many successive thin layers of material via a computer-controlled printer (3D Printing Industry, 2017). 3D printing is a little more complex for low-fidelity and high-fidelity prototyping. It may require knowledge of CAD programs and 3D printers. This section explores the basics.

The 3D printing workflow involves locating a 3D model on a website like Thingiverse. com or building a file on a platform likeTinkercad.com, modifying the file in a CAD program, exporting the file to an STL or OBJ file, loading the file into the native software for the printer, and finally printing it.

You must have a design developed from a CAD program or reuse an existing design available on a free online repository. There are dozens and dozens of different CAD programs available online for free, and you can find most of them through a simple Google search. The one program we recommend for individuals who have just started prototyping is Autodesk's Tinkercad. Tinkercad offers a manageable platform that allows anyone to dive into 3D modeling. Free and easy to use, Tinkercad introduces novice designers and engineers to the foundations

Figure 5.6 3D Printing

of innovation: 3D design, electronics, and coding (Autodesk Tinkercad, 2021). No matter what program you choose, be sure to export your design into the correct export file, like an OBJ, STL, or GLTF file. You will need this file at some point to print your design.

Once you have experimented with a design, you can print your design. There are many different types of 3D printers, and they are becoming more and more affordable. Brands like Prusa, Makerbots, and Utilmakers are commonly used with early prototypes because they work quickly and efficiently (fun fact: Prusa printers are shipped disassembled, and their parts are 3D printed!). There is another advantage to 3D printing: if a printer fails to print a particular part, it indicates what part of the design might need additional work.

The 3D printer work by heating materials known as filaments, allowing the filament to be extruded from the machine. The most common material is PLA, polylactic acid, which is used to make simple prototypes. The versatility of 3D printers means they can print materials of different types and qualities, from plastic to metals (see Table 5.2 for the most used materials). Environmentally friendly filaments are available and should be preferred to nonbiodegradable plastic.

One final concern if you choose to 3D print a prototype is how to access a printer. One option is to buy a printer. Printers range in price from a few hundred dollars to thousands, depending on the type of materials they support, their size, and speed. For students or faculty, another viable option is to ask your university IT department if there are any 3D printers you can use. Finally, if you're working independently, you can use an online, on-demand 3D printing service such as Shapeways (www.shapeways.com). Typically, you can send these companies the 3D file with your design and have it printed at one of their facilities and shipped directly to you.

Table 5.2 Commonly used filament materials for 3D printing. Adapted from (ALL3DP, 2021).

Material	Pros	Cons
PLA (polylactic acid): known as the king of materials in 3D printing. Most commonly used.	Easy to print, wide variety of colors/styles, biodegradable	Brittle, lackluster mechanical properties
ABS (acrylonitrile butadiene styrene): moderately superior to PLA, most commonly used in household goods	High strength, high durability, resistant to high temperatures	Warps easily, hazardous fumes, requires a high-temperature print nozzle
PET (polyethylene terephthalate): a very commonly used plastic, best known for applications in water bottles, clothing fibers, etc.	Flexible, durable, easy to print	Susceptible to moisture, surface scratches easily
TPE (thermoplastic elastomers): plastics with rubber-like qualities, extremely flexible and durable, mostly used in automotive parts, household appliances, and medical supplies.	Extremely flexible, perfect for parts that bend or compress	Difficult to print, requires tight filament path and slow print speed
Nylon: a popular family of synthetic polymers used in many industrial applications, it is a go-to in powder-fusion methods of 3D printing. It excels in 3D printing where strength, flexibility, and durability are key requirements.	High strength, high flexibility, high durability	Typically expensive, susceptible to moisture, requires high nozzle and print bed temperature
PC (polycarbonate): one of the strongest filaments, it is extremely durable and resistant to both physical impact and heat, able to withstand temperatures of up to 110°C. It's also naturally transparent.	Extremely strong, resistant to heat and physical impact	Susceptible to moisture, requires very high print temperature

5.5   High-fidelity prototyping

High-fidelity prototypes are built to appear and function similarly to the actual product that will be available to the public (Babich, 2017). Like low-fidelity prototyping, high-fidelity prototyping focuses on visual design, content, and interaction. What differs is the level of detail and functionalities the prototype offers. A high-fidelity prototype is typically developed after several iterations of low-fidelity prototypes have been tested. As shown in the double-diamond design model, you must iterate and alternate divergent and convergent thinking when creating high-fidelity prototypes. The difference between low- and high-fidelity prototyping is that you have an excellent understanding of the problem in this process stage, and the prototyping iterations are needed to perfect the solution.

High-fidelity prototypes should exhibit the following characteristics (Babich, 2017, Pernice, 2016):

1. **Meaningful Feedback:** With a high-fidelity prototype, it is possible to get "raw," natural reactions from users who see an almost final product.
2. **Easy Buy-In from Clients:** You present this prototype to shareholders and stakeholders to get buy-in.

There are a few issues with high-fidelity prototyping. High-fidelity prototypes are time-consuming and costly. As mentioned, high-fidelity prototypes typically come after several iterations of low-fidelity prototypes. Depending on the complexity, getting to a high-fidelity prototype can take a long time. Building high-fidelity prototypes often requires dedicated funding, additional knowledge, and coding or engineering skills. Before engaging with building a high-fidelity prototype, ensure you can procure the necessary financial and technical resources.

5.6   Conclusions

Prototyping is one of the most engaging activities in the Human-Centered Design process. When building a prototype, we examine what elements are essential to our customers. In this case, we must connect with our customers emotionally, understanding their problems and how our product or service would solve their problems. There are many ways to develop a prototype. We must be willing to rapidly prototype with the tools in front of us. Paper and 3D printing offer us different routes to building a low-fidelity prototype, and with the rise of no-code tools and software, we can start prototyping digitally. As we attempt to develop a high-fidelity prototype, we must prepare the resources needed to achieve our goal. We can all build prototypes, and just like Tony Stark, we can start with our Mark 1.

Key takeaways for this chapter

Lesson learned	Implications for your entrepreneurial project
Find the maker superhero in you	• Do not be scared about building things. Making is a way to express your ideas so that others can have better access to them. Do not be intimidated by a lack of skills or quality concerns. Early-stage prototypes do not have to work; they are just a way to better understand the problem you are trying to solve. • Making is exciting! Building tools is part of human nature and it is one of the most powerful ways through which we interact with the world and learn. • Technology is a means to an end; tools can be acquired and skills can be learned.
The right prototype at the right time	• Early-stage prototypes are not designed to see if your solution works but to test if you understand your users' problems. Do not overdesign them; instead, adopt a very low-cost approach to their implementation. Use them to have more informative conversations with your prospective users. Remember that in this stage, the objective is *designing the right thing*. • High-fidelity prototypes can be designed when you have a very good understanding of the problem and to test if your solution works as it should. Details are now important, and more financial and technical resources may be necessary to build them. This is when you need to *design the thing right*.
Learn prototyping skills and tools	• There are many tools available; some are free. Pick the right tool for the right phase of your development. • Do not underestimate the importance of acquiring prototyping skills. Do not be scared to venture into domains with which you are not familiar. Again, technology is a tool, and skills can be learned.

References

3D Printing Industry. (2017). The free beginner's guide. *3D Printing Industry*. https://3dprintingindustry. com/3d-printing-basics-free-beginners-guide/

ALL3DP. (2021). Best 3D printer filament – The ultimate guide. *ALL3DP*, June 21. https://all3dp. com/1/3d-printer-filament-types-3d-printing-3d-filament/

Autodesk Tinkercad. (2021). Tinkercad | Create 3D digital designs with online CAD. *Tinkercad*, September 1. Tinkercad.com

Babich, N. (2017). Prototyping 101: The difference between low-fidelity and high-fidelity prototypes and when to use each. *Adobe Blog*, November 29. https://blog.adobe.com/en/2017/11/29/ prototyping-difference-low-fidelity-high-fidelity-prototypes-use.html#gs.9kgg47

Björklund, T., Laakso, M., Kirjavainen, S., & Ekman, K. (2017). *Passion-based co-creation*. Aalto University.

Dam, R. F., & Siang, T. Y. (2020). Design thinking: Get started with prototyping. *Interaction Design Foundation*. www.interaction-design.org/literature/article/design-thinking-get-started-with-prototyping

Fandom.com. (2020). Iron Man Mark I | Iron Man Wiki | Fandom. *Iron Man Wiki*. https://ironman. fandom.com/wiki/Iron_Man_Mark_I

Formstack. (2021). Rise of the no-code economy | Formstack. *Formstack*, June. https://resources. formstack.com/reports/rise-of-the-no-code-economy

Ingold, T. (2013). *Making: Anthropology, archaeology, art and architecture*. Routledge.

JUSTINMIND. (2021). Low vs high fidelity prototypes: A complete breakdown. *JUSTINMIND*, February 1. www.justinmind.com/blog/low-fidelity-vs-high-fidelity-prototypes/

Langley, H. (2014). Nintendo Wii U review. *TechRadar*, May 16. www.techradar.com/reviews/ gaming/games-consoles/nintendo-wii-u-1113919/review

Leroi-Gourhan. (1964). *Le geste et la parole. Technique et language*. Albin Michel.

Marvel Studios. (2021). Iron Man (2008) | Cast, release date, Villians. *Marvel*. www.marvel.com/ movies/iron-man

Narayan, K. L. (2008). *Computer aided design and manufacturing*. Prentice Hall of India.

Nintendo. (2012). Iwata asks: Wii U: Miiverse: The producers: A browser made for a gaming console. *Nintendo.com*. https://iwataasks.nintendo.com/interviews/#/wiiu/miiverse2/0/0

Norman, D. A. (2004). *Emotional design: Why we love (or hate) everyday things*. Civitas Books.

O'Grady, A. (2015). Designing with emotion means being brave. *UX Magazine*, July 15. https:// uxmag.com/articles/designing-with-emotion-means-being-brave

Passera, S. (2017). Show, don't tell!: Conceptualizing and sharing abstract knowledge. In: Bjorklund T, Laakso M, Kirjavainen S, et al. (eds) *Passion-Based Co-Creation*. Espoo: Aalto University, pp. 38–49.

Pernice, K. (2016). UX prototypes: Low fidelity vs. high fidelity. *NN/g Nielsen Norman Group*, December 18. www.nngroup.com/articles/ux-prototype-hi-lo-fidelity

Weick, K. E. (1984). Small wins: Redefining the scale of social problems. *American Psychologist*, 39(1), 40–49. https://doi.org/10.1037/0003-066X.39.1.40/

Chapter 6

The agile entrepreneur

Iterate, iterate, and iterate again!

[The] process took six months, with breaks the whole recording took one year, most of which went for a single song, "Born to Run." Sometimes from 9 am to 6 am. We spent days just in trying the sound of instruments and amplifiers. He [Springsteen] would just pick up the guitar, stare at the floor and say "Again . . . again . . . again."

—Nils Lofgren, interview in Springsteen (2005)

6.1 The ambiguity challenge

Born To Run was the disc that launched Bruce Springsteen into rock stardom when he was only 26. Released in 1975, the album was an instant success, but it had a long gestation period, one whole year of extended rehearsals and recording sessions, and multiple creative crises made worse by significant and unexpected changes in the production team and the band (Springsteen, 2005).

The inspiration for the album came from Springsteen's interest in old B-movies, from which he took the song titles "Born to Run" and "Thunder Road." Most recording sessions were spent refining the initial musical "hunch" through intense remixing and editing. Springsteen reports that the music was composed "very, very meticulously, [and] so were the words. I wrote, then I rewrote it, then I rewrote it. . . . What I kept stripping away was cliché, . . . until it started to feel like emotionally real." Bassist David Sancious, a member of Springsteen's E Street Band who participated in the recording of the album, said that the lyrics "went from being very dense verbally" to "more sparse, more concise . . . [to] say the same things but using less words." Springsteen went from the convoluted and manneristic lyrics of his earlier songs such as *Blinded by the Light* (1973) to the epic poetry and immediacy of "Thunder Road."

Springsteen was trying to solve a fundamental design dilemma: escaping cliches by creating something novel and fresh while offering people familiar feelings and mental imagery they could understand and relate to.

The music of *Born to Run* was composed through layering, a technology that is today seldom used. Through this method, instrumental layers are laid one over the other (over-dubbing). The arrangements were made by adding and removing sounds, allowing for a lot of instrumental experimentation (e.g., drums, acoustic and electric guitars, bass, piano and keyboards, glockenspiel, saxophones, even a little piece of an orchestra) and including sounds such as car racing. David Sancious states, "The idea was to build a wall of sound by adding and removing."

This trial-and-error process took six months; with breaks, the whole recording took one year, most of which went for a single song, "Born to Run." The band and the technicians

DOI: 10.4324/9781003346463-7

would relentlessly work every day, sometimes in monster sessions going from 9 a.m. to 6 a.m. the next morning and spend days trying the sound of various instruments and amplifiers. Springsteen asked bassist Gary Tallent and drummer Max Weinberg to play very simply, but also very solidly. This was a major change because, as guitarist Nils Lofgren recalls,

> We were a band for which hyperactivity was a business. Our way of playing in the first two records was wildly eccentric, a fabulous style that perfectly fitted the eccentric qualities of those two records. Still, by the time we came to 'Born to Run,' everything on 'Born to Run' was lining down: lyrics, rhythm sections, the whole thing was pulled down in a slightly more aesthetic direction.
>
> (Springsteen, 2005)

The same obsessive compositional attention was given to each part of the song. To create the magnificent saxophone solo in "Jungleland," Clarence Clemons spent sixteen hours standing at the microphone, working on every single note.

The making of *Born to Run* is an exemplary and familiar story of how creativity unfolds behind the scenes, with many lessons learned that can be applied to creating innovative products. In this chapter, we focus on a few, and specifically on how much iteration is crucial in transforming a potentially good idea into an actual product. With iteration here, we refer to the need to add and remove complexity from our design while we repeat the ideate-empathize-prototype-test cycle several times. In this chapter, we provide you with more detailed and structured advice on bringing your products to the required level of complexity and show that this objective can be achieved when we walk the fine line between novelty and familiarity.

6.2   The fundamental trade-off: how complex should our product be?

Aesthetics and complexity are surprisingly related. British-Canadian psychologist Daniel Berlyne (1974) found that aesthetic pleasure tends to peak in the presence of stimuli of intermediate complexity (Figure 6.1). According to this finding, people seem to enjoy some level of complexity. In contrast, too little or too much complexity harms customers. The absence of complexity signifies that the design is dull, obvious, and uninspiring. Too much complexity equates to impenetrability and leads to confusion and information overload.

While this finding may seem like a quirky academic discovery, it is essential for product design. Designers know it all too well. Don Norman says that users want some complexity (Norman, 2010). John Maeda frames the complexity problem as a trade-off between novelty and familiarity: too much novelty scares people, and too little is underwhelming. More specifically, our customers want novelty and performance in situations they perceive as familiar. This makes a lot of sense from the point of view of fundamental human psychological needs (Berghman & Hekkert, 2017).

On the one hand, we strive for safety by finding comfort in the familiar. On the other, we are excited by new possibilities and novel outcomes. How much and when should we explore and risk versus how much and when we should find shelter and rest is a fundamental evolutionary trade-off that surfaces in everyday and long-term decisions. Should I try the new restaurant or stick with the usual lunch place? Should I accept the new job or persist in my current career? Pursuing safety pushes us toward the familiar and the safe, while searching for novelty can lead us to discover better solutions.

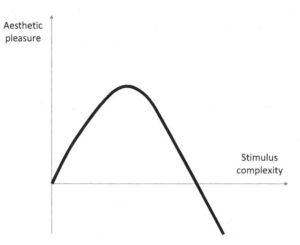

Figure 6.1 **Complexity and aesthetic pleasure**. In a series of empirical studies, Berlyne (1974) found that aesthetic pleasure and complexity are related through an inverse U-shaped curve: subjects perceived a stimulus as uglier if it was too simple or too complicated.

When potential customers are confronted with a product or a service they have never seen or experienced, they are subject to similar psychological needs and constraints. They want some complexity, and the ideal level of complexity is an intermediate one that aligns well with both the complexity of the task and the complexity that the users are willing or able to absorb. For instance, a beautifully curated and information-rich website may be too complex if the users only need a limited subset of the same information and do not have the time to search for it or to enjoy the beautiful visuals.

However, when entrepreneurs create something novel, they typically do not have an easy or direct way to assess this ideal of desired complexity. Two opposite cases are likely: the product needs to be more complex for the task and the users, or the design needs to be simplified because it overshoots the complexity target with too many unnecessary features and functions.

Even the best companies may get this wrong. In their article titled "How Apple Is Giving Design a Bad Name," Norman and Togazzini (2015) assert that Apple sacrificed learnability, usability, and productivity in its quest for beauty and simplicity:

Good design should be attractive, pleasurable, and wonderful to use. . . . But the wonderfulness of use requires that the device be understandable and forgiving. It must follow the basic psychological principles that give rise to a feeling of understanding, control, and pleasure. These include discoverability, feedback, proper mapping, appropriate use of constraints, and the power to undo one's operations.

In other words, eliminating context-sensitive menus and readable fonts to craft a less cluttered and more visually pleasant design risks making our design ineffective in terms of usability.

The opposite mistake, stuffing our products with unnecessary functionalities and components, is more frequent. The design of the weather apps available on our smartphones is becoming increasingly cluttered because the developers provide us with a lot of information about the weather—such as wind speed, humidity, pressure, UV index, and rainfall amount—that, arguably, few average users care about. They just want to know what to wear and where to go.

To identify the right amount of complexity to incorporate in the design of a new product or service, entrepreneurs have no choice but to develop and test design alternatives characterized by higher or lower complexity. While iteration can help, it may be expensive and time-consuming. To minimize iteration costs while hedging the risk of developing the wrong product, in the following sections, we propose a method based on the dual design mindset and the adoption of design heuristics that can be used to simplify or complexify a design.

6.3   Iterating between co-creating and testing

There are two fundamental types of uncertainty. The first type includes known unknowns. This is a fancy way to say that, in this case, we know the question but do not know the answer. We can deal with this type of uncertainty by using methods for rigorous tests of market hypotheses. A market hypothesis sounds like this: "Customers prefer a subscription model for listening to music on the go instead of downloading and listening offline." The rigorous testing of a hypothesis like this requires unambiguous definitions and the development of objective metrics. The test must be conducted following sound methodologies akin to the ones scientists use in scientific research. Entrepreneurs must learn to think like scientists (we illustrate this process and recommend tools in detail in Chapter 9).

The other type of uncertainty includes unknown unknowns. These are relevant questions that we need to be aware of. When we figure out one of these good questions, we can generate hypotheses to test.

The iteration cycle is illustrated in Figure 6.2 and is based on the dual design mindset described in Chapter 1.

Typically, the cycle starts with a low-fidelity prototype. Low-fidelity prototypes (LFPs) are early-stage, underspecified designs used to interact creatively with the team of developers

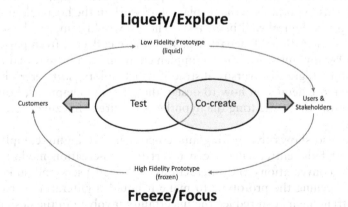

Figure 6.2 **Reducing uncertainty by iterating across co-creation and testing**. Liquid, low-fidelity prototypes are made to support co-creation and uncover good questions. High-fidelity prototypes can then be designed for rigorous testing with prospective customers.

and, more importantly, to co-create with customers and stakeholders (see Chapter 5). In this phase, we characterize LFPs as "liquid" because they lack a finalized shape and can be morphed based on what the development team is creating and discovering. The other reason for which LFPs must be underspecified is that entrepreneurs cannot afford to invest significant resources at a time when customers' needs and competition may still be poorly understood.

Co-creation with users and stakeholders and prototype transformation are predominant in this phase. Entrepreneurs can rely on the customer discovery techniques we illustrated in Chapters 3 and 4. It is okay in this step to open the prototype as much as possible toward different uses and to pursue alternative designs. The logic should be like the organization of a search party: you need enough people, and they should be well spread out to explore a large and unknown area.

Using open artifacts as LFPs can generate ambiguity and introduce additional complexity, but this is far from an inconvenience at this stage. First, by working with open and underspecified prototypes, we save money and time in designing a possibly inadequate solution in detail. Second, the LFP becomes a tool that can help entrepreneurs better understand the problems users are dealing with and pursue serendipitous innovation. In this way we aim to find good problems and relevant questions to define the hypotheses we will test in the next step.

Once co-creation and transformation activities help us clarify the users' needs, discover promising leads, and discard irrelevant design alternatives, we can focus on the definition of hypotheses that we will subject to rigorous validation. We must identify the associated prototype features and the hypotheses we want to test. Finally, we must establish metrics to assess whether the test is successful.

For example, some hospitals are experimenting with ways to make the hospital environment more welcoming and psychologically comforting for their patients. The Agostino Gemelli hospital, located in Rome, Italy, established a new department called Gemelli ART (Advanced Radio Therapy), in which works of art are displayed in patients' and doctors' rooms and radiotherapy labs. In this case, the hypothesis could be formulated as follows: more welcoming spaces will improve patients' well-being; the prototype feature associated with this hypothesis is the display of artwork in the hospital, and the metric is represented by psychological well-being tests. The test would compare the scores obtained by patients in the Gemelli ART department with those collected from patients treated in ordinary radiotherapy units. Alternative implementations can be assessed this way, such as what type of art (figurative versus abstract), which colors (soft versus bright), and so on. We provide more details on how to design these tests in chapter 9; however, this example clearly shows that validating the hypothesis requires "freezing" certain features of the prototype.

The example also shows that testing and co-creating are highly complementary processes. If the test fails, entrepreneurs can revert to a co-creation mode by engaging in a new round of conversations and interactions with lead users and stakeholders. This step requires reopening the prototype to make it liquid. By iterating across co-creation and testing, entrepreneurs can reduce the uncertainty involved in the design of their new product. By leveraging the dual mindset iteration model presented in Chapter 1, they can more effectively and efficiently generate good hypotheses and subject them to rigorous field validation.

6.4 Iterating between simplicity and complexity

When iterating between co-creating and testing modes, entrepreneurs will inevitably deal with the fundamental trade-off we presented at the beginning of this chapter: what is the level and type of complexity users need and want? In practical terms, an entrepreneur will have to create alternative designs characterized by different levels of complexity. Some will turn out to be too simple to address the user's problem; others may exceed the desired level of complexity. In principle, the search for the ideal design can proceed by trial and error, as illustrated in Figure 6.3, in which the zigzagging dashed line represents moving back and forth between too much and too little complexity.

Berlyne's curve (Figure 6.1) shows how users' aesthetic pleasure peaks in the presence of an intermediate level of complexity. This result implies that users dislike too obvious or too complicated designs; the emotional response to obvious and predictable designs is typically associated with boredom, while an exceedingly complex design produces anxiety, confusion, and cognitive overload.

If a design is too familiar, developers must find ways to add novelty, which can be done by adding new information. Conversely, if a design is perceived to be overwhelming and complicated, entrepreneurs must operate by subtraction. In the following two chapters of the book, we will present design strategies to simplify or complexify a prototype.

For now, it is essential to clarify that the ideal level of complexity must be understood in relative terms. In other words, there is no universal way to assess this level, which must be evaluated in terms of alignment between the complexity of the design, the complexity of the task the product is supposed to be used for, and the complexity our users can tolerate or

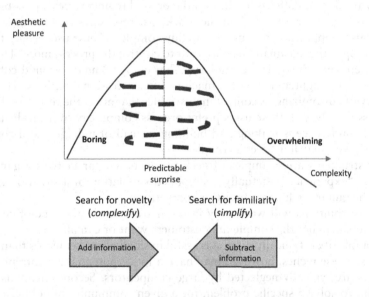

Figure 6.3 **Reducing uncertainty by iterating across simplification and complexification**. The optimal level of complexity can be found by trial and error by designing prototypes that err on either end of the spectrum. When a prototype is too simple for the task, we must complexify it by adding information. When it is too complex, we must simplify it.

afford. This search often boils down to understanding the complexity users want and enjoy. While marketers and companies glorify the advantages of simplicity and convenience, the message that we must develop simple solutions may be misleading for product developers. For instance, some successful products are deceptively simple.

The one-button espresso machine, initially designed by Nespresso and now available from many manufacturers, strips down the coffee-making experience to a few easy moves: slide in the coffee pod and push a button. So, where is the complexity of a product like this? In part, it is invisible, hidden in the technology inside the machine. The machine must produce sufficiently high pressure at the right temperature to get the perfect espresso. Developing the technology that reliably achieves this result in such a small device is not trivial, and the Nespresso system was protected by more than 1,700 patents, according to Bloomberg News (2013). However, while users who buy the one-button espresso machine want to avoid the complexity of crafting the perfect cup of coffee, they are not willing to sacrifice the taste of a good espresso. They enjoy aesthetic complexity more than process complexity: the variety of high-quality coffee choices, the colors of the pods, the use of luxury touches, the boutique-like design of the Nespresso coffee stores, and the elegant shape of the machine. Nespresso successfully shifted the complexity of user experience to where users wanted it.

The one-button coffee machine could not be more different than the Blossom coffee high precision brewer (Seifert, 2012). Astronomically priced at $11,111, this appliance, developed by an MIT startup, used aeronautics parts, a lab-grade filter, and sophisticated software and microprocessor to create the ideal physical and chemical conditions for the perfect cup of coffee. The machine is a high-precision brewer designed to reduce thermal gradients so that every particle of coffee is as close to the desired temperature as possible. While this coffeemaker is no longer available on the market, it represents an extreme example of a product that users appreciate because it is highly complex. These users enjoy the craft, can be experts or sophisticated amateurs, and want to control the process more. They may want to grind their coffee to the desired granularity; they enjoy filling the ground-coffee holder to the desired level and tightening it in the machine like professional baristas. They appreciate the possibility of customizing or controlling variables that affect the result, such as temperature and pressure. Overall, these users prefer process complexity over product complexity; their aesthetic preference is making and building instead of indulging and contemplating. Using a cliché, we can call it "geek's complexity."

Musical instruments are examples of geek products. Guitar Hero is a gamified virtual guitar-playing "experience"—actually a simplified simulation of a situation in which you would play the guitar, such as a concert or competition.

Any of these solutions will work only in the market where the type of complexity the product delivers matches the complexity customers want or can afford.

Process complexity is typically more successful in smaller market niches than in generalist mass markets. These niches, however, may have a lot of potential for entrepreneurs. First, small markets are typically neglected by large competitors. Second, many aspiring entrepreneurs want to solve a specific problem for a given community of hobbyists, DIYers, or specialists. Gamified complexity typically works well with younger customers and in entertainment or educational applications.

Iterating between simplicity and complexity is answering questions such as: how much complexity do our users want? Where do they want it? How much are they willing to pay for it? To answer these questions, entrepreneurs must iterate design solutions characterized by different levels and types of complexity and subject these variations to user validation via testing and co-creation, as illustrated in Figure 6.2. Simplification and complexification can happen in both phases, but co-creation will likely generate more complexity, while simplification will drive testing.

In the co-creation step, our LFP is quite simple, and the interaction with users can open our minds to new possibilities and options. As a result, co-creation may increase the complexity of the design. In this step, entrepreneurs work with users and stakeholders to answer questions such as: what if we add feature X? How might we do Y? Wouldn't it be nice if our product would do Z?

In the testing step, ideas and design choices identified through co-creation must be implemented into testable features. For instance, if we want to make our coffee shop more welcoming to our customers, we could test the effectiveness of furnishing the space in a certain way or adding background music. The need to implement ideas into product features will freeze, at least temporarily, some design choices. It will bring some simplification because only some of the creative ideas identified in the co-creation phase will be technically or economically sound.

6.5   Conclusions: the pursuit of elegance

This chapter offers several arguments for why ambiguity and complexity can be leveraged to identify innovation opportunities.

Iterating between testing and co-creation helps entrepreneurs identify good problems and transform these opportunities into questions and testable product features. Co-creation helps product developers open their initial design to alternative interpretations and uses. The low-fidelity prototype becomes a tool to explore customer needs and solicit their input regarding alternative uses and whether the proposed prototype is a good solution for the problems they are dealing with. Rigorous testing helps entrepreneurs focus on and optimize product features and gives them valuable insight into why most solutions won't work. As stated earlier, Thomas Edison famously said, "I have not failed; I have only found 10,000 ways in which my idea won't work." This form of negative knowledge is essential because it helps to question assumptions, prejudices, and stereotypes. It may not be pleasant to find that something is not working as we expected, but what will be the price of failing to recognize in advance that an idea is not as good as it seems?

Contrary to mainstream thinking, users enjoy some complexity. The amount and type of complexity they are happy with changes depending on the task and the user preferences. Typically, aesthetic complexity and technical simplicity of use are more sought after in generalist mass markets. In contrast, higher technical complexity is more appropriate for niche markets populated by more specialized, demanding, and sophisticated users.

Thus, iterating between simplicity and complexity helps entrepreneurs to explore different potential markets and to find the right fit between the complexity of the design and the complexity customers want. The right level of complexity is associated with elegant design (Iandoli & Zollo, 2022). The same product, such as a coffee machine or a barbecue station can be designed to serve markets on either end of the complexity spectrum. A critical mistake entrepreneurs must avoid is creating products that are either too simple or too complicated for the customers they plan to serve.

In the following two chapters, we will provide actionable and general design guidelines to help entrepreneurs experiment across the complexity spectrum illustrated in Figure 6.3 to identify the ideal level of complexity their customers are happy with. We start in the next chapter with ways to simplify your products.

Key takeaways for this chapter

Lesson learned	Implications for your entrepreneurial project
Complexity	• Complexity is not something to avoid. Sometimes we must pursue it if our product is too obvious or uninspiring for our customers. Customers enjoy some complexity. The challenge is to provide them with the complexity they want. We can achieve this result through trial and error by adding and removing information.
Iteration	• By alternating creative co-creation with testing, we can generate and tame complexity in our design. Co-creation helps open our design and mind to ideas and ways to achieve a goal. Testing helps us to freeze our design to measure whether certain features work. • One way to iterate is by adding and removing complexity. • The ideal level of complexity is associated with aesthetically pleasing design.
Elegance	• Elegance is achieved when we find the best solution to manage the trade-off between familiarity and novelty. Elegant design is deceptively simple, familiarly novel, and predictably surprising.

References

Berghman, M., & Hekkert, P. (2017). Towards a unified model of aesthetic pleasure in design. *New Ideas in Psychology*, 47, 136–144.

Berlyne, D. E. (1974). *Studies in the new experimental aesthetics: Steps toward an objective psychology of aesthetic appreciation*. Hemisphere.

Bloomberg News. (2013). *Nestle loses patent on a Nespresso single-serve coffee machine*. https://financialpost.com/legal-post/nestle-loses-patent-on-a-nespresso-single-serve-coffee-machine

Iandoli, L., & Zollo, G. (2022). *Elegant design: A designer's guide to harnessing aesthetics*. Bloomsbury Publishing.

Norman, D., & Togazzini, B. (2015). How apple is giving design a bad name. *Fast Company*. www.fastcompany.com/3053406/how-apple-is-giving-design-a-bad-name, last accessed August 2023.

Norman, D. A. (2010). *Living with complexity*. MIT Press.

Seifert, D. (2012). Can an $11,111 coffee pot turn out a better cup of joe? *The Verge*. www.theverge.com/2012/10/1/3432980/blossom-one-limited-coffee-maker-11111, last accessed August 2023

Springsteen, B. (2005). *Wings for wheels: The making of born to run*. Sony Music.

Chapter 7

Make it simpler
Design strategies for smart simplicity

It seems that perfection is reached not when there is nothing left to add but when there is nothing left to take away.

—Antoine de Saint-Exupéry

7.1 Simple but not simpler

Google.com was registered on September 15, 1997, and it changed the search engine business and the experience of millions of internet users for good. A significant factor in this success was the invention of its intelligent search algorithm. However, Google also revolutionized the design of the search interface. At the time, well-known search engines—"web portals"—such as Yahoo! and Altavista, had visually busy pages. They were cluttered with information and advertising displayed through hyperlinks, banners, and pictures. Google's choice was counterintuitive in a competitive space where an abundance of digital information was exalted. It was thought that people wanted a gateway to the cybersphere. In a brilliant deduction, Google's software engineers resisted this temptation and understood that users wanted to quickly find what was relevant to their search, rather than be presented with too much information. Google delivered all of that through a white and simple, uncluttered webpage where the main visual elements were a search bar and the company logo.

Google simplified users' digital lives. Google search engine's interface, however, is deceptively simple. It includes, in fact, a mix of simple and complex, novelty and familiarity. We defined this ideal mix as elegance in chapter 6. In this chapter we show that intelligent simplification can be achieved through thoughtful reduction and better information visualization.

The underlying principle of intelligent simplicity—that more information equals better decisions and happier users—does not hold when the information to absorb is too much or too complex. Here we will show that less is not always better and that the design of our product or service should be as simple as possible but not simpler, borrowing the saying, "Everything should be made as simple as possible but not simpler," attributed to Albert Einstein. As we pointed out in the previous chapter, the real question is not to abandon complexity but make our design complex enough to deliver the expected performance and excitement while still being usable and enjoyable. This aspect is highly critical for entrepreneurs as well. You can have the most sophisticated entry strategy, in-depth market analysis, and innovative business models, but if your product sits on the shelves because customers find it unnecessarily complicated or disappointingly simplistic, you clearly need more than

DOI: 10.4324/9781003346463-8

that. In that spirit, this chapter demonstrates that smart simplicity can be achieved through the following product design strategies:

1. Subtract details: Remove unnecessary complexity by focusing on what users need and do the most
2. Split: Displace necessary complexity so that it can be accessed at the user's discretion and uncovered gradually
3. Symmetry: create physical or conceptual symmetry to help users navigate more smoothly and efficiently
4. Group: Create familiar patterns and easy-to-recognize forms of order

7.2 Subtract details

This design strategy is essential in interface design. All products and services have an interface, not just digital devices. We can define an interface as a layer connecting the internal complexity of your offering to the customers. This complexity may result from the technology used in the product or, your company's organization, compliance, or bureaucracy. Inevitably, this internal complexity tends to surface at the interface, and most of it is unnecessary or unwanted. For instance, the architecture of a product can be determined by the company's organizational chart that makes the product or by the characteristics of the different technologies combined in the design. Whatever the source of this complexity, we should do our best to avoid the mistake of having this complexity determined by internal factors and instead focus solely on the complexity that the users want. Entrepreneurs must remember that the user experience is the independent variable; the rest, including the entrepreneur's ideas and mental models, should be molded around the user.

Here are a few ideas on how to implement user-centered simplification via thoughtful subtraction in a bottom-up hierarchy originating from the users' immediate reactions and moving through the way they interact with a product and find deeper meaning associated with owning and using it (see Figure 7.1):

1. Work with the five senses.
2. Identify fundamental patterns of use.
3. Remove information and add meaning.[1]

Let's see a few examples.

7.2.1 Simplifying through the senses

We tend to overstate the importance of rational thinking and language. We must remember that our senses carry more data that is processed and understood more quickly than words. Sensory input talks first and foremost to our emotional brain, which is faster than its logical counterpart and primes how we reflect on and articulate our thoughts. The emotional brain is responsible for creating first impressions. Sloppy visuals, the use of the wrong colors, or an unpleasant voice tone would do a big disservice to the best business idea or the most brilliant design.

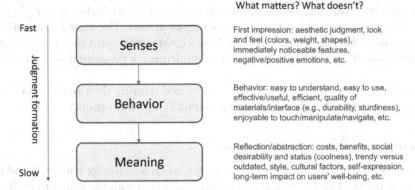

What matters? What doesn't?

First impression: aesthetic judgment, look and feel (colors, weight, shapes), immediately noticeable features, negative/positive emotions, etc.

Behavior: easy to understand, easy to use, effective/useful, efficient, quality of materials/interface (e.g., durability, sturdiness), enjoyable to touch/manipulate/navigate, etc.

Reflection/abstraction: costs, benefits, social desirability and status (coolness), trendy versus outdated, style, cultural factors, self-expression, long-term impact on users' well-being, etc.

Figure 7.1 **The formation of customer judgment.** Inspired by the theory of emotional design (Norman, 2004), this model assumes that customer judgment is determined by a hierarchy of levels: aesthetic (senses), behavioral, and cultural (meaning).

When designing our product, we should do our best to understand how users perceive it when asked to use it. What do they notice first? What elements in the appearance of our design are immediately detected? What emotions do they trigger?

While the repertoire of human emotions can be very nuanced, there are two fundamental types of reaction: joy and fear. Joy opens the mind and makes the user feel safe and ready to engage and experiment. Fear pushes us to narrow our focus and instigates either aggression or the impulse to flee. Therefore, the first simple test is to collect data via observation and interviews to answer these questions: what goes unnoticed? What gets noticed? What are the immediate emotional reactions, and which parts or aspects of our design trigger them?

What goes unnoticed is emotionally neutral, so it is a candidate for subtraction. Similarly, we should remove features that scare users by generating confusion, information overload, or any practical inconvenience or difficulty.

Simplification driven by the senses primarily aims to identify the elements that create a pleasurable user experience. The impact can be both practical and psychological. When Google decluttered the crowded home page design of the early search engines, the empty whiteness sent both a functional and psychological message to users. The practical message was that we are here to help you focus on the critical information. The psychological message was to reassure users and protect them from the anxiety of being inundated by too much information and noise.

Another example is to stimulate the user's senses in a pleasurable way so that our customers will associate that sensation with the experience of using our product. Gutteridge, an Italy-based men's clothing retailer, uses its signature perfume in its stores; not only does the scent attract the attention of casual customers who pass by the stores, but it sticks with us and makes the brand and its product more memorable because of the powerful effects of odors on our ability to remember things.

Decluttering the appearance of our design can also go a long way to producing positive first impressions. Information overload typically generates anxiety. Our brain longs for order, any order that we can easily recognize. The more time we spend looking for this order, the higher the stress and the cognitive fatigue. Minimalist designs such as the ones adopted for Apple devices, IKEA furniture, and Tesla cars are popular not only because they are fashionable but also because a clean design makes space available in our physical and mental world, a space that we can use for other tasks or uses. The same logic works with a negative approach: Which elements in your design create unpleasant emotional reactions or are just distractions? This test can help you to implement a thoughtful subtraction design strategy.

These examples prove that engaging with users and trusting their senses and emotional reactions can give you valuable insights about simplifying your product.

7.2.2   Identify fundamental patterns of use

Part of the joy of a well-designed product emerges when we interact with it. Good interaction is a mix of physical and cognitive ergonomics sprinkled with the ability to easily predict or discover what the product can do for you. Think of a product you love and why you do; a big part of your attachment is likely determined by the joy of using it and how it smoothly solves the problems you use it for.

A straightforward way to identify how to streamline and optimize your design to achieve smart simplification is to observe how users interact with it or a similar one already available on the market.

The Nest thermostat provides excellent lessons on creating well-designed and successful products (see Figure 1.1). This thermostat stands in strong contrast to traditional ones for its minimalistic and aesthetically pleasing design. It is a round knob that users can turn clockwise to increase the temperature or counterclockwise to lower it. A colored ring shows how long it will take for the room to achieve the desired temperature and provides a little chromatic accent to the plain dark color of the knob. A number at the center tells you the temperature, and a little green leaf indicates that your heating system is efficient. The Nest also has easy installation and streamlined packaging that reduces waste and helps customers quickly identify the various parts of the product and the installation kit.

One of the key insights behind the design of the thermostat was the observation that all most users do with a thermostat is set the temperature to a desired level of comfort while ignoring most of the more complicated functionalities that traditional thermostats offer. What is one of the most familiar, intuitive, and ergonomic shapes to perform this task? A knob. Thus, the whole design started with creating a beautiful and easy-to-use knob that would display only the most essential information a user would want to see right away: what is the temperature setting and how far am I from where I want to be.

Another design optimization for the Nest was the creation of a simplified installation kit and procedure, achieved by designing and patenting special screws and attachments. Again, this idea came from the observation that some user pain points were the difficulties arising from identifying the parts, procuring the tools, and finally attaching the device to a wall.

With older models, people could figure out these things only by observing someone using an existing thermostat. However, this requires time and patience, and it is instead easier to adopt a dominant standard design by inertia and dump its internal complexity on customers.

The Nest example also helps clarify another attribute of intelligent simplification. Not only should the design appear simple, but it should suggest to users what to do with it. A knob tells us, "Grab me and turn me," a sizeable red button on a yellow background says, "Push me in an emergency," and so on. This ability of an interface to speak to us and facilitate interaction and information processing so that users can quickly figure it out without instructions or manuals is also called fluency (Reber et al., 2004).

Thus, a very effective way to know where to focus is to list the dominant behavioral patterns with which customers interact with a product and leverage that pattern as a source of inspiration for designing a low-fidelity prototype.

7.2.3   Remove information, add meaning

Emotions influence human decision-making by working as filters. They help us to get an initial appraisal of whether given clues trigger pleasure or fear (first impression). At a higher level, emotions kick in, enabling us to appreciate a specific behavior (indulgence). Finally, emotions also play a role in helping us evaluate whether purchasing and using a product fit with higher-level constructs such as cultural norms, status, and how others see us when we pursue specific consumptions and behavioral patterns. The more we abstract from the immediacy of appearance and clues, the more culturally and socially situated the evaluation becomes. Welcome to the realm of meaning!

Here is a sweet example. Think of a premium chocolate brand, such as Godiva. Chocolate lovers buy chocolate because they enjoy its consumption, so the visceral and behavioral elements in the chocolate design are apparent. These involve the way the chocolate looks, the nuances in aromas and tasting experience, and the texture of the chocolate (smooth, crunchy, etc.). What can we say of the higher-level meaning consumers attribute to chocolate consumption? Is eating chocolate meaningful beyond indulging in the physical pleasure of having it? The answer is yes. In many countries, chocolate (or other types of dessert) is a gift offered in particular circumstances. It could be a romantic gift for Valentine's Day, or something sent to express sympathy for those who lost a dear one. How chocolate is presented in these situations matters; hence, ornamental aspects such as packaging are fundamental. A more eccentric packaging could help with a romantic gift but would be inappropriate for a funeral.

Another example of meaning associated with chocolate is the idea that indulging is not bad if it is a reward for hard work and a stressful day. This aspect is often emphasized in chocolate commercials that typically show characters fully immersed in their chocolate-tasting experience while entering some chocolate-induced nirvana.

This type of analysis can be done for any product; the three levels are always present, although their relative importance may change from case to case. Even at the third and highest level of the user experience, a level Don Norman defines as reflective (Norman, 2004), there may be aspects that need to be exalted, communicated, or eliminated.

7.3   Split information to displace complexity

As mentioned throughout this book, a certain amount of complexity is intrinsic to the need, task, or application we are designing for, so it is unavoidable. Our objective is not to eliminate this complexity but to make it accessible and understandable to the user most efficiently and effectively. A design strategy that we can adopt to accomplish this result is a split strategy. Splitting consists of allocating information in different layers and locations that are easily accessible for the users when they want or need it. The opposite of splitting is giving customers a lot of the information and functionalities on the interface, even if they do not need it immediately.

Here is an example. The design of a traditional TV remote is unanimously considered very confusing, a case of information overload. We are presented with a few dozen buttons and controls whose meaning is challenging to grasp. Yet most users end up using only a tiny subset of those buttons, such as on/off, increase/decrease volume, or switch channels. It is not that users cannot understand more sophisticated functionalities; the reality is that they do not need to perform those tasks frequently, so why bother? On the other hand, many, if not most, of those more complex/less frequent functions are good to have, so we do not want to eliminate them.

The splitting design strategy helps to deal with this problem. How about distributing the information into hierarchical layers so that the information and the frequently needed functionalities are immediately available at the interface, and the rest is hidden in other layers that can be accessed when needed?

The designers of the Nest thermostat followed this approach. The thermostat shows the essential information and the only type of controls frequently needed: the desired temperature, the difference between the current temperature and the desired one, and a knob to increase/decrease the desired temperature. The more complex or unusual functionalities are available in a phone app that can be used in exceptional cases or by more demanding or technically savvy users. This type of design is now widespread, thanks to the diffusion of smart digital devices that can be controlled remotely through an app from our smartphones.

There is another crucial aspect of splitting. Once we allocate information across different levels, we should also make this information easily discoverable and help users navigate back and forth across the layers to avoid getting lost. This is why splitting is not just about creating hierarchy and directories but has a dynamic aspect. An analogy is the "undo" or "return" button present in many applications.

While splitting information seems more important for digital design and applications, it may also apply more broadly to physical products and services. Questions about whether you are providing too much information up front or how users can navigate the complexity of your offering are always worth asking. Information overload can come in many forms. It could be improper packaging, complicated installation instructions, a poorly designed restaurant menu, a frustrating customer service workflow, verbose and unfocused advertising, or cluttered websites and apps. In all these and other cases, we should always test our product to ensure the minimally complete set of information is accessible, no more, no less.

7.4 Symmetry

The importance of symmetry and other aesthetic principles of "good form" is well known. There is plenty of evidence in research on human perception and cognition and studies on art appreciation showing that our minds tend to like clean and ordered representations of information. People prefer symmetry for many reasons. Some are associated with objectively better performance, as in evolution, where symmetrical organisms have proven more efficient or effective than asymmetrical ones. Our brain likes symmetry because it can use only half of the data to process new information.

However, we can look at symmetry beyond the physical properties of a design or layout, that is, in a more conceptual perspective, as a mechanism to confer equilibrium, fairness, and balance.

One of the design choices that made Airbnb's fortune was the double review system that assigns equal importance to customers' and hosts' reviews. If you rent a place through the platform, you can write a review on the facilities and your host. Likewise, your host will review you and give you so many stars, depending on whether you are a good guest. In this way, Airbnb rebalanced the relationship between these two parties, a relationship traditionally skewed in favor of the guests.

Why was this choice so crucial for Airbnb? Because the value proposition that Airbnb offered its users was primarily about reassuring users that the stranger equals danger equation would not be valid for the platform customers. Airbnb created a business where trust is foundational and symmetric. This solution is popular among many other companies in the sharing economy, meaning any digital platform that connects providers with clients, such as car sharing or freelance and small-gig work.

We advise entrepreneurs to seek different aspects and places of their business and check if a more symmetric redesign could help. Do you need a more symmetric layout of your spaces? Is there an imbalance in the workflow? How is power distributed between providers and customers? Are there any functions that have a symmetrical counterpart that customers will look for? For instance, if there is a control to switch a device on, there must be one to switch it off; if there is a delete button, there must be an undo one; if there is a save button, the possibility to revert to the previously saved versions should be available. Similarly, if there is an online sale, there must be a smooth and quick return process; if there is a way for customers to express their complaints and suggestions, there should be an immediate feedback and resolution system.

Looking at the world with different eyes, you can find many more examples of symmetry (or lack thereof) and redesign your idea more symmetrically.

7.5 Group

Grouping things is another example of good form through the rational organization of information, and our minds do that intuitively and spontaneously. Grouping can occur physically, by placing objects or elements in distinct groups, or conceptually, by assigning individual items to abstract categories. Gestalt psychologists identified a set of universal principles through which our minds organize complex information, known as the law of perceptions (Table 7.2). All these laws relate to how we collect information into clusters—for instance, based on physical or conceptual proximity, perceived similarity, or by filling a gap and enclosing various items into a shape that is easier to recognize.

These laws describe how we perceive things and make sense of the physical world. Therefore, product designers should consider them when designing the interface of their product/service. For instance, controls or functions frequently used together should be close to one another. It is supermarket logic: people want pasta, condiments, and sauces to be displayed contiguously because people tend to buy them together.

You can also use these laws to reverse-engineer an existing design. Are the laws correctly applied? When and where are they violated? Is there a reason for such exceptions, or is it just a design mistake?

Like symmetry, grouping can be used conceptually or metaphorically.

One way to do that is to categorize your offering correctly. To which group does your product belong? The example of Starbucks is quite telling (Raz, 2017). Starbucks started in Seattle after its founder, Howard Schultz, partnered with an existing store that sold coffee beans. After a while, Starbucks began to serve brewed coffee, but it wasn't the quality of their coffee that made Starbucks a powerhouse. It was an "aha!" moment that Schultz had

Table 7.2 Gestalt laws of grouping. Adapted from Iandoli and Zollo, 2022.

Law	Objects, concepts, and ideas tend to be grouped together when . . .	Examples (e.g., fast food)
Proximity	they are close to one another	Products or functions that are jointly purchased or performed should be co-located (e.g., design a menu in which complementary products are displayed together)
Similarity	they are similar based on certain criteria	Products or functions that are considered similar should be grouped together (e.g., create categories that are relevant to the users such as "Healthy corner" or "Food for fun" or "Share alike")
Closure	connecting them helps to fill the gaps and create a new form	Facilitate the creation of a personalized mix of functions or choices (e.g., build your own burger)
Continuation	they guide our eyes to find connection among them	Use physical or digital clues to guide users toward the next step
Connectedness	are explicitly related	Items that fit together in a standard menu (e.g., breakfast menu)

while traveling in Italy and observing people hanging out in espresso bars to socialize with friends or colleagues. He started to think of his coffee store as a special place where people would spend time having their coffee instead of just buying it. Starbucks thus capitalized on the idea of the "third place," a public space in which we spend part of our life in addition to our first place (home) and second place (work). Schultz transformed coffee from a product into an experience, from a drink into a space. The design of the Starbucks coffee stores was consequential: a welcoming environment with warm colors, comfortable seating, and free Wi-Fi, where customers could buy expensive drinks. Since the profit margin on these drinks is very high, Starbucks can tolerate the apparent inefficiency of wasting precious real estate on customers spending hours in the store. Thus, they can sell less but still make money thanks to the high margin. However, since takeaway and online delivery are always available, Starbucks makes money with significant sales volume and high margins, a hard-to-achieve combination in many businesses.

The last and final way to use grouping is to frame customer behavior as a narrative. A story is a sequence of events with an understandable purpose. Some changes, such as an action by the protagonist or one of the characters, a crisis, or environmental circumstances, can trigger the end of an episode and the beginning of another. Finally, a good story has moments of tension, a peak, and a happy problem resolution.

Applying this narrative model to user experience analysis can be helpful (Lupton, 2017). You can observe potential customers while they work on their problem. What are the steps? Where do they encounter challenges? How can you help?

This approach was adopted to solve a business problem in which a fast-food chain was trying to increase the sales of milkshakes (Christensen, 2009). Various ways to improve the sale of milkshakes were tried, such as increasing the variety of choices, experimenting with new recipes and flavors, creating healthier drinks, targeting different customer groups, or simply reducing prices. None of these ideas worked. The company then engaged in more thorough customer research based on observing the typical routine of their customers. Note that this research was done by observing customers, not asking whether they wanted healthier or different drinks, questions to which customers would probably answer "yes."

It turned out that the customer routine could be described through the following narrative: Customers drive to work in the morning and stop and buy a milkshake they consume while driving to work. Sipping their drinks is one way to make their commute more pleasant and absorb some extra calories that will keep them going until lunchtime.

While this is certainly not the most exciting story ever heard, it is particularly informative about what one could do to improve sales. The company understood that the critical attribute of the milkshake was not taste or nutritional properties but its density, something physicists call viscosity. If the shake is too liquid, it will "end" too soon, before the commute ends; additionally, it may be spilled in the car or on clothes. But the drink will be difficult to sip and unappealing if it is too dense.

The story also tells us what we should not waste our time on. Customers do not need more or different tastes, are not looking for a healthier snack, and are okay with paying the price they pay.

By segmenting the story into episodes, we can find other ways to make the whole experience smoother (pun intended). The entire point is that the story helps us put a product into context; in the example, the product is the milkshake, and the context is commuting to work in your car. Understanding the context can give us a better comprehension of the user's needs and offer clues about how to perform thoughtful simplification. The story also highlights what emotions are relevant in the experience: boredom, maybe some anxiety about work, and willingness to indulge in a tasty shake to compensate for the workday ahead of us. How can we help our users by soothing negative emotions and amplifying positive ones?

For instance, given that buying a drink while commuting to work is a habit, how can we transform this habit into a pleasant routine? Since customers will do the same every day, can we customize the experience in some way so that it feels more personal and faster? Can we add a motivating quote on the cup that may energize them? Can we create a driver-friendly loyalty program? These ideas show how the power of "storifying" the user experience in a practical and emotional context can go a long way to help generate creative insights and unconventional solutions.

We recommend visualizing the story through a diagram like the one in Figure 7.2.

7.6 Conclusions

In this chapter, we have sung the virtues of pursuing simplicity in our design. We have also warned entrepreneurs that simplicity is easier said than done because it may not be obvious what we should eliminate from our design and what we should keep and improve. We have provided some practical guidelines and multiple examples of design strategies that can help us perform a thoughtful reduction.

The subtraction of useless details can be performed by analyzing how customers react to and form a judgment on our product at different levels (first impression, behavioral, and reflective). Complexity can be hidden by allocating more complex functionalities away from the interface so that they can be accessed quickly, at the user's discretion. Symmetry and balance help to create equilibrium and redistribute power between users, technology, and

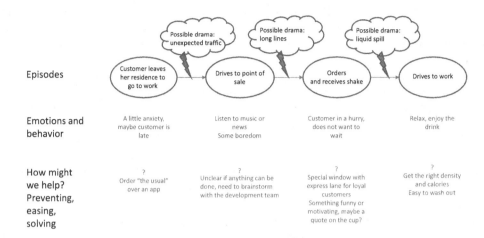

Figure 7.2 **Narrative grouping**. A story diagram to help visualize the story episode, events, and ideas to help our customers navigate their experience in a pleasant way.

Key takeaways for this chapter

Lesson learned	Implications for your entrepreneurial project
Apply intelligent simplification	• Less is better; what does not add value should be eliminated. To identify what to remove and what to keep, distinguish information from meaning. If information leads to some meaning (emotional, functional, cultural), keep it; if not, get rid of it. • Users want simplicity but also want performance. Be careful about what you remove.
Simplify by subtracting information	• Simplification requires the perception of an understandable order, so it must be aligned with your users' mental models. • Any product or service has an interface where the product/organizational complexity meets the user's complexity. Do not let internal complexity dictate your design choices. These choices should be solely determined by the complexity users want and can handle. • Subtract information in one of the four ways illustrated in this chapter: 1) remove unnecessary details; 2) split information at different levels and hide complexity; 3) find opportunities for symmetry and balance; 4) cluster into appropriate market categories or narratives describing your customer journey.

other stakeholders. Finally, grouping information through creative recategorization and storifying the user experience can help us identify creative solutions.

If we err too much on the side of simplification, our product can underperform and be emotionally underwhelming. If that is the case, it is time to spice things up by adding complexity to the recipe. We will show ways to do that in the next chapter.

Note

1 See Maeda (2006)

References

Christensen, C. M., Grossman, J. H., & Hwang, J. (2009). *The innovator's prescription*. McGraw Hill.

Iandoli, L. (2022). When solutions are in search of problems: New venture creation in the booming market of digital speech recognition. *SAGE Business Cases*. https://sk.sagepub.com/cases/new-venture-creation-booming-market-digital-speech-recognition

Iandoli, L., & Zollo, G. (2022). *Elegant design: A designer's guide to harnessing aesthetics*. Bloomsbury Publishing.

Lupton, H. (2017). *Design is storytelling*. Cooper Hewitt Smithsonian Design Museum.

Maeda, J. (2006). *The laws of simplicity*. MIT Press.

Norman, D. A. (2004). *Emotional design: Why we love (or hate) everyday things*. Civitas Books.

Raz, G. (2017). Starbucks: An interview to Howard Schultz. *How I Built this Podcast, National Public Radio*. www.stitcher.com/podcast/how-i-built-this/e/51626348, last accessed April 6, 2023.

Reber, R., Schwarz, N., & Winkielman, P. (2004). Processing fluency and aesthetic pleasure: Is beauty in the perceiver's processing experience? *Personality and Social Psychology Review*, 8(4), 364–382.

Chapter 8

Design strategies to complexify your product

Everything should be made as simple as possible but not simpler.

—Attributed to Albert Einstein

8.1 Good complexity

Online content streaming is a flourishing business and a medium that has revolutionized the broadcasting and entertainment industry. Digital content can be seamlessly distributed over online channels, generating revenue through subscriptions, pay-per-view, and advertising. This revolution has affected virtually every branch of the publishing and broadcasting industries, including television, film, music, books, and teaching materials. However, the design of the streaming interfaces differs significantly depending on the type of content. Let's contrast the streaming of videos by services such as Netflix, Hulu, or the Disney Channel with music streaming by companies like Spotify. One can't help noticing that the design of video streaming interfaces is simpler than that of music.

Video streaming services all look the same, and videos are categorized based on type (series, movies, documentaries, etc.) or genre (family, thriller, comedy, etc.). The search mechanism is straightforward, just a bar where we can input a title or names of actors and directors. We often do not even look for a video; instead, the algorithm offers options based on our past views and preferences.

Let's now look at Spotify's music app. The app offers many functions to help its users to engage with content. There is a personal library, daily mixes, a list of concerts that your favorite artists are giving nearby, ways to discover new music, the possibility to share music with friends and even listen to it together, thematic playlists by artist or genre, a function to build or join playlists by authors, genre, places, mood or moment of the day, a list of your all-time favorite songs, a lyrics function, and so on. Its latest addition is an artificial intelligence–enabled personal DJ that plays music by mixing and matching from your favorites and similar artists.

Why did a company like Spotify add more complexity to its users' experience? The answer is simple: its users want that complexity. Listening to music is more complex and nuanced than passively consuming video entertainment. One aspect is that music is more performative: when we listen to it, for instance, we may sing, hum along, or dance. We can listen to the same music repeatedly because it connects directly with our emotions and memories. Music is social. Different songs can be assembled to build a narrative in a playlist, and nobody does any of that while watching a movie.

The point of the example is that customers want something other than simplicity when they enjoy having a complex experience. The design of the product or service must then

DOI: 10.4324/9781003346463-9

align with the level of complexity that the users are asking for. Spotify understood this, and continuously developed new ways to provide such complexity in listening to music. Compare Spotify to the old interface of Apple iTunes, which was essentially just a music catalog. That design needed to be more complex to capture the complex pleasure of navigating, discovering, listening, performing, and sharing music.

This chapter explores how we can add complexity to our design when our products are underwhelming and underperforming. We present four design strategies that can be applied to virtually any product or service. All these strategies help complexify your design by adding information and novelty to it, namely:

1. The power of the center: reorganize the design around visual centers to create more expressive configurations.
2. Emphasize: pursue novelty by making your design more extreme and, in this way, more exciting, intriguing, and original.
3. Remix: recombine existing ideas and information in novel ways determined by an overarching narrative.
4. Contrast and balance: manage tensions by working with opposites to create pleasurable but dynamic equilibrium.

8.2 The power of the center

In his book *The Power of the Center*, psychologist Rudolf Arnheim (1983) analyzed and explained the importance of visual centers in representing and understanding visual information. Our eyes and attention are attracted by dominant visual elements that provide structure and coherence to the whole. Additionally, visual centers are dynamic elements that create a scaffolding around lines of force emanating from them as from a magnetic field. Centers possess visual weight, help to anchor an image, and create equilibrium by balancing each other out.

An example of visual centers in artworks is Van Gogh's *The Starry Night*, in which the centers are the bright moon and an air vortex in the sky (Figure 8.1). Notice how the two centers create dynamism: the two circles are not positioned at the same level, but the vortex sits a little lower than the moon.

We can trace an ideal diagonal line connecting the two (Figure 8.2). Diagonals have a powerful psychological effect by moving our gaze across the image. The result of this composition is that the whole landscape seems to be in motion. As a further test, imagine raising the vortex to the same height as the moon, and you will find out how the image suddenly becomes much more static and less interesting.

We can use the power of the center theory to analyze any image in terms of visual centers and their visual weight and interaction. Let's apply these ideas to the visual analysis of an interface: the control panels of microwave ovens (see Figure 8.3), sketched from actual microwaves. Some are free of visual centers, except for the digital display at the top, like the first model on the left. The interface is very flat and confusing; all the buttons have equal visual importance, nothing strikes our attention, and we will have to spend much time figuring out how to operate this appliance. Compare now the first and the second models. Introducing a knob makes the interface more balanced and pleasant to look at. Note how the knob adds visual weight at the bottom of the panel and drags our gaze from the top down. Since users are familiar with a knob and what it does (regulate the intensity of something), most

Figure 8.1 *The Starry Night* (Vincent Van Gogh, 1889).

Source: By Vincent van Gogh—bgEuwDxel93-Pg—Google Arts & Culture, Public Domain, https://commons. wikimedia.org/w/index.php?curid=25498286

people will intuit the connection between the two centers of the image: the knob controlling quantity or power and the display showing their values. The other buttons are perceived to be in the background, and we can speculate that they execute specific and possibly more sophisticated commands.

The last two images on the right are variations in which knobs are mixed with buttons or in which they are eliminated. Notice how the two knobs of equal size and shape are a little confusing in the third model, while the choice of two different sizes in model number four creates a more dynamic image, in which the knobs do two other things, namely, setting power and time.

You can also think of centers for the design of spaces and services. For instance, if you are designing the layout of a space where customers are supposed to move, such as a store, you can create centers to which customers would gravitate or hubs from where they would be directed toward other points of service. The proper distribution of such centers would make the workflow smoother and more efficient and, at the same time, make the layout more visually pleasant. This happens because centers add extra structure and meaning to a complex

Figure 8.2 **Visual analysis of *The Starry Night*.** The image is scaffolded around two visual centers: the central vortex and the moon on the right. The diagonal emphasizes the direction and speed of rotation and creates a relationship between the two centers that appear to move together.

Source: (Iandoli & Zollo, 2022, courtesy of Bloomsbury).

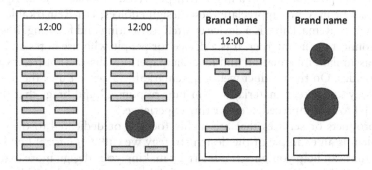

Figure 8.3 **Visual centers in interface design**. The arrangement of information on an interface can benefit from the use of visual centers, as in this example, in which a few microwave oven control panels are illustrated. Prominent elements such as big knobs and displays can work as visual centers to guide perception and interaction.

display. When customers easily recognize and identify such patterns, positive emotions are triggered, and negative ones, such as anxiety and confusion, are kept at bay. Remember that emotional judgment kicks in before the slower rational elaboration of a message and that it primes understanding. An emotionally positive and safe perception pleases the eye, relaxes tensions, and thus makes your customers' attitude more open and friendly.

Finally, centers can also be interpreted from a metaphorical and rhetorical perspective. Think of good slogans and taglines. What these short statements have in common is the ability to communicate in a few words something we can easily connect to the value proposition of a brand or product. BMW's "Ultimate Driving Machine" is probably one of the longest-lasting slogans ever invented. Created by Ammirati & Puris, a leading advertising agency in the 1980s and 1990s, the sentence immediately focuses on the core of BMW's value proposition, which centers on delivering the latest state-of-the-art automotive technology (St. John's University, 2023).

8.3   Emphasize

The proliferation of digital text has left little room for handwriting and paper notes. However, while digital text is highly convenient for many well-known reasons, there is something lost when we give up handwriting and manual drawing entirely. Taking notes or drawing a picture are ways to record content and to express our ideas and focus. Many digital devices and software have been developed to support digital handwriting, with mixed results, from the Palm Pilot handheld notebook released at the end of the nineties with its original approach to capturing handwriting on a screen to recent writing and drawing apps on Apple and Android tablets.

An issue with tablets is that they typically introduce many distractions, such as notifications, multitasking, and hyperlinks. The designers of the Remarkable tablet took an entirely different approach. The company was launched in 2013 through a crowdfunding campaign to finance the development of a tablet designed to recreate the handwriting experience in a digital, paperless world. The whole set of design choices derived from this focus, almost an obsession, on enabling a distraction-free, digital note-taking experience on a device that felt like paper while providing many of the conveniences of digital documents. Remarkable tablets do not offer functionalities made available by their competitors, such as an internet connection or the possibility of reading DRM-protected e-books (digital rights management). You may or may not appreciate these design choices, but Remarkable critics often don't get the point. Remarkable is a device created for writing and focusing. It is not a tablet designed to connect to the internet. It is a device for people who use notes and drawings to capture and assimilate information and love the paperlike, distraction-free experience Remarkable provides. On the product website, Remarkable asserts it uses the most advanced e-ink technology and screen material for "instant response," and brags that the "textured surface make[s] for an unprecedented writing experience."[1]

Creating products or services that are highly focused or dedicated to the solution of a specific problem is an example of the design strategy we call *emphasize*. Emphasis is a design strategy that can help you pursue novelty by making your design more extreme and, in this way, more exciting, intriguing, and original. These results can be achieved by adding deliberate distortion to your design to give prominence to a critical user need or message. Once you embrace emphasis, you are on your way to making your products highly specialized and distinct from more generalist competitors. The main object of the emphasis will require you to shadow or even eliminate some design features that your competitors may offer. It is like you are realigning the design of your solution to one or a few dimensions in which every element is supposed to be subservient to the focus.

In the example of the Remarkable tablet, developers used e-ink technology to make the screen highly responsive to the touch of the pen. At the same time, this choice allowed them to avoid retro-illuminated screens that are bad on the eyes and rapidly discharge batteries. The material used for the screen feels a little rough, like actual paper, and you can hear the typical scratch noise produced by a pen on a paper when writing on the device. On the subtraction side, if the value proposition is about offering a distraction-free experience, you will have to limit the possibility of being interrupted and distracted. Hence, the choice of restricting how the tablet connects to the internet or other applications, such as your email.

8.4   Remix

Novelty often emerges from the recombination of existing parts or elements. Sometimes, recombination happens spontaneously, as in evolution, through the recombination of genetic materials and the filters determined by the adaptation to a changing environment. Sometimes, this recombination occurs as a deliberate attempt to question an existing approach, structure, or mental model. In this book, we are more interested in the second point of view. Remixing is a design or problem-solving strategy that relies on the availability of the following ingredients:

- Parts to recombine (e.g., ideas or physical components)
- "Liquid" work environment favoring smooth but partially constrained action
- Surplus (e.g., wealth, time, and energy to support movement and recombination)
- Narrative polarization, i.e., a storytelling attempt to orient change towards the "right" direction.

Cooking provides a compelling analogy to understand how remixing works. The parts include recipe ingredients, kitchen tools, cooking techniques, and existing knowledge on combining them. The liquid work environment is your kitchen, a lab where rules exist but you have discretion in solving problems and accomplishing the final output. Surplus means you have enough resources and time for experimentation and to let your imagination pursue an alternative course of action if needed. The narrative is your story about why you are creating the dish, for whom or for what occasion, what the dish is supposed to convey or communicate to your guests, and so forth.

Many breakthrough products, such as the Sony Walkman or the 3M Post-it, resulted from a similar remixing approach (Nayak & Ketteringham, 1986). The parts were incomplete or even failed products or technologies. In the Walkman case, the failed stereo recorder and the invention of a lightweight headphone did not make much sense as standalone products. In the 3M case, it was a failed project that led to the development of a glue that did not glue. Sony and 3M gave employees some freedom and extra time to experiment with innovation. This can happen deliberately or by oversight when companies are loose on the control side. Many companies nowadays follow the 3M policy of allowing employees to use a portion of their time, perhaps 15%, to pursue a personal innovation project. Both companies had a surplus that allowed them to provide their employees with abundant know-how, financial resources, labs, technologies, and human capital to be allocated to new projects. Finally, both products were the result of a biased narrative. In the case of Sony, this narrative was created top down, through the vision of two charismatic leaders who could see a future for portable entertainment. In the case of the Post-it, the narrative emerged bottom up by observing what potential users would do with the yellow sticky notes. One key result of this observation was that people used the Post-it as a sort of external memory. The choice of bright colors also helped, since it made the Post-it emotionally relevant in an environment, the workplace, that was notorious for being austere, boring, and deprived of colors and emotions.

Easy-to-access and affordable digital technologies make remixing more frequent and pervasive. In chapter 5, we showed how 3D printing technology combines affordable printers and software, online repositories of existing designs that can be reused and recombined in different ways, and online communities of makers where these designs and other issues are discussed and solved. AI-enabled bots can support recombination by giving us an initial assembly of ideas and pieces we can edit and improve.

8.5   Contrast and balance

Patagonia is a well-known active and casual wear brand. Yvon Chouinard, an avid climber, established the company in 1973, transforming his passion and will to create better climbing apparel and accessories into a business (Raz, 2017). Patagonia has been growing steadily for 50 years and represents a best-in-class example of achieving environmental and business sustainability. While there are many reasons behind Patagonia's achievements, a few key ideas stand behind its successful growth.

First, Chouinard realized that climbing and outdoor clothing designers were not concerned about fashion. The idea was that all customers needed was something practical and reliable. It was then that Patagonia started to market apparel in various bright colors. However, the attention to fashion was balanced by an uncompromising attitude toward sturdiness and performance, even when that was the cause of higher costs. For instance, one of the company's first products was a new type of climbing pitons that were much more robust than the existing alternatives and cost two or three times more. However, these new pitons were designed so that climbers could remove them after use instead of leaving the tools in the rocks, one of the early signs of Patagonia's attention to the environment.

The interest in fashion was combined with encouraging customers to repair their apparel when it was damaged. Patagonia not only created garments that were highly durable but also made repair centers available to its customers. The company message was counterintuitive: do not buy clothes; fix them if you can.

The ability to work with opposites and combine contrasting attributes in the value proposition is an example of the design strategy we call *contrast and balance*. This strategy that works in two steps: create elements of distinction by questioning existing stereotypes or assumptions, then balance this tension to develop sustainable equilibrium. Think about sustainability: isn't it often the outcome of a well-balanced system where opposite forces compromise or collaborate for the common good?

Patagonia's approach to fashion strongly contrasts with many clothing companies' fast fashion business models based on frequent purchases and quick disposal of "old" and "outdated" clothes, no matter what the implications are for the environment.

As with the other strategies illustrated in this and the previous chapter, they can be applied literally or metaphorically. For instance, contrast and balance can be applied to the display of visual information in a device or a store by using contrasting shapes, colors, and physical layout that is both visually pleasant and easy for customers to understand. Contrast improves the readability of information and the identification of critical command functionalities; balance helps users to easily find and operate commands and controls doing opposite things, such as start/stop, forward/rewind, accelerate/brake, and so on.

Contrast and balance also help to handle the novelty/familiarity trade-off. When a product or a technology is genuinely new, it is also unfamiliar to most customers. While we are excited by novelty, we also find comfort in the well-known and the familiar; we saw in chapter 6 that managing this trade-off is one way to achieve the ideal level of complexity that customers enjoy. The history of technology is full of examples in which old and new characteristics were blended into the design of new products. The first cars had a lot in common with horse carriages, computers looked like typewriters, and mobile phones looked like portable phones (it could have been designed differently, perhaps in today's keyless, black mirror form, but customers wouldn't have been ready to understand that design yet). It is not surprising that Blackberry, the first successful smartphone, came with a little keyboard.

Finally, contrast and balance can be used rhetorically to promote a controversial or provocative statement. Consider iconic campaigns, Apple's 1984 Super Bowl spot and L'Oréal's "I am worth it" campaign. These are good examples of how contrast and balance can be leveraged to market unique products or implement revolutionary marketing strategies.

Apple's 1984 ad by famous movie director Ridley Scott is a stunning video in which a female athlete breaks into a theater where hundreds of men, all dressed similarly, listen to a dictator on a colossal screen (Apple, 1984). The Olympian athlete then smashes the screen by throwing a hammer, and the narrating voice mentions, "On January 24th, Apple Computer will introduce Macintosh, and you'll see why 1984 won't be like *1984.*" The commercial is full of contrast. The colors in the athlete's outfit and her blond hair contrast with the dominant gray of the image. Apple positions itself as a rebel rising up against a giant and alludes to the Big Brother concept from the novel *1984*. The tone of hope and the fanfare of a brand-new day balances the gloom of the video.

L'Oréal's "I am worth it" campaign revolutionized marketing communication in the cosmetic industry. It attacked the conformism of the existing ads in which women would make themselves beautiful to please their men. The French company, riding the growing protest and positions of the feminist movement in the late 1960s, told women to buy cosmetics for themselves, for their enjoyment and pleasure, because they deserved it, and not to please men's whims and stereotypical feminine beauty ideals.

8.6 Conclusions

While marketers and customers alike celebrate simplicity, we must remember that users want some complexity. The ideal level of complexity is achieved when the design's complexity matches the task's complexity. If we are any shorter than that, our product will look underperforming and underwhelming. This is why we should not fear adding complexity. It is a legitimate design choice to help us create a more innovative, emotionally, and technically sound product. Adding complexity is also a way to respect our users and stop treating them as passive consumers of content and goods.

Finally, adding complexity helps us rethink our design to consider what we had initially neglected or underestimated in terms of expected performance and user satisfaction and sources of external complexity, such as the impact of our design on individual well-being, society, and the environment.

The next chapter will conclude the second part of this book, dedicated to the challenging step of fleshing out an idea into a prototype. One essential requirement of our prototype is that it must be testable. We need testing for external validation and additional input for our ideation and making process. While we have recommended entrepreneurs think like designers to transform ideas into working prototypes, we now ask you to wear the scientist hat to achieve rigorous and critical validation of whether your prototype is a great solution to the users' problems. We will also illustrate how entrepreneurs should deal with failure, a likely scenario when you set out to critically assess your assumptions and working hypotheses.

Good scientists have a great way of dealing with failure. The scientific method provides entrepreneurs with a solid methodology to test their products, but it also demystifies failure by promoting emotional detachment from our ideas. While a test producing negative results may be a source of disappointment, it should also be a cause of joy if we consider that what we learned has prevented us from wasting time and resources on the wrong development path. To paraphrase Edison's comment on failure: we don't fail, we only find out how it won't work."[2]

Key takeaways for this chapter

Lesson learned	Implications for your entrepreneurial project
Complexify	• The omnipresent mantra that things must be simple results from a misunderstanding. What it means is that people do not want *unnecessary* complexity. Thus, do not be afraid of adding complexity to your products. Customers will be disappointed if they are short of the complexity they would like to have. The real question is how much complexity they want, what type, and where.
Complexify by adding information	• A lack of structuring or powerful visual or narrative centers may be the source of confusion. Users need anchors and grounding. Adding one or more centers to the design can help. Remember that a center is not just a visually dominant element but a source of structure that can guide understanding and user behavior. • Add emphasis to your product through some deliberate distortion that magnifies your message. It is sometimes okay to be loud if loudness communicates something meaningful and is not just about showing off. Be consistent and realign everything else towards the emphasis. • When your product feels underwhelming and dull, try to scramble things up. Remix parts and ideas based on a different and more powerful narrative. Allow yourself and your team to experiment and keep building surplus and redundancy as long as it leads to learning. Short-term inefficiency may result in huge future gains. Leave people the necessary levels of autonomy and freedom to experiment and ideate. The glue is not the rules but the story. • People understand opposites and like to play with them. Aesthetic pleasure often results from tension generated by these opposites. Add contrast to make your product more intriguing, like a chef mixing savory and sweet or crunchy and velvety. This tension helps us to enjoy the two qualities at a deeper level. For this to happen, a balance must emerge from this tension so that these different qualities may coexist and reinforce each other instead of canceling each other.

Notes

1 Quotes from https://remarkable.com/?gclid=CjwKCAjw586hBhBrEiwAQYEnHRhUPAHq0K23S_OLKRay-fCerHQmn44voUBqaqNlTj4am5ZENdRmrhoC7KEQAvD_BwE (last accessed April 10, 2023)
2 As quoted in: [J. L.] Elkhorne. Edison—The Fabulous Drone, in 73 Vol. XLVI, No. 3 (March 1967), p. 52. Thomas Edison made a similar statement in 1890 in an interview to *Harper's Magazine*, available through paid subscription at https://harpers.org/archive/1890/02/talks-with-edison/

References

Apple. (1984). *1984 Super Bowl commercial.* www.youtube.com/watch?v=ErwS24cBZPc, last accessed August 2023.

Arnheim, R. (1983). *The power of the center: A study of composition in the visual arts.* University of California Press.

Iandoli, L., & Zollo, G. (2022). *Elegant design: A designer's guide to harnessing aesthetics.* Bloomsbury Publishing.

Nayak, P. R., & Ketteringham, J. M. (1986). *Breakthroughs!* Rawson Associates.

Raz, G. (2017). Patagonia: Yvon Chouinard. *How I Built This, NPR Podcast.* www.npr.org/2018/02/06/572558864/patagonia-yvon-chouinard, last accessed August 2023.

St. John's University. (2023). *Martin Puris works online exhibition.* https://www.stjohns.edu/academics/schools/college-professional-studies/ammirati-puris-archive-st-johns-university

Chapter 9

The scientist entrepreneur

Learning from failure

9.1 The heroic entrepreneur

The hero's journey is a popularized narrative framework developed by Joseph Campbell, which outlines the unique stages of a hero's adventure from when they venture into their world, witness various challenges, and transform themselves, leading to success and a triumphant return with newfound wisdom and growth (Campbell, 1949). The hero's journey can be seen in various books and movies, for example, *Star Wars*, with its main character Luke Skywalker, the Harry Potter books, and even *The Hunger Games* and its protagonist Katniss Everdeen. The entrepreneur's journey often follows a similar path, from identifying the opportunity to having the courage to create your prototypes, challenges, and failures throughout the process, ultimately leading to an eventual form of success (Price, 2022; Toren, 2014).

Tables 9.1 and 9.2 draw parallels between the hero's and entrepreneur's journeys. Table 9.1 shows the downward spiral, the part of the story when things get worse and everything seems lost. Table 9.2 shows how the heroes' resilience and determination help them rebound and succeed.

What is similar in both versions of the journey is that the concept of failure is embedded within the journey. The fear of failure can exist as initial hesitation and doubt about solving the problem. Actual failure can occur when faced with a challenge or obstacle that hinders progress. There is an expectation that the hero/entrepreneur should overcome failure, eventually, reaping rewards from the work invested in the process.

Essentially, the hero's journey is a metaphor for the challenges and transformations that occur throughout the product development process, which is the entrepreneur's journey. This includes the inevitable encounters with failure. Embracing failure as a stepping-stone toward growth and improvement is a crucial aspect of both narratives. Just as heroes learn from their setbacks, entrepreneurs and product developers can leverage failures to iterate, innovate, and ultimately achieve success. When thinking about failure, we need to frame failure as a part of the extended product development journey. Failure is not something we necessarily avoid, but rather something that can be critical in creating improvements in the product development process. We intend to orient everyone who reads this book to accept failures as a part of the product development process. When viewed from a learning and growth perspective, failure can offer abundant knowledge to young or new entrepreneurs. It can support the refinement of a product or even an entirely new approach to reaching a brand-new product. In this chapter, we spend significant time discussing the concept of failure. We examine failure within the entrepreneur's journey and offer some recommendations

DOI: 10.4324/9781003346463-10

Table 9.1 Dealing with failure through the hero's journey metaphor: the downward spiral.

The Stage	The Hero's Journey	The Entrepreneur's Stage	The Entrepreneur's Journey
The Call to Adventure	The hero is presented with a challenge that disrupts their life.	Identifying Opportunity	Within product development, the entrepreneur is identifying a market need or an opportunity for a new product.
The Refusal of the Call	In some cases, the hero may be reluctant to answer the call due to fear of failure.	Hesitation and Doubt	Entrepreneurs may hesitate to answer the call due to a fear of failure.
Meeting the Mentor	The hero meets a mentor who provides guidance, advice, and support.	Seeking Guidance	Just as heroes meet mentors, product developers and entrepreneurs seek advisors and mentors.
Crossing the Threshold	The hero commits to the journey and crosses from their familiar world into an unfamiliar and often dangerous realm.	Committing to the Journey	The moment when an entrepreneur commits to building a prototype is a moment when failure could become a real possibility. This is when they go from the known to unknown.
Tests, Allies, and Enemies	The hero faces trails, has allies that help them and confronts adversaries	Challenges and Obstacles	The product development process also contains challenges, setbacks, and obstacles. Failures can manifest as technical issues, design flaws, or failure to gain traction in the market.
Approach to the Inmost Cave	Heroes eventually must confront their fears in	Confronting Failure	Product developers face failures head on to deal with the issue.
Ordeal	The hero faces their most challenging test or ordeal, often confronting their inner demons or a powerful enemy. This experience often pushes them to their limit.	Major Setback	In product development, this is a major setback or failure, it can lead to a reevaluation of the prototype approach.

on how to rise above the moments of failure on our prototyping and entrepreneurial journey, positioning failure as the first step to success. Failure, however, can be devasting psychologically and economically. The negative consequences of failure are at their worst when failure happens when we do not expect it or are not prepared to deal with it. Our objective in this chapter is to help entrepreneurs avoid these problems by developing:

1. a mindset to mentally frame failure in the proper perspective and be psychologically prepared to cope with it when it happens

Table 9.2 Dealing with failure through the hero's journey metaphor: resilience, rebound, and victory.

The Stage	The Hero's Journey	The Entrepreneur's Stage	The Entrepreneur's Journey
Reward	After successfully overcoming the ordeal, the hero receives a reward, which could be knowledge, an object, or insight.	Learning from Failure	Product developers can extract valuable insights from failure. This may lead to refining a product, adjusting strategy, or even looking for new opportunities.
The Road Back	After receiving the reward, the hero begins the journey back to the world.	Iterative Process	Product developers go back to the drawing board and refine their product based on what they have learned from failure.
Resurrection	The hero transforms, faces a final challenge, and embraces new abilities. The challenge tends to be bigger than the first ordeal.	Transformation and Adaptation	Product developers evolve through the process, adapting to challenges and setbacks, ultimately emerging stronger and more resilient.
Return with the Elixir	The hero returns to the ordinary world, bringing back the "elixir," or the lessons learned during their journey.	Success and Contribution	For product developers, the elixir could be a successful product launch or prototype or the publishing of lessons learned from the journey.

2. a method to plan for intelligent failure. You got it right! Instead of waiting for failure to fall on our heads, we can design experiments to subject our ideas and prototypes to stress tests and see if and how they fail under controlled conditions. This is what scientists do: the scientific method.

9.2   The fear of failure and the spirit of innovation: intelligent failure

One of the first critical decisions a product developer must make is whether they even want to take the plunge and work on building a product. If you are reading this chapter, you may have already made that decision. However, there are often many considerations that occur within that process. These decisions may include how much time and money we can invest in this prototype. While these questions are reasonable, they can also bring up a fear of failure.

Imagine investing all these resources into a prototype, and it fails. The idea of failure can be almost paralyzing. However, is that fear unavoidable? Rita McGrath (2011) posits that organizations can undertake the risks necessary for innovation only if they are comfortable with the idea of failure. She further points out that while failure can waste money, destroy morale, and even damage reputation, it is necessary to build anything worth building. Failure is a necessary mechanism in product design. Researchers like Kerrigan et al. (2020) argue that there is an almost symbiotic relationship between failure, creativity, and innovation. They identified that creativity and innovation often result in twists and turns and even a few failures. Individuals need to accept that a risk of failure is inevitable and that there is a clear possibility that one can learn from such mistakes. Great ideas are rarely pursued when we are risk averse and fearful of failure.

If managing fear is a part of the product development process and almost critical for innovation, how do we harness this fear into a vehicle for success? Sim Sitkin (1992) popularized an approach that looked at failure as a science. This approach is known as "intelligent failure"—failures that "arise from thoughtful actions or experiments" (Cvrlje, 2021).

The process of intelligent failure consists of a cyclical loop that contains four steps:

1. Detecting failure: learning to recognize failure and understand how to speak up about it
2. Learning from the failure: become curious about what went wrong and hypothesize what could be improved
3. Improving: capture what we learned and apply it to revise our prototype
4. Iterating: launching a new version of the prototype.

This process is done in a loop, so once a new iteration of a product is launched, the four steps are repeated on a new instance of the prototype. Throughout this process, however, there are several moments where fear may increase:

1. Detecting failure: There may be embarrassment, blame, self-criticism, and even defensiveness, which may hinder an individual from reporting a failure. The lack of reporting may put an entire project at risk.
2. Failing to learn: Sometimes, even after a failure is detected, we choose not to apply what we learn to avoid it again. There are also times when we learn the wrong lesson or make the same mistake again.
3. Failing to improve: While a goal may be to perfect everything, this may lead to longer lead times to retesting a prototype.
4. Failing to innovate: At the final stage, feedback may not have been heard, seen, or understood.

While the concept of intelligent failure appears to support being more methodical and strategic about failure, our instincts may encourage us to ignore this process or repeat the same mistakes. Siktin (1996) and Cvrlje (2021) argue that there are several things we can do to ensure we embed a "failing forward" mentality into our work:

1. Accept that failure is inevitable; the goal is to embrace that failure and lead to better performance.
2. Detect and accept any failure quickly.
3. Analyze why the failure occurred and maximize anything you can learn.
4. Apply anything you learn to change your mindset and behavior.
5. Continue taking intelligent risks and innovating; don't be afraid to make new mistakes.

The very concept of intelligent failure is a learned skill and only sometimes something that comes naturally (Fail Forward, 2022). Many of the greatest innovators of the current generation often showcase their failures as an almost natural part of the design process. An excellent example we encourage you to watch is the engineer, Mark Rober. Through his

YouTube channel, Rober demonstrates how building engineering products is a process of trial and error (Rober, 2022).

9.3   Using a scientific approach with intelligent failure

In this section, we argue that for intelligent failure to be implemented, we must rely on an excellent methodology: the scientific method. The scientific method is one of the key factors that determined Europe's scientific and industrial revolutions, starting at the end of the 17th century. The method is based on a few cornerstones. First, something is true until proven contrary (falsifiability). Second, hypotheses must be subject to empirical validation through rigorous and transparent experiments and objective metrics.

As we begin the prototyping process, the rate at which a failure can occur increases exponentially. Sometimes, it is not so much whether failure will occur; it is more like when it will and how prepared we are to confront it.

At this stage, it is not about testing whether a solution will work but about discovering when it can fail. Identifying potential failures may seem like attempting to doom a project, but attempting to anticipate problems leads to refinements and improvements.

Low-fidelity prototypes (LFPs) are the objects of our experiments. As discussed in chapter 5, LFPs are a perfect medium to discover the problems within a product or service. They offer a low-stakes investment whereby individuals can test their prototype, make errors, and refine it into a high-fidelity prototype closer to the final product. Discovering problems with LFPs is traditionally done in 4–5 steps.

1. Design experiments for customer tests—think strategically about what you want to discover about your problem.
2. Build an LFP to execute tests and design them to focus only on the problem.
3. Contact your target audience/potential customers.
4. Test the LFP with your customers to assess whether the LFP is a satisfying solution for them.
5. Revise the LFP.

9.3.1   Designing experiments for customer tests

When designing customer tests, we must focus on designing tests that can validate hypotheses we identified during customer discovery. We can ask ourselves: "What is our theory about the prototype and the problem? How can we validate it?"

A theory can be described in terms of if/then statements linking the prototype's features to customer satisfaction, for instance:

If Prototype's feature X is present, then Customer will be happy.

Validation is obtained through the design of simple pass/fail tests. To design a test, we must carefully plan its execution and identify metrics to measure customer satisfaction. We must repeat these experiments with a sufficiently high number of customers. The test will help us understand which features work and which must be redesigned or eliminated. We can obtain additional insights by observation. To guide you, Table 9.3 outlines the process

Table 9.3 Elements to design customer experiments.

Question(s)	Prototype features to be tested	Test and measurement	Results and Insights
Hypothesis 1	Feature 1 Feature 2	Response metric	. . .
Hypothesis 2	Feature 3	Response metric	. . .

Table 9.4 An example of customer experiment design.

Question(s)	Prototype features	Test and Measurement	Results and Insights
How can we make hospitals more child-friendly? (Theory/Hypothesis: more welcoming, playful spaces will improve hospitalized children's well-being)	Indoor playground (which toys/games?)	Test different toys to know which one kids use/like the most (build the playground and test with hospitalized kids) Measure well-being (How? Use observation checklist.)	Needs to be modular to adapt to the available spaces Needs to facilitate interaction, since playing is a social activity
	Doctors and nurses wearing costumes (which costumes?)	Test different characters (ask doctors or actor to wear costumes and observe kids' reactions) Measure well-being (How? Observation)	Some kids found clowns scary

Table 9.4 presents an example of how this approach can be used in a case in which the design question is: how can we make hospitals more friendly for children?

9.3.2 Build low-fidelity prototypes to execute test

Once there is an understanding of the problem, we test a problem/solution by producing rapid prototypes that help to validate the problem and solution. Chapter 5 mentions several ways to create an LFP (drawings, wireframing, computer-aided design, 3D printing). Table 9.3 guides us to ensure we incorporate all the features we need to test in the LFP as determined by the theory we want to test.

9.3.3 Contact your target audience/potential customers

The next phase requires that we reach out to customers to engage them to test our prototypes. Reaching out to customers may require us to find ways to reach out to them. Three methods exist to obtain customers as testers for our experiments. We can "push" customers towards us through invitations, referrals, and social media. We can "pull" customers in by advertising our need to test a product. Finally, we can pay customers to try our prototype by offering a monetary incentive (Blank & Dorf, 2012).

9.3.4 Execute test and revise the low-fidelity prototype

Once you have your testers, you can invite them to the testing space and run the test. The test can be done in person or online, depending on the case. Metrics can be collected by observing or measuring the LFP's performance and customer reactions. You can also consider indirect measurements, such as survey or interview questions. Indirect measures are less robust and objective because they are based on what customers perceive or think happened, as opposed to direct metrics and observations that detect what happened.

The measurements must be defined before starting the experiment, regardless of your metric type. In addition to metrics, it is also essential to obtain less structured and open feedback from your testers. The feedback obtained in all these different ways must be used to refine the prototype.

It is also essential to understand the difference between analytic and aggregate feedback. Analytic feedback is based on specific aspects and features of your product. Aggregate feedback is about whether your customers like your product (or not) in its entirety. It is reasonable to expect that analytic and aggregated judgments are consistent, but this is not always the case. For instance, customers may like certain features, so the test on those features will be successful. However, they may find the overall design a little bland.

An easy way to measure aggregate customer satisfaction is the net promoter test (Blank & Dorf, 2012; Carpenter, 2022). The net promoter test measures the likelihood of a customer using a product or service (Carpenter, 2022). The NPS calculation is:

Total % of promoters - total % of detractors = net promoter score

The test is a simple one. After every test, ask your customer:

"How likely would you be to recommend our product to a friend or colleague? Use a 0–10 scale, where 10 is 'extremely likely' and 0 is 'not at all likely.' "

Based on their responses, customers are categorized into one of three groups:

- Promoters (9–10 rating)
- Passives (7–8 rating)
- Detractors (0–6 rating)

A generally accepted guideline says that if your net promoter test score is above 50, customers like and would probably use your product.

9.4 Exploring the emotions behind failure: the stages of failure

Now that we have a systematic method to help us fail cheaply, quickly, and correctly, we want to return to the psychological impact of failure. After all, you can engage in experimentation and testing only if you develop the right mindset and psychological resilience to deal with failure.

Failure is generally associated with what we may define as a catastrophic event: an event that forces the hero, or in our case, the entrepreneur, to question everything they knew about the problem they are facing. It can often bring up hard-to-manage emotions, such as sadness, frustration, and even moments of regret. While it may be easy to remain in those feelings for some time, there is an expectation that entrepreneurs/innovators will eventually confront the problem or challenge they are facing. Joseph Campbell (1949) believed that when a hero is confronted with an insurmountable challenge, there may be a moment of failure, and in some ways, something dies within the hero. The concept of death, in this case, does not necessarily mean to die, but rather a retirement of old habits, old techniques, and even a shift of our old mindset. In that same way, when innovators and entrepreneurs are faced with failure, there is an expectation that they must rethink their approaches, modify their expectations, adapt, and ultimately change.

When we examine our potential shortcomings in product development, entrepreneurs are often oriented toward two different mindsets. The first orientation is solely focused on performance. Performance-driven entrepreneurs often look at failure as a reflection of themselves; they take failure hard, hold back on efforts, and, on rare occasions, step back from projects. The second orientation is focused on learning and growth. In this orientation, failure is seen as an opportunity to learn and a part of the process. At the same time, accepting that failure is a part of learning and growth doesn't necessarily mean a product will be successful. In fact, a product can still be considered a failure even if you continuously work on it. A great example of this, discussed in chapter 5, is the Wii U. The Wii U was considered a commercial failure, but the learning and growth obtained in the process made the following product, the Nintendo Switch, a commercial success. In other chapters, we provided additional examples of failed products that were reinvented and repurposed for a different use or market, such as the Sony Walkman, the 3M Post-it, and Slack. In all these cases, learning occurred because companies repeatedly tested these products. Even if those tests technically failed, they produced insights and "aha" moments that would not otherwise have happened.

Steve Blank argues that failure is like dealing with grief (Blank, 2013) and proposes a staged model to deal with it. Within the stages, the entrepreneur goes through a series of emotions with the hope that they and their product will be ransformed at the end of the process. In his view, there are two phases to failure: the failure itself and the redemption. These two phases can be broken up into the following six stages: Shock and Surprise, Denial, Anger and Blame, Depression, Acceptance, and Insight and Change. If we expand the stages to include Joseph Campbell's hero's journey, we can draw parallels between what the hero and entrepreneur may feel on their journey.

1. *The Ordeal: Shock and Surprise.* In the hero's journey, the ordeal is a pivotal moment when the hero faces their most challenging test. Similarly, for entrepreneurs and product developers, a major setback or failure can often feel like a sudden shock, almost a moment of disbelief, leaving them surprised and disoriented. This initial stage is marked by a struggle to comprehend what went wrong. In many cases, an entrepreneur must confront their inner doubts and insecurities, just as a hero faces their inner demons.
2. *Denial: Holding onto Hope.* Denial is a common response to failure. Just as heroes might initially deny the magnitude of their task, entrepreneurs can often deny the extent of the failure's impact. Denial is often the first defense mechanism, a way to hold onto hope in the face of looming disappointment. Denial can also hinder progress by preventing a moment of honest evaluation and learning from those mistakes.
3. *Anger and Blame: Battling Frustration.* Anger and blame are emotions that often arise when the hero encounters obstacles. In the entrepreneur's journey, these emotions manifest as frustration directed at oneself or others. The entrepreneur might feel anger at the circumstances or blame others for the failure. It is important to channel these emotions

constructively, using them as fuel to initiate change, rather than allowing them to consume energy that could be better spent on adaptation. In this case, it is vital to focus on cognitive conflict, which focuses on the problem, versus A-type conflict, which focuses on interpersonal issues (Williams, 2022).

4. *Depression: Navigating Darkness.* The hero's journey often features a moment of despair or darkness. Similarly, entrepreneurs may experience a period of sadness following failure. The emotional low point can be a time of self-doubt, questioning one's abilities, and feeling overwhelmed by the challenges. However, this dark moment can also catalyze introspection and self-discovery, setting the stage for growth and transformation. We often recommend that entrepreneurs seek a mentor to support them in these moments.

5. *Acceptance: Embracing Reality.* Acceptance is a turning point in both the hero's journey and the entrepreneur's experience of failure. It involves acknowledging the reality of the situation, even if it's not what was hoped for. Entrepreneurs must come to terms with failure, recognizing that it's an inherent part of the innovation process. This stage paves the way for accepting personal responsibility and the need for change.

6. *Insight and Change: Transformation.* In Joseph Campbell's monomyth, the hero emerges transformed from their journey. Similarly, entrepreneurs who navigate the stages of failure can experience profound insights. These insights drive changes in mindset, strategy, and approach. In many cases, they can build new prototypes and ideas. By embracing failure as a learning experience, entrepreneurs can refine their products, pivot their strategies, and adapt to new opportunities.

The hero's journey is not linear; failure is also not rigidly sequential. We often cycle through various emotions within the iterative process. The key is recognizing and acknowledging that failure is a necessary part of the process, and the emotional experience is key to creativity and innovation. The emotions behind failure are a complex and transformative journey for entrepreneurs, much like the hero's journey in mythology. By drawing parallels between these narratives, entrepreneurs can find solace in knowing that setbacks are a natural part of innovation (see Table 9.4).

9.5   Conclusions

The journey of an entrepreneur mirrors the hero's journey, as both entail embarking on transformative quests with challenges and failures that pave the way to some form of ultimate success. Just as heroes often face unique trials and adversities, entrepreneurs encounter obstacles and setbacks. The fear of failure is a common thread in both narratives, but embracing failure as a catalyst for growth and improvement is crucial. The "intelligent failure" concept presents a systematic approach to learning from mistakes and iterating on prototypes, leading to innovation. Like scientific experimentation, this process involves detecting failures, learning from them, improving, and innovating. By harnessing the power of failure, entrepreneurs can refine their products, enhance their strategies, and ultimately achieve success.

Emotions play a pivotal role in the entrepreneurial journey, much like the emotional stages of grief. Like heroes who face adversity, shock, denial, anger, depression, acceptance, and insight on their journeys, entrepreneurs face similar emotions as they navigate failures and setbacks. However, these stages of failure can ultimately lead to transformation and change, propelling both the entrepreneur and their product forward. Just as heroes return from their quests with elixirs of wisdom, entrepreneurs who embrace failure as

Table 9.5 The stages of failure in the hero's journey framework.

The Stage	The Hero's Journey	The Entrepreneur's Stage	The Entrepreneur's Journey	Steve Blank Stages of Failure	The Journey through failure
Ordeal	The hero faces their most challenging test or ordeal, often confronting their inner demons or a powerful enemy. This experience often pushes them to their limit.	Major Setback	In product development, this is a major setback or failure. It can lead to a reevaluation of the prototype approach.	Failure	Stage 1: Shock and Surprise Stage 2: Denial Stage 3: Anger and Blame Stage 4: Depression
Reward	After successfully overcoming the ordeal, the hero receives a reward, which could be knowledge, an object, or insight.	Learning from Failure	Product developers can extract valuable insights from failure. This may lead to refining a product, adjusting strategy, or even looking for new opportunities.	Redemption	Stage 5: Acceptance Stage 6: Insight and Change

Key takeaways for this chapter

Lesson learned	Implications for your entrepreneurial project
The parallel between the hero's journey and the entrepreneur's journey	• The narratives behind Joseph Campbell hero's journey and the journey of the entrepreneur involve challenges, transformation and the fear of failure. The process of prototyping is a journey. The journey is designed to challenge you, and, in some cases, you may feel like giving up. Resist the urge to give up. The design thinking process is designed to be a challenging process where you may constantly learn and adapt. • If you ever feel like giving up on a product, review Tables 9.1 and 9.2 and define where you may be on your journey.
Embrace failure as a stepping-stone	• Failure is a natural part of the product development process. Accept that failure is inevitable, and apply anything you learn to change your mindset and behavior. As you continue to iterate prototypes, be bold and continue to take smart, calculated risks. Don't be afraid to make new mistakes, as this is one of the ways we learn.
Intelligent failure and the scientific approach	• We need to learn from failure in order to keep improving and innovating our prototypes. Test your prototype using Table 9.4 to ensure its features align with its purpose.

a stepping-stone to success can reap the rewards of their perseverance, adaptability, and resilience.

Essentially, the hero's journey and the journey of an entrepreneur are interconnected narratives of growth, transformation, and triumph over challenges. The ability to confront failure with a growth mindset, adopt the principles of intelligent failure, and navigate the emotional stages of failure sets successful entrepreneurs apart. By viewing failure as an integral part of the process, entrepreneurs can harness its power to innovate, iterate, and ultimately succeed, bringing valuable lessons and contributions to the world of product development.

References

Blank, S. (2013). *Failure and redemption*, February 26. https://steveblank.com/2013/02/26/failure-and-redemption/

Blank, S., & Dorf, B. (2012). *The startup owner's manual: The step-by-step guide for building a great company*. John Wiley & Sons.

Campbell, J. (1949). *The hero with a thousand faces* (1st edition). Bollingen Foundation.

Carpenter, A. (2022). What is NPS? Your ultimate guide to net promoter score. *Qualtrics*. www.qualtrics.com/experience-management/customer/net-promoter-score/#:~:text=NPS%20survey%20template-,How%20do%20you%20calculate%20Net%20Promoter%20Score%3F,be%2070%2D10%20%3D%2060

Cvrlje, T. (2021). The "intelligent failure" concept. *Linkedin*, July 2. www.linkedin.com/pulse/intelligent-failure-concept-tom-cvrlje/

Fail Forward. (2022). *Smart risk taking and maximum learning, welcome to intelligent failure*. https://failforward.org/intelligent-failure#what-is-intelligent-failure

Kerrigan, S., McIntyre, P., Fulton, J., & Meany, M. (2020). The systemic relationship between creative failure and creative success in the creative industries. *Creative Industries Journal*, 13(1), 2–16. https://doi.org/10.1080/17510694.2019.1624134

McGrath, R. (2011). *Failing by design*, April. https://hbr.org/2011/04/failing-by-design

Price, W. (2022). *Joseph Campbell, hero's journey and lessons for entrepreneurs*, March 29. www.linkedin.com/pulse/joseph-campbell-heros-journey-lessons-entrepreneurs-will-price/?trk=articles_directory

Rober, M. (2022). Egg drop from space. *YouTube*, November 25. www.youtube.com/watch?v=BYVZh5kqaFg

Sitkin, S. (1992). Learning through failure: The strategy of small losses. *Research in Organizational Behavior*, 14, 31–266.

Toren, A. (2014). *Entrepreneurship as the hero's journey*, June 21. http://entrepreneur.com/leadership/entrepreneurship-as-the-heros-journey/234889

Williams, C. (2022). *Mgmt 12: Principles of management (Twelfth)*. Cengage.

Chapter 10

From prototypes to businesses

Design your business model

Entrepreneurs do not usually fail from circumstance; they fail from what I call entrepreneurial rigidity—a fixed mindset and unwillingness to change the business model.

—*Richie Norton*

10.1 Designing successful business models: align and scale

This is the story of Better Place, an Israeli startup that attempted to revolutionize the electric vehicle (EV) business during its existence. Despite the auspicious name, the company went bankrupt in 2013, but its story provides excellent lessons learned for business model (BM) design (Wikipedia, 2023).

EVs are the future of the automotive industry. Batteries and electric engines are expected to replace gas-powered cars and constitute critical technologies to fight climate change.

Better Place's idea to support and monetize this transition was brilliant. Many of us know that the main EV inconveniences stem from the battery. Batteries are still expensive, slow to charge, and have limited autonomy and life. Shai Agassi, the Better Place founder, designed a system to liberate EV users from battery problems: a battery swapping station where drivers could replace their exhausted battery with a fully charged one in a few minutes. These stations would replace the existing networks of traditional gas stations. Drivers would not need to own a battery; they would swap an empty battery with a recharged one anytime they needed to "refill."

By solving EV customers' problems of buying, recharging, and replacing expensive batteries, Better Place also identified novel ways to profit from the new EV-powered car market. The company figured out a revenue model for drivers based on mileage plans, like subscription models used in the mobile phone market, which are based on minutes or gigabytes of data. The battery cost was subsidized in the same way phone companies let you buy a phone at a reduced price when you purchase to a multiyear subscription. By eliminating the need to buy the battery up front, EVs would become competitive in price with their gas counterparts, leading to mass EV adoption. Battery charging, maintenance, and disposal would be handled by Better Place at a reduced cost per unit thanks to centralization and economies of scale. Charging the batteries would be supported by an intelligent grid connected to the electric grid to produce additional efficiency gains. Energy would be supplied by renewable sources such as wind and solar. The economies of scale and the efficiency and environmental improvements created by this green grid would create additional cost savings and revenue opportunities for the company.

DOI: 10.4324/9781003346463-11

The idea was piloted in a few countries through agreements with local governments and some car manufacturers, who developed EVs compatible with Better Place's service stations. However, despite its promising beginnings and the enthusiasm of early investors, the company went bankrupt in 2013. Among the reasons behind the bankruptcy were the high cost of building the swapping station networks, the lack of standardization in EV development to make cars compatible with the system, the low market penetration of EVs, and the fast development of alternative technologies such as fast charging and less expensive/more capable batteries. Better Place's BM was too ambitious regarding the scale of the business. It required many more EVs on the road than those available then and too much standardization in the EV development platform to be economically sustainable. None of these variables were under the control of the company. While brilliant on paper, Better Place's BM had two significant issues—capital sins of a poorly designed business model: *it was not scalable and did not align with the industry.*

* * *

The approach we propose in this chapter to BM design is a scalable and iterative discovery process inspired by the same design-driven principles outlined in the previous chapters for transforming an idea into a prototype. The process's exploratory and experimental nature aims to introduce scalability and alignment in the design of the business model to reduce uncertainty progressively and sustainably. We also explore how the research and experimentation that has gone into the development of the prototype can be helpful for BM design. Let us start by revisiting, from a business model angle, the value proposition concept illustrated in chapter 4.

10.2   A value proposition approach to business model design

A business model describes how an organization creates, delivers, and captures value (Osterwalder & Pigneur, 2010). In more concrete terms, a BM describes how your organization makes money. According to Clayton Christensen (Johnson et al., 2008), a BM can be described through four building blocks (definitions provided in Figure 10.1):

- A value proposition
- A set of critical resources and activities needed to embed and deliver the value proposition into a product or service

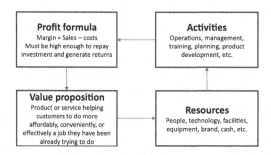

Figure 10.1 **The building blocks of a business model**. A well-functioning business model exhibits internal consistency, reinforcing these four elements.

Source: (Johnson et al., 2008)

- A profit formula to cover the cost of operations, repay the investment, and generate additional profit.

These components work together in a self-reinforcing cycle (Figure 10.1) in which a positive profit formula will strengthen the value proposition and provide the financial resources to procure the resources and implement the activities. The cycle also shows that a BM can fail in any or more of these blocks. It could be a flawed value proposition, the lack of adequate resources, the mismanagement of critical activities, or a faulty profit formula based on inaccurate estimations of costs and revenues.

To apply this framework to the Better Place case, we can contrast Better Place with the BMs of existing competitors, for instance, EV battery manufacturers such as A123 Systems or Sanyo (Figure 10.2).

The BM on the top is typical of manufacturing companies, batteries producers in this case. Manufacturers develop proprietary designs and technology, procure and assemble inputs, distribute the outputs through a supply chain, and make money by charging a profit margin to the cost of making one unit of output.

In this BM, the manufacturer's value proposition is about delivering better capacity and autonomy at an affordable cost; the essential resources include the raw materials and the

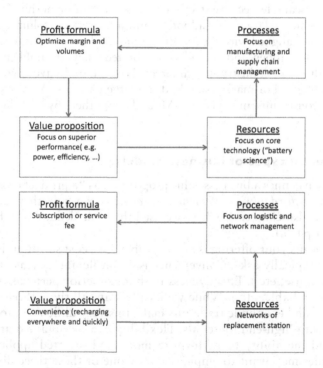

Figure 10.2 **Business model comparison.** In this picture we use Christensen's definition to compare Better Place to EV batteries manufacturers. The top picture shows the BM of a battery manufacturers such as A123 Systems or Sanyo; the bottom picture describes Better Place's BM. It is evident that Better Place was entering the EV market adopting a service network approach focused on energy distribution instead of adopting an added value BM that is typical of manufacturing companies.

battery engineering know-how, and the critical activities include the making and distributing of EV batteries. The profit formula is positive if the unit margin and the sale volume are high enough to cover the engineering and supply chain costs, repay the investments in the fixed assets such as manufacturing plants and technology, and generate profit for the company.

In the Better Place case, the BM is quite different. The value proposition is based on convenience and EV affordability for EV drivers. The essential resources include the swapping station, the smart grid technology, and strategic partnerships with automakers and utility companies. The key activities are focused on managing the station networks and the grid. A subscription model drives the profit formula.

A post-mortem analysis of Better Place's BM reveals its flaws. The cost of building and interfacing the station networks with the utility grid was significantly higher than anticipated. This cost is fixed, meaning it does not increase with the volume of service and is incurred even if no customers show up at the "pump." To cover that huge, fixed cost, the company would need a sale volume that could be achieved if EVs were a significant share of the automotive market. This was not the case at a time when the EV market share was less than 1% and did not show any sign of significant growth.[1] Additionally, Better Place was supposed to secure industry standardization to ensure a sufficiently high number of compatible cars would be circulated.

The BM was not scalable because it was based on an "all or nothing" logic: either the company rapidly achieves large-scale adoption and huge service volume, or it goes bankrupt. The BM was not aligned with the industry trends and the competitors' dominant BM. While revolutions do happen and should be celebrated, they are unlikely. In most cases, a startup cannot drive the industry in a different direction and have negotiation power to impose new technological or market standards on large partners. A safer strategy is to understand industry constraints and existing BMs and adopt them by introducing incremental modifications.

10.3 Fundamental types of business models

Clayton Christensen defines a business value proposition as "a product or service that helps customers do more *affordably*, *conveniently*, or *effectively* a 'job' they have already been trying to do." (See also chapter 3, where we used the same definition to help you build a successful elevator pitch.)

Affordability means your offering is an accessible, low-cost solution (lower than what your competitors typically ask). Convenience is about flexibility (easy to access, learn, use, portable, multiuse, etc.). Effectiveness is about superior performance (faster, prettier, greener, more reliable, etc.). While we ideally want all these three dimensions in a product, technical and economic trade-offs make this very difficult. A low-cost solution cannot be built with high-end materials. Flexibility can be obtained at the expense of specialization and the ability to perform in more sophisticated applications. Finally, different companies may want to emphasize only one of these three dimensions to acquire a distinctive competitive advantage. IKEA's ability to create low-cost, attractive designs is an example of emphasis on affordability. This focus differentiates IKEA from companies like Design Within Reach, which, despite its name, sells designer furniture at a very high sticker price. This observation does not imply that IKEA is "better" than Design Within Reach, only that these companies position themselves to serve different types of clients.

It's important to emphasize that our product must address a "job" the customers have already been trying to do. If affordability is their primary concern, your value proposition should address that problem. If customers want portability, they may not be concerned about affordability and be ready to pay more for a great portable version of a product.

The design of a BM should answer two questions:

1. Where should the emphasis be?
2. What is the BM type that aligns best with our entrepreneurial idea?

The answer to the first question lies in the research you have done so far to build your prototype. The Human-Centered Design approach proposed in this book provides much information to understand what your users need and want. At this point, you should be confident in knowing whether your prospective customers primarily need a low-cost solution, convenience, or better performance. The answer is also in the value proposition definition previously reported. It is about helping customers to do "a job they have already been trying to do" (see the milkshake example in Chapter 7). This means identifying a problem that is relevant to them and that they are trying to solve on their own, but with less than satisfying results.

Christensen's definition can also be used to identify a classification of fundamental types of BMs by using the four building blocks as classification criteria (Johnson et al., 2008). This classification is reported in Table 10.1.

Table 10.1 Fundamental types of business models. Adapted from Johnson et al., 2008.

	Value Proposition	Critical Resources	Critical Activities	Profit Formula	Examples
Solution shops	Diagnoses and recommend solutions	Highly qualified experts	Not very standardized; based on experts' knowledge, expertise, and intuition	Fee for service	Most consultancy and professional services firms (accountants, doctors, etc.)
Value adding process	Transformation of lower-value inputs	Materials, equipment, people, facilities	Highly standardized processes not relying on hard-to-replace individual skills	Fee for outcome	Manufacturing companies, distributors, and retailers; standard service providers
Facilitated users' networks	Assist transactions in networks of participants	Network infrastructure and communication channels	Network or platform management	Fee for transactions or subscription (to cover the fixed costs of infrastructure building and maintenance)	Real estate agencies, matchmaking services, online platforms such as Uber, LinkedIn, TaskRabbit, etc.

"Solutions shops" are typical of consulting firms. An architecture consulting company's value proposition is diagnosing problems and recommending solutions in a specific domain (e.g., designing premium residential units in a particular area). Its key resource is well-paid, highly specialized experts with high-level academic credentials and technical training and expertise matured through many years of experience (architects). The development of solutions is typically highly customized. Experts tend to charge for the service rather than for the outcome. For instance, the architecture company will charge you for the blueprints of the house, not the house.

Value-adding BMs are typical of manufacturers, distributors, and retailers. Following the building example, this is the typical BM of a construction contractor. The contractor will procure the materials and build the house following the specs provided by the architect. The key resources, in this case, are excellent construction materials and good carpenters. The key activities include building processes, procurement, and project management. Contractors do their best to standardize these activities to avoid reinventing the wheel each time they build a new house. The contractor's profit will be based on the price of the outcome minus the cost borne for its making (worked hours, pounds of materials, square feet of built surface, etc.).

The third type of BM is the facilitated user network. Still following the same example, a real estate company would adopt such a BM. Facilitated user networks' value proposition is to connect demand and offer in a market. They do so by building a platform where such a match can occur. This platform can be a network of contacts, a physical marketplace, or, more and more frequently, a digital network. Network operators traditionally charge by asking for a finder's fee. In the digital world, the finder's fee has been replaced by or coexists with a subscription model or advertising. For instance, LinkedIn adopts all these revenue models. It charges employers for posting job announcements (pay per outcome). It makes money on job seekers wanting access to premium services (subscriptions). Finally, it makes money through advertisements posted on the website. Subscription models often follow a "freemium" approach. Customers can access essential services for free, which helps create the critical mass these networks need to function. Some customers then are open to paying to get more sophisticated functionalities.

Table 10.2 also helps to clarify what business model innovation is. Better Place, the case study presented at the beginning of the chapter, tried to innovate the EV market by implementing a facilitated users' network BM in contrast with the value-adding process BM adopted from battery manufacturers. Better Place did not reinvent EVs or batteries; they just figured a different way to deliver and facilitate EV mobility.

Early-stage entrepreneurs should spend time designing alternative BMs before investing significant resources in implementing a particular model. This research can be based on brainstorming sessions, expert investors' feedback, user studies, and industry benchmarking. Table 10.2 provides a checklist of diagnostic questions to help you identify the correct type of BM for your company.

10.4   The business model canvas

The BM canvas is a one-page document that helps entrepreneurs to visualize the essential building blocks of their BM and their connections (Osterwalder & Pigneur, 2010). Through the past decade, the canvas has gained massive popularity among entrepreneurship educators, and the concept of business model innovation has revolutionized the way strategy is

Table 10.2 **A preliminary checklist to assess the alignment and scalability of your business model**

A BM design checklist to assess alignment and scalability

1. Is your model aligned with the industry?

   a. What is the dominant BM among your most immediate competitors?
   b. Can you describe the four building blocks for a generic competitor in the industry?
   c. What is the dominant BM among your indirect competitors?
   d. Are these models stable or have they changed during the last five years?
   e. Which of the three models shown in Table 10.1 seems to fit better with your business idea?
   f. Where is the emphasis in your value proposition? Where is the emphasis in the industry? Do you need to be different? Can you afford to be?

2. Is your model scalable?

   a. If not, what can prevent scalability?
   b. Can the profit formula be positive even with a low volume of sales?
   c. Can you claim a high margin?
   d. Can you identify the critical resources and activities you need?
   e. Can you acquire these resources and implement these activities in small quantities and steps?
   f. Can your BM support different ways of revenue generation?
   g. Can your BM be digital or digitalized?

taught in business schools. In a few words, business model innovation is based on the idea that business success is driven by the "what" as much as by the "how." While a great value proposition is at the foundation of any great organization, "how" the value proposition is delivered can make a difference. This "how" is your BM; when you change the "how," you pursue business model innovation.

Let us look at an example offered by one of the canvas inventors, Alex Osterwalder (Osterwalder, 2016). The example refers to the Nespresso system developed by Nestlé in the early 2000s. (A YouTube video is also available, and the canvas template and other free tools are available at www.strategyzer.com (Strategyzer, 2023).)

The value proposition is the keystone around which the whole BM is built. Following this principle, the value proposition building block is at the center of the canvas (Figure 10.3).

The canvas includes eight additional building blocks, four to the left and four to the right of the value proposition block. The left-right direction represents the flow of inputs from suppliers to customers. Left-side activities, such as procurement and operations, will generate costs, while right-side activities, including sales and customer relationships, will shape the company revenue model.

Nespresso's value proposition hinges on two different products: a coffee machine and coffee pods. It is easier to understand how these products work together by splitting the BM into two canvases (Figures 10.3 and 10.4). It is not infrequent for a large company to adopt multiple BMs simultaneously. Following Osterwalder's example, we use virtual Post-its to highlight Nestlé's crucial business choices to build the business.

The Nespresso coffee machines were designed to frame the "making an espresso" experience to be as seamless and pleasant as possible. No more complicated procedures and messy coffee powder spill on your counter! You only need to snap the pod into the machine and push a button. The technology inside the machine sets the right temperature and pressure. The design of the coffee machine and the pod was consistent with the Nespresso system value

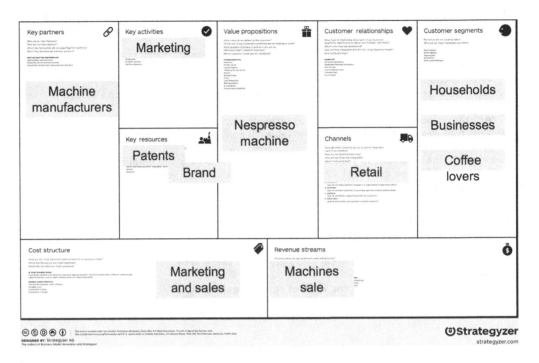

Figure 10.3 **Nespresso business model canvas for the Nespresso coffee machine**. Notice how the value proposition shapes the other building blocks when a BM has internal consistency.

Source: Adapted from Osterwalder, 2023; originally published in Iandoli & Zollo, 2022.

proposition in that it sported a contemporary, sleek design based on higher-quality plastic and steel details, and the coffee pod was designed like a deluxe chocolate bonbon box.

Nestlé made significant investments in patents and brand building (its patents are now mostly expired, which is why today we have compatible pods and machines built by other producers; see chapter 11). Production was outsourced since Nestlé did not have manufacturing capability internally, and it was not critical from the strategic point of view.

As for the downstream part of the model, the company decided to distribute the machine through traditional retailing channels (e.g., department stores). Revenues are generated by selling the machines to final customers. Thus, the coffee machine is an example of a value-added process BM.

Once we account for the high manufacturing and marketing costs and the relatively low sticker price of the coffee machines, the profit margin on each sale is very small or even negative. Why would Nestlé build such an unattractive BM? Because its objective is to make money through repeated sales of the coffee pods. Nothing new under the sun here: it was a version of the razor and blade BM, invented by Gillette more than one century ago. Companies in effect subsidize purchasing the razor so customers will purchase the blades repeatedly. This model is popular in digital applications. E-booksellers subsidize their e-readers so that you will buy many e-books from them. Phone companies will get you a deal on a smartphone so that you will buy data and voice services for at least a few years.

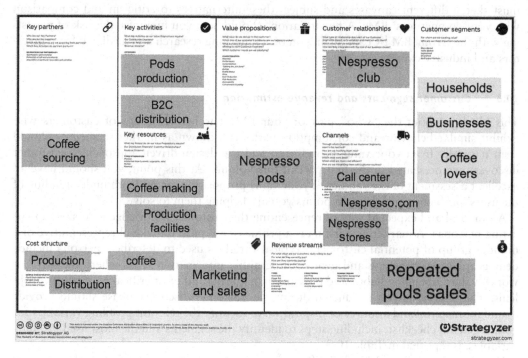

Figure 10.4 **Nespresso business model canvas for Nespresso coffee pods** (our adaptation. Notice how a change in the value proposition originates a very different BM compared to the one depicted in Figure 10.3

Source: Authors' adaptation from Osterwalder, 2023, originally published in Iandoli and Zollo, 2022, for Bloomsbury Publishing.

The profitable part of the model is making and selling pods (Figure 10.4). Nestlé is not an appliance manufacturer but a food company, so it made sense for them to focus on their core skills of mass-producing, distributing, and branding alimentary products on the global market.

Sourcing good-quality coffee from selected producers was imperative, since Nespresso is marketed as an upscale, high-quality product. Then Nestlé decided to be directly responsible for producing and distributing the coffee pods. The channels to reach the final customers included online and dedicated brick-and-mortar outlets, including the Nespresso website, the exclusive Nespresso stores, and a dedicated call center. Revenue is generated by consumers held captive through a proprietary platform (the coffee machine) engaging in repeated and frequent purchases (the pods). In this way, Nestlé transformed a commodity (coffee) into a high-margin product.

10.5   Design ideas block by block

In the following sections, we walk you through the most critical building blocks of the canvas and provide checklists and examples that can help you build canvases for your BM. The plural here reminds you to consider alternative ways to deliver your value proposition. You must sketch different canvases and subject these alternatives to criticism and comparison with your competitors' BMs. A few iterations should help you minimize the risk of persisting with the wrong BM by capitalizing on benchmarking research and feedback from investors and industry experts.

10.5.1 Customer segments and revenue estimation

This block is about the "who" part of your BM. The list of groups of customers who exhibit similar behavior and consumption patterns—known as market segments—should stem naturally from your value proposition and the design-driven approach to customer discovery we presented in the first part of this volume. At this point, you should have an excellent assessment of the validity of your value proposition, an in-depth understanding of the users' problems, and the pain points you are helping them to solve.

A practical and expected way of representing this customer knowledge is to sketch marketing personas. A marketing persona is a profile of a typical individual representative of a broader group of potential customers. Typical variables used to describe a persona include demographics such as age and gender, geographic information (e.g., where they live or work), values, spending habits and purchasing patterns, and most critical pain points/problems. The interviews you conducted during the customer discovery phase should provide abundant material and a source of inspiration to identify the relevant profiling variables for you. A general checklist, including steps to identify the segments and the most used profiling variables, is reported in Table 10.3.

You should identify at least 3–5 different user profiles. The next step is to make an initial assessment of the viability of these users in terms of their capability to generate revenue for your business. The analysis should focus on three critical tests (Meyer & Crane, 2013):

1. What is the size of the market segment?
2. How much do they spend on a product like yours, and how frequently do they purchase it?
3. How much would it cost you to reach out to them?

Table 10.3 Suggested profiling variables to describe your marketing personas and a card-on-the-wall approach to generate them

---

Typical variables to profile marketing personas
- Name the persona (Rachel)
- Job/profession (communication manager)
- Demographics such as age, gender, residence, marital status, income (35, female, suburban zip code 12345, single, $90,000)
- Goals/pain points (as described in the customer discovery analysis)
- How we can help (as described in the customer discovery analysis)

A card-on-the-wall method to optimize the definition of the market segments
- Create a Post-it for each of the user types you have identified through your customer discovery research.
- Try to expand the list by adding other types of users connected to the ones you identified or that you had not considered during customer discovery.
- Stick the Post-it on the wall and see if you can group these users into broader groups: users in the same group should have the same consuming and purchasing behaviors and overlap in many profile characteristics.

Regarding point 1, you could find out that certain groups are too small to consider. When you add profiling variables, you exclude all people who do not fit the profile and discover that the market is too small to be profitable. For example, the number of families with three kids and an income of $150,000 in a given neighborhood can be too small to make sense as a prospective market. These demographic data can be retrieved via existing market studies or, for U.S. markets, the Census.gov website. The Small Business Administration web site also offers great advice on procuring or performing market research (SBA, 2023). This check would immediately rule out these marginal groups from your consideration.

Let us say, however, that the group is not that small but that, on the other hand, their expenditure for similar services is limited and infrequent. It is also possible that these customers are pretty happy with what they have and are likely to keep using the same product. This information can be easily collected via a market survey. This second test will help you to eliminate other unattractive customer groups. In both of these cases, the segment will not generate enough revenue for you.

Finally, let us say the number of customers is high, they spend enough money, and they are not particularly satisfied with the product they are using. It is time for the third test: how hard do you have to fight to capture these customers and, once captured, to retain them? To answer this question, you should have an estimate of the cost of entering this market. For instance, do you have to spend much on advertisement and branding? Can you afford the distribution channels that your prospective customers typically use? Large-scale distribution through wholesalers and big retailers such as Walmart can be expensive and unfriendly to small businesses. Large-scale distribution will cost you money, and you will not have any negotiation power.

Table 10.4 suggests how to perform these three tests. These suggestions help you execute an initial screening of your prospective customers so that you can exclude unattractive or too expensive segments and focus on the ones that are affordable and have potential. Once you identify the promising segments, a complete market study with extensive data collection

Table 10.4 Three tests to identify your target market segments

Test	Tools
What is the size of the market segment?	Use the demographic variables of your personas to estimate the number of subjects fitting the profile in a geographical area. For example, how many dog-lovers families of 4–5 members of a certain age and income range live in the suburbs of a given city?
How much do they spend on a product like yours, how frequently they purchase, and do they like what they buy?	Survey prospective customers to learn about their expenditure patterns (see Meyer and Crane, 2013, for a list of questions). For instance, how much does Persona X spend on dog food each month? Do they buy in supermarkets, small stores, or online? Do they get information about the product from advertising available on which media? Are they happy with the dog food they are already using?
How much would it cost you to reach out to them?	Where can customers find your product? Where do they find information about the product? Do your competitors buy a lot of offline or online ads? Do you need to be on supermarket shelves?

can be done. As always, in the spirit of the approach proposed in this book, the key is scalability. You must prune a tree's dead branches before focusing on the ones you can grow.

10.5.2 *Estimating your revenues*

Once you have identified your target segments and estimated their size, you have an initial base to estimate your revenue. The target market size is your potential demand. Only a fraction of those customers will switch to your product.

Let us say you are opening a new restaurant in a neighborhood with 50 restaurants and have estimated the number of customers dining there. It is reasonable to assume that each restaurant has a small market share, slightly higher or lower than the average 2%. Since your restaurant is new, you can estimate you will be able to capture only half of that at the beginning, which is 1%. If 10,000 customers dine in the neighborhood every night, you can count on average on 100 customers per night (not great, but a good start!).

If your market survey tells you that the average customer spends $70 on a meal, you have a potential $7,000 in revenue per night, about $200,000 per month. The average customer's expenditure on each purchase is the average price for your product. You can be more or less affordable, but in that neighborhood, you will have to keep your menu price in a range, say, between $50 and $100 for most customers.

The example shows that in establishing the price of your product, you must consider many factors, but the starting point is the analysis of your competition and your target market. Once you understand who your competitors and customers are, you can establish the price range in which your offer will have to be confined.

The only way you can escape these brackets is to offer a value proposition that is so unique and distinctive that your customers will be glad to pay a premium price. Even then, you should expect imitation or innovation by your competitors, which in the long term can erode your margins.

Startups often fail to appreciate their competitive advantage and how much customers are willing to pay for a great product. As a result, they make the mistake of underpricing their products. Startups are also likely to need to pay more attention to their costs. The combination of underselling your product and underestimating your costs will be fatal.

We will look at cost in the next section; here, we focus on revenues and pricing. Another way to price your product is to use cost as a basis:

Price = costs + mark-up

This approach may not take into consideration costs that are not under your direct control such as distribution, sale costs, and any other cost you are not even aware of. A rule of thumb is to use a multiplying factor between 2 and 3 of your cost per unit to make a safer estimate, such as

Price = 2.5 × (costs) + mark-up

A way to increase your revenue is to find additional sources. In the restaurant examples, these sources could be food delivery, catering services, special events, or sales of certain products. You could also consider revenue models that promote customer loyalty, such as points and rewards or discounts to specific categories of repeat buyers. Finally, a significant source of additional revenue can be obtained by selling complementary products. For instance, hair or nail salons can make significant additional revenue by selling hair care or nail care products on the side.

Let's put everything together:

1. Establish price: P = average market price + premium price, or Price = 2.5 × (costs) + mark-up
2. Estimate revenues for each segment S_i: R_i = P × segment size S_i × market share
3. Estimate additional revenues AR
4. Compute total revenue: TR = R_1 + R_2 + . . . + R_n + AR

10.5.3 Estimating costs

Your cost estimate should be based on a careful analysis of all the building blocks of the canvas, especially those at the left of the value proposition. The activities you must perform and the resources you need to acquire or develop to execute them are the primary drivers of your costs.

Here is a general list of activities that apply to many companies:

• Production costs include direct labor and materials to make a product or deliver a service. In the restaurant example, these include the money you need to buy the ingredients and pay your servers and cooks.
• Marketing costs include money you must spend to acquire customers, such as advertising and online presence (website, search engine optimization, online advertising, etc.). The money you spend to develop your brand also falls in this category.
• Development costs include any cost you must pay to design and test new products, or research and development to improve your product. These include expenses to create and test prototypes (e.g., new recipes).
• Distribution includes all the costs to bring the product to your customers: in the restaurant example, you have no distribution costs for the customers who dine in, but you have distribution costs for deliveries.

For each of these activities, you must estimate the personnel costs—the cost of the people you need to hire. The number of employees you will have to hire will be a function of the volume of activity you have planned. How many customers can a server attend at a given time? How many cooks do you need to serve X meals per hour? Based on the number of customers and shifts, how many managers do you need?

In addition to the employees in charge of providing the service, you may need other indirect employees, such as administrative and security staff, janitors, and managers.

Other costs are determined by the capital you need to start your business. This capital includes both financial and nonfinancial sources. Financial sources are loans and debts. Nonfinancial sources include physical assets, such as buildings and equipment, and nonphysical assets, such as intellectual property. Capital goods are used for an extended period, typically over multiple years, so accounting rules establish that the initial cost of these goods must be distributed across all the years during which the capital goods will be used. For instance, if you buy a piece of equipment for $10,000 and plan to use it for five years, you could spread the initial amount over the five years at $ 2,000 per year.[2] The same applies to

Table 10.5 P&L statement for the year 2024

Revenues	Description and notes
Sales	Sales from all market segments
Additional revenues	Sales from other sources
• **Operating costs**	
Materials & Direct labor	Production/service delivery
Administrative expenses	Administration & management
Research and Development	Costs to design, test and innovate the product
Distribution & Sale	Costs to deliver the product to the final customers
Capital cost (depreciation and	such as marketing costs and distributors mark-ups
amortization)	Yearly fraction of the capital costs
Other operating costs	May include insurance, security, legal fees, training, and extraordinary expenses
Operating profit	
• Financial costs	Loan yearly repayment and other financial obligations
Profit before taxes	
• Taxes	Federal and local government
Net Profit	

financial resources you acquire from others, such as banks. A loan must be repaid through periodic installments along with the interest it generates.

You can summarize all your estimates into a yearly simplified profit and loss statement, or P&L, as illustrated in Table 10.5.

The P&L starts from the revenues your company generates. You will have to subtract all the costs of your activities or the mere fact that your company exists to estimate your profit. In the P&L all the expenses can be grouped into three categories:[3]

- Operating costs include all the operations your company performs to make and sell a product or service.
- Financial costs include the cost of your debts, typically interest arising from loans or mortgages you must repay. If the debt extends over multiple years, the P&L will report only the installments paid in the year.
- Fiscal costs include taxes to federal and local governments.

10.6 Conclusions

In this chapter, we have introduced BM design. Visualizing a BM for your product or service is the first step to assessing the viability of building a sustainable business around your idea. The various building blocks force you to think about the additional complexity of making and selling your product, understand the industry, and identify some rudimentary but crucial economic estimates regarding the sources of revenues and costs.

You can think of a BM canvas as a low-fidelity prototype of your company. Leveraging your design mindset, you can use these prototypes in the same way you used your product prototype: as an effective way to deal with uncertainty by iterating and scaling your design.

A well-designed BM will go a long way to prove to potential investors that you have a good grasp of the business fundamentals and the industry constraints. It will provide a solid foundation to write a complete business plan when such a plan is required. Writing a business plan is beyond this book's scope; you can find many tutorials, manuals, and tools to help you. Most likely, however, you do not need a plan when you are still trying to

Key takeaways for this chapter

Lesson learned	Implications for your project
Understand and design the logic of your business	• A BM describes how you plan to make money out of your product. Designing your BM will help you to understand the complexity around making and selling your product and will force you to look into the industry where you will compete. • A well-designed BM is scalable and aligned with the industry. Scalability means you can expand your business in sustainable steps, without risking too much up front. Alignment means you know the BM that is dominant among competitors and that you understand if and to which extent it is a good idea to differentiate your BM and where you can stand out. BM innovation is a way of improving on existing BMs, but the more you change, the more you risk.
Map your BM's building blocks	• A BM canvas is a low-fidelity prototype for your business, so use it as such. Get feedback, design alternatives, and do little experiments if you can. • Always start from the value proposition and build around it. • Each building block comes with a set of questions that you should be able to answer. How will you reach out to your customers? How will you procure what you need?
Understand sources of revenues and costs	• A preliminary quantification of revenues and costs will give you an educated guess about whether your business is financially viable. • It will also help you to identify the causal links between how you run the business and how your BM can generate revenues and costs. Such causal analysis can be leveraged to anticipate risks and bottlenecks and will provide you a basis for more sound and in-depth financial analysis.

address more fundamental questions regarding your business's viability and logic. For now, a well-thought BM will help you to address some burning questions from your partners and investors.

Another question you are likely to receive at this stage is whether you have sufficient protection for your idea in terms of intellectual property (IP). Investors want to know whether your idea is sufficiently novel and does not infringe on existing IP, what can prevent others from appropriating or imitating the idea, and if you have some form of IP protection or are at least aware of what you need (whether you are planning for it). This is the subject of the next chapter.

Notes

1 According to the International Energy Agency (IEA), the market share of EVs in the US jumped from 4% to 14% between 2020 and 2022, after being well below 1% in the previous decade (IEA, 2023). The recent incentives provided by governments to promote the transition to clean energy are accelerating both adoption and the development of better EV technology.
2 The loss of value of an asset per year of use is called depreciation. Your accountant will use the methods that the law allow to compute these values. These methods can depend on the type of assets. Even if you do not really pay this money out, you treat it as a cost, and this will translate into a tax saving. You should set aside some of your profit to be able to refresh your equipment when it gets worn out or obsolete.

3 The P&L format presented in this chapter and based on classifying costs by their nature is only one possible format. Accountants and budget directors use other formats depending on the information they want to emphasize.

References

Christensen, C. M., Grossman, J. H., & Hwang, J. (2009). *The innovator's prescription*. McGraw-Hill.

Iandoli, L., & Zollo, G. (2022). *Elegant design: A designer's guide to harnessing aesthetics*. Bloomsbury Publishing.

IEA. (2023). *Trends in electric light-duty vehicles*. www.iea.org/reports/global-ev-outlook-2023/trends-in-electric-light-duty-vehicles, last accessed September 2023.

Johnson, M. W., Christensen, C. M., & Kagermann, H. (2008). Reinventing your business model. *Harvard Business Review*, 86(12), 50–59.

Meyer, M. H., & Crane, F. G. (2013). *New venture creation: An innovator's guide to entrepreneurship* (2nd edition). Sage Publications.

Osterwalder, A. (2023). *Nespresso business canvas*. www.youtube.com/watch?v=_UECTWQCYxQ last accessed July 2023.

Osterwalder, A., & Pigneur, Y. (2010). *Business model generation: A handbook for visionaries, game changers, and challengers* (Vol. 1). John Wiley & Sons.

SBA. (2023). *Market research and competitive analysis*. https://www.sba.gov/business-guide/plan-your-business/market-research-competitive-analysis

Strategyzer. (2023). *Build an invincible company*. www.strategyzer.com

Wikipedia (2023). *Better Place (company), definition*. https://en.wikipedia.org/wiki/Better_Place_(company), last accessed September 2023.

Chapter 11

A primer on intellectual property

If people had understood how patents would be granted when most of today's ideas were invented and had taken out patents, the industry would be at a complete standstill today.

—Bill Gates, Challenges and Strategy Memo (1991)

11.1 A man walks into a Starbucks

Try this exercise next time you go to Starbucks for a cup of coffee. Look around you and see if you can spot anything unique and distinctive about the coffee shop that Starbucks may want to protect or leverage as intellectual property (IP). Try to do this before you even read this chapter. The only thing you need, if you are not familiar with IP, is the following definition:

Intellectual property refers to the creations of the mind, such as inventions, artistic works, designs, symbols, and names used in commerce. It grants exclusive rights to creators and innovators, protecting their creations from unauthorized use and ensuring they can benefit from their work (Melman, 2023).

Do you have your tentative list? Great job! Now, let's look at some numbers and examples. First, Starbucks owns almost 1,000 patents, of which more than half are still active (however, patents do expire; more on this later). Patents are a specific form of IP that typically protects material functional or aesthetic inventions. These patents have been acquired through the years, on average 59 per year from 2011 to 2021, of which only 32 per year were, on average, approved (Insights, 2023). These numbers show that innovation is nonstop and that even large companies with a lot of resources and legal support, such as Starbucks, can get rejections from the U.S. Patent and Trademark Office (interestingly, the approval rate was only 10% in the first year, but it went up to 60%, an evident sign that even Starbucks had to go over a little bit of a learning curve).

Let's look at examples to understand what kind of inventions Starbucks protects. We can use the number of citations they received to identify the most famous patent. A patent looks a lot like an academic paper. If someone creates an invention for a similar task, the inventor will add a reference to other patents to show how her invention is related to the prior art. Hence, the more impactful a patent is, the more citations it receives.

The most popular Starbucks patents include:

- A chewing gum tin
- An insulated beverage container and lid assembly
- Instant beverage cartridges and methods

DOI: 10.4324/9781003346463-12

- A machine for brewing a beverage such as coffee and related method
- A music user interface
- A disposable beverage cup lid
- Method and apparatus for automatically reloading a stored-value card
- System for brewing and serving a hot beverage
- Beverages with enhanced flavors and aromas and methods of making same

This list is very informative. Some of the items are expected. Of course, Starbucks would invent and protect devices to make and store beverages. However, Starbucks also patented the drinks and the methods to make them. Some patents are crucial to improving the customer experience beyond consuming a beverage. That is the case for the music player, since music is an essential aspect of the Starbucks coffee experience (up to some years ago, Starbucks also sold music CDs to satisfy customer requests to buy the music played in the stores).

It is also essential to notice that patents can have a "negative value." With this, a patent may effectively prevent a competitor from doing something. The Starbucks disposable lid is functional, but we doubt anyone would mention the lid design as a determinant of excellent customer experience. More likely, patenting that design is primarily a way to prevent competitors from developing something similar. Instead, they will have to design a more costly or less effective one, or they will have to pay royalties to Starbucks. Or maybe Starbucks had to patent its lid so as not to pay royalties to other inventors. We will see later in the chapter that this is tricky: there are many criteria a patent must fulfill, among which one is that you cannot patent the obvious and you cannot appropriate common knowledge.

Patents are not the only way to acquire and protect IP. There is much more to notice in a Starbucks store regarding copyright, trademarks, and, possibly, trade secrets.

Before we dive deeper into the different forms of IP and how to acquire them, we will illustrate why acquiring IP is critical for entrepreneurs.

11.2 What intellectual property is and why it matters

Intellectual property (IP) refers to a set of legal mechanisms to ascertain ownership and control of creations of the mind, such as inventions, artistic works, designs, symbols, and names used in commerce. It grants exclusive rights to creators and innovators, protecting their creations from unauthorized use and ensuring they can benefit from their work. A property can be exclusively owned and accessed. It can be donated, leased, or sold. IP is, however, an intangible asset, unlike the physical capital you may own or need for your business, such as office space and machines. It is a legal title whose value is enforced by the government.

The reason why IP was invented was to give inventors an incentive to profit from their creations. IP is a cornerstone of modern capitalism. Creating something new and useful requires a lot of work and significant investments, so it is fair that those investing effort in creating something new are given the possibility to get a return on that investment.

However, regulators do not give inventors the perpetual right to profit from their creations. That is an essential difference with other types of properties: in the United States, IP expires after a certain number of years, for instance, 20 years for a utility patent or 70 years after the author's death for copyright. The expiration terms may differ in other legal systems, but IP will expire sooner or later. While inventors or entrepreneurs may not be happy to lose their monopoly, regulators must reconcile incentives to individual creativity with

Table 11.1 Fundamental benefits of IP for early-stage entrepreneurs

Key Advantage	Why It Matters
Protection	IP safeguards your unique ideas and products from unauthorized use or copy.
Competitive Advantage	IP can help you differentiate in the market: IP tells investors and customers that a company owns and is capable of developing technology or distinctive branding. For instance, you can build brand equity by developing strong trademarks and leveraging their reputation to attract customers and establish a distinct market position.
Capital	IP is an asset, i.e., a form of capital, that entrepreneurs can leverage to create revenues or attract additional capital through a third party's investment. A startup in its early stages typically has limited capital assets: IP helps close that gap and reassure prospective investors that, at least potentially, the company has unique and defendable assets.
Additional revenues	You can license your IP to others in exchange for licensing fees or royalties. Franchising is another option, whereby entrepreneurs grant others the right to operate a business using their brand and business model.
Partnership	IP can be an asset when forming strategic partnerships or collaborations. By sharing or combining intellectual property with other businesses or individuals, entrepreneurs can access new markets, leverage complementary expertise, and accelerate innovation.

the common good. A perpetual right would prevent society from benefiting from an invention forever. This would create a powerful disincentive to future innovation and an unfair profit for the inventor. For instance, why should humanity be deprived of freely listening to Mozart or reading Mark Twain's works to compensate their descendants who had no part in creating that beautiful music and literature?

Besides, technology and science are built on previous knowledge, often by reusing existing inventions and discoveries. Governments would severely hinder technological progress and economic development by blocking others from building on prior knowledge.

The fact that IP expires instead incentivizes inventors to keep innovating and build new solutions by reusing knowledge that other human beings have previously created. We summarize the benefits of acquiring IP for entrepreneurs in Table 11.1.

A key benefit of IP is often overlooked: learning. As we show in this chapter, investigating what kind of IP your business needs, assessing which IP your competitors own, and finally acquiring IP comes with an immense amount of learning about the relevant technology and the competition in your target market or industry. Whether you secure it or not, pursuing IP makes you much more knowledgeable and competent, and the value of this knowledge can even outgrow the value of the IP you will eventually develop and acquire.

11.3 Types of intellectual property

IP law identifies different objective criteria to determine what can be protected and what cannot and provides various ways to secure and enforce IP, depending on the type of "creation" of the mind. A simple tool to determine what kind of IP you need can be found, along with plenty of information, advice, and other great resources, on the website of the US Patent and Trademark Office (see USPTO, 2023 in the reference list at the end of the chapter).

As much as regulators try to define clear criteria, there will always be some level of ambiguity and room for legal disputes (a famous, multiyear patent battle occurred between Apple and Samsung concerning the development of smartphones).

In the following sections, we review the existing mechanisms and outline the process to secure IP. Securing IP will typically require you to consult with an IP lawyer. Good legal counseling will help you to maximize the chances of obtaining IP, safeguard you from future legal action in case of possible infringements, and create well-designed IP that is hard for your competitors to overcome.

11.3.1 Patents

Patents typically protect physical inventions and new technologies. They grant inventors exclusive rights to make, use, and sell their inventions for a limited period. Patents encourage innovation by allowing inventors to monetize their creations and recover research and development costs.

Not everything can be patented. A fundamental requirement for a patentable invention is that the idea must be embedded into some physical device or form. This physical form includes any apparatus, process, composition of matter, or manufactured product. For instance, drugs can be patented because the chemical formula is embedded into a molecule. You can also patent a plant. Given its intangible nature, software is typically not patentable, but if you embed an algorithm into a device (physical product), the software component will be included in the patent. You can patent an original invention, improve on the prior art, or repurpose an existing patent for a different use or application.

Two types of patents are available: utility patents cover useful products, processes, or machines, while design patents protect ornamental/aesthetic aspects of an invention. Utility patents are about how it works, and design patents are about how it looks. Examples of design patents include jewelry, packaging, fonts, and computer icons. Examples of utility patents include most patented devices, ranging from simple (e.g., coffee cup lids) to complex (e.g., the formulation of a vaccine).

Design patents are less expensive and easier to obtain but don't last as long (15 years versus 20 for design patents) and are easier to be "designed around" by competitors, who may create a similar product that looks different only from the aesthetic point of view.

To be patentable, an invention must satisfy the following three criteria:

• Usefulness: must support a practical task
• Novelty: not identical to (or sufficiently different than) anything in the prior art
• Nonobviousness: obvious improvements over the prior art are not patentable; a test for this criterion is whether a person skilled in the art will likely come up with the same idea through logical deduction and minimal effort.

The process to acquire a patent includes three steps:

• Patent search
• Patent application preparation and filing
• Deliberation and approval or rejection by the IP government authority (USPTO in the United States)

The process of filing a patent requires the support of a specialized lawyer. While paying a lawyer is expensive, it is recommended since a well-written patent application will substantially increase your chances of approval. A ballpark estimate of the cost to file a patent for a startup or small entity is $3,000–4,000 for a design patent and $10,000–15,000 for a utility patent (SBIR, 2023). However, this average cost can depend on the technology's complexity, the applicant company's size, and whether you are applying to have your patent approved internationally. The price includes government and attorney's fees.

However, this book is written for early-stage entrepreneurs, and we recognize they may not have the money to invest in a patent. We want, however, to reassure you that a DIY approach to creating a successful patent application is entirely possible (see Box 11.1).

Box 11.1   Mini case study: A do-it-yourself approach to patent application (courtesy of Dr. John DiMarco; see also DiMarco, 2023)

Lessons for applying for a patent without a lawyer

While it is more complicated, applying for a patent without an attorney is not impossible. If you apply independently, follow the guidelines at USPTO.gov, which provides a wide range of resources for "pro se" (on one's own behalf) applicants.

We asked Dr. John DiMarco, a professor of digital advertising at St. John's University and an entrepreneur, to share some tips for preparing and filing a patent. His passion for golf led him to design a novel stretching bar. During his journey as an inventor, he acquired different types of IP, including one design patent and copyright on digital content developed for the invention (Figure 11.1). You can read more about this case study in DiMarco (2023).

RESEARCH

- Research both utility and design patents regardless of the application type (the examiner will be looking for that—see Figure 11.1 for the references in the stretching bar patent).
- Examine classifications of goods and keywords on previous patents.
- When looking at previous patents that are close to your idea and in the same categories, highlight claims to look for that have similar and novel relationships.
- Create a list of keywords and identify the classification of goods category (SIC code) based on your research.

APPLICATION PREPARATION

- Hire an experienced draftsperson to create drawings; they are critical for provisional and design patents (see Figure 11.2).
- Show all technical views and the invention "in the environment" of how it would be used.
- Write broad claims for a utility and a single-encompassing claim for a design application.

- Have your most trusted colleague or an attorney (if you can afford it) review the document (pay attention to typos; they are not allowed in final patents, and the USPTO doesn't edit).

FOLLOW-UP

- Use the term "patent pending" on investor and industry presentations after your application is acknowledged by the USPTO.
- Be prepared to amend claims or drawings based on examiner's feedback.
- Don't be afraid to make a telephone conference with the examiner to clarify how to respond to "actions." (i.e., requests of changes from the evaluators)
- Always explicitly follow the examiner's instructions.

Before you decide to invest any money, you can start with an initial search to understand how your invention compares to similar ideas already patented. You can perform a keyword search for existing patents using Google Patent or the USPTO tool. Most of the time, inventors are surprised to discover how many inventions are already available that differ little, if not at all, from what they were thinking to patent. A good search can give you some solid insights about the state of the art in the field and provide you with ideas on improving existing solutions. It is important to remark that patents do not recognize independent discovery: this means that if you come up with a great idea on your own but an existing and very similar version of your invention already exists, you will not be able to patent your idea even when it has been independently discovered.

A patent application is a document that includes the following parts (see Figure 11.1):

- An abstract
- Drawings and specifications (including background section, list of drawings, and detailed description)
- Claims describing what aspects of the invention the applicant believes deserve protection
- Citations of prior art, typically through the references to similar patents and technical/academic literature.

Once filed, the patent will be examined by the patent authority of the country where the request is filed. Experts appointed by the authority will finally determine whether the request is accepted or denied. The process can take up to a few years, with 22 months being the average processing time, as reported by the USPTO. Figure 11.1 shows the patent for the invention mentioned in Box 11.1.

When you submit your application, your invention will be patent-pending for 12 months. This status does not guarantee legal protection and only informs potential competitors that a patent may be on the way and that they can be sued for patent infringement after the patent is granted. Alternatively, if you are not ready to file yet, applying for a provisional patent will give you one year before a nonprovisional patent will be filed. A provisional patent is an inexpensive placeholder that will signal your intention to patent without committing to doing so immediately.

US00D910126S

(12) **United States Design Patent**   (10) Patent No.:   **US D910,126 S**
DiMarco   (45) Date of Patent: **   Feb. 9, 2021

(54) **BODY STRETCHING BAR**

(71) Applicant: **John DiMarco**, Massapequa, NY (US)

(72) Inventor: **John DiMarco**, Massapequa, NY (US)

(**) Term: **15 Years**

(21) Appl. No.: **29/651,881**

(22) Filed: **May 29, 2019**

(51) **LOC (13) Cl.** **21-02**

(52) **U.S. Cl.**
USPC **D21/691**; D21/679

(58) **Field of Classification Search**
USPC D8/14; D6/349; D32/42; D25/67;
D21/694, 691, 690, 689, 688, 686, 685,
D21/684, 682, 681, 680, 679, 662;
D14/209.1; 482/95, 93, 91, 83, 8, 51, 5,
482/49, 45, 44, 41, 40, 38, 36, 34, 25,
482/148, 146, 142, 141, 139, 138, 132,
482/131, 121, 111, 108, 107, 106, 104,
482/100
CPC A63B 23/1236; A63B 21/4035; A63B
21/00047; A63B 23/12; A63B 2210/50;
A63B 21/068; A63B 23/03541; A63B
23/0211; A63B 21/0004; A63B 23/1218;
A63B 23/1227; A63B 21/4049; A63B
2208/0219; A63B 2208/0295; A63B
23/1209; A63B 1/00
See application file for complete search history.

(56) **References Cited**

U.S. PATENT DOCUMENTS

2,666,640 A *	1/1954	Jennings, Sr.	A63B 3/00
			482/141
2,817,347 A *	12/1957	Hilt, Sr.	A61H 3/00
			135/65
2,919,918 A *	1/1960	Horn	A63B 21/00047
			482/142

3,016,267 A *	1/1962	Cones	A47C 16/02
			297/423.41
3,077,347 A *	2/1963	Nova	A63B 21/00054
			482/142
3,809,393 A *	5/1974	Jones	A63B 22/20
			482/132
4,103,887 A *	8/1978	Shoofler	A63B 21/0602
			482/106
4,126,308 A *	11/1978	Crumley	A63B 22/20
			482/148
4,176,835 A *	12/1979	Aziz	A63B 23/0211
			482/140

(Continued)

OTHER PUBLICATIONS

Pink by Shape Stretch dated no date given. Found online [Oct. 27, 2020] https://shapestretch.com/products/mystretchbar-commercial-stretching-equipment-with-guide-videos-1.*

Primary Examiner — Ryan Harvey

(57)   **CLAIM**
The ornamental design for a body stretching bar, as shown and described.

DESCRIPTION

FIG. 1 is a perspective view of the body stretching bar;
FIG. 2 is a front elevation view thereof;
FIG. 3 is a rear elevation view thereof;
FIG. 4 is a left side elevation view thereof;
FIG. 5 is a right side elevation view thereof;
FIG. 6 is a top plan view thereof;
FIG. 7 is a bottom plan view thereof; and,
FIG. 8 is an additional perspective view of the body stretching bar in a typical environment.
The broken lines of FIG. 8 depict environment and form no part of the claimed design.
The claimed design is shown with a symbolic break in its length. The appearance of any portion of the article between the break lines forms no part of the claimed design.

1 Claim, 8 Drawing Sheets

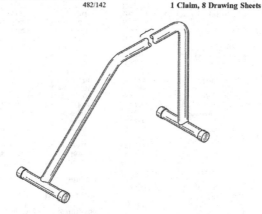

Figures 11.1a and 11.1b **Example of a design patent.** The cover page has crucial information about the invention, description, and claims, and then a list of other patents is cited. Citations are critical because they help the patent examiner to relate the new invention to the prior art.

Source: Courtesy of Dr. John DiMarco

US D910,126 S

Page 2

(56)   **References Cited**

U.S. PATENT DOCUMENTS

4,185,816	A	*	1/1980	Bernstein A63B 21/1645
				482/140
4,212,458	A	*	7/1980	Bizilia A63B 21/1654
				482/140
4,232,863	A	*	11/1980	Roach A63B 21/00047
				482/141
4,327,907	A	*	5/1982	DeVries A63B 21/00047
				482/141
4,351,525	A	*	9/1982	Rozenblad A63B 23/12
				482/141
4,380,231	A	*	4/1983	Rocha A61H 15/00
				482/79
D269,691	S	*	7/1983	Ornstein D21/691
4,406,450	A	*	9/1983	Regan A63B 3/00
				482/41
D277,218	S	*	1/1985	Hinds D21/687
4,539,977	A	*	9/1985	Schneider, Sr. A47C 16/02
				297/423.41
D281,006	S	*	10/1985	Durushia D21/687
4,666,154	A	*	5/1987	Lipscomb A63B 21/00047
				482/142
D301,361	S	*	5/1989	Harlan D21/691
4,850,589	A	*	7/1989	Block A63B 21/00047
				482/36
4,854,573	A	*	8/1989	Johannson A63B 23/12
				482/141
4,923,194	A	*	5/1990	Montgomery ... A63B 21/00047
				482/141
D315,003	S	*	2/1991	Huang D21/682
5,102,124	A	*	4/1992	Diodati A63B 21/0605
				482/106
5,180,349	A	*	1/1993	Marcus A63B 7/08
				434/258
5,181,897	A	*	1/1993	Agan A63B 23/12
				482/141
D332,981	S	*	2/1993	Poli D21/686
5,230,684	A	*	7/1993	Wallisch A63B 23/12
				482/141
D339,836	S	*	9/1993	Wallisch D21/692
5,266,069	A	*	11/1993	Thorne A63B 21/0084
				482/106
D345,468	S	*	3/1994	McVicker D6/349
D352,540	S	*	11/1994	Harger D21/691
D354,100	S	*	1/1995	Tsay D21/686
5,466,206	A	*	11/1995	Fleming A63B 23/12
				482/141
5,527,252	A	*	6/1996	Sather A63B 21/00047
				482/131
5,607,380	A	*	3/1997	Duty A63B 21/00047
				482/141
D381,714	S	*	7/1997	Easley D21/694
D382,610	S	*	8/1997	Maycock, Jr. D21/684
5,697,875	A	*	12/1997	Stan A63B 21/00047
				482/141
5,752,903	A	*	5/1998	Chang A63B 21/00047
				482/140
D403,036	S	*	12/1998	Ashcraft D21/686
D410,050	S	*	5/1999	Matte D21/691
6,117,054	A	*	9/2000	Soltanpour A63B 69/0079
				482/148
D432,603	S	*	10/2000	Bullard, Jr. D21/662
6,203,473	B1	*	3/2001	Atwood A63B 21/00047
				482/142
6,248,048	B1	*	6/2001	Zuckerman A63B 21/00047
				482/141
6,406,406	B1	*	6/2002	Onorati A63B 21/0004
				482/44
D460,507	S	*	7/2002	Stewart D21/688
D479,289	S	*	9/2002	Turner D21/662
D480,772	S	*	10/2003	Washington D21/686
6,773,379	B1	*	8/2004	Bing A63B 22/20
				482/132

D525,668	S	*	7/2006	Payne D21/691
D536,753	S	*	2/2007	Rongo D21/685
D562,016	S	*	2/2008	Tomasch D6/349
D580,998	S	*	11/2008	Lin D21/686
D585,947	S	*	2/2009	Royster D21/662
D593,169	S	*	5/2009	Storch D21/686
7,637,855	B2	*	12/2009	Bizzell A63B 21/0004
				482/142
7,651,449	B1	*	1/2010	Balentine A63B 23/12
				482/95
7,658,702	B1	*	2/2010	Harms A63B 21/0029
				482/141
7,662,067	B2	*	2/2010	Payne A63B 21/00047
				482/38
7,780,575	B1	*	8/2010	Goodwin, III A63B 21/169
				482/34
D631,560	S	*	1/2011	Merritt, Sr. D25/67
7,892,158	B2	*	2/2011	Varga A63B 21/4017
				482/141
D635,622	S	*	4/2011	Martin D21/681
8,075,425	B2	*	12/2011	Conwright A63B 69/0071
				473/447
8,088,052	B1	*	1/2012	Sprague A63B 21/00047
				482/141
D653,714	S	*	2/2012	Meininger D21/662
D654,545	S	*	2/2012	Richard D21/662
D662,997	S	*	7/2012	Su D21/662
D666,684	S	*	9/2012	Meininger D21/662
D686,287	S	*	7/2013	Boatwright D21/691
D695,364	S	*	12/2013	Khalil D21/662
D701,581	S	*	3/2014	Heitzman D21/686
D703,773	S	*	4/2014	Henry D21/691
D704,779	S	*	5/2014	Boatwright D21/686
8,876,677	B2	*	11/2014	Meininger A63B 23/03541
				482/132
D725,725	S	*	3/2015	White D21/682
D744,051	S	*	11/2015	Anderson D21/682
9,205,295	B2	*	12/2015	Williams A63B 21/4035
9,308,416	B1	*	4/2016	Oliverio A63B 23/1236
D764,607	S	*	8/2016	Beckford D21/679
9,409,049	B1	*	8/2016	Brunelo A63B 21/0726
D774,605	S	*	12/2016	Summers D21/680
9,630,054	B1	*	4/2017	Russo A63B 21/4034
9,713,745	B2	*	7/2017	Rogers A63B 21/4035
9,717,948	B1	*	8/2017	Hsu F16B 7/00
9,770,614	B1	*	9/2017	Sudeith A63B 69/0048
D799,610	S	*	10/2017	Ho D21/681
D823,405	S	*	7/2018	Roepke D21/694
10,099,082	B2	*	10/2018	Kravchenko A63B 23/0482
D839,365	S	*	1/2019	Martinez D21/662
D841,746	S	*	2/2019	Fazzari D21/691
D841,915	S	*	2/2019	Cira D32/42
10,207,142	B2	*	2/2019	Le Nguyen A63B 21/068
10,213,640	B2	*	2/2019	St. Jeor A63B 21/4035
D843,520	S	*	3/2019	Thompson D21/691
D844,075	S	*	3/2019	St. Jeor D21/662
D844,078	S	*	3/2019	Salomone D21/691
10,220,252	B2	*	3/2019	Jackson A63B 23/1218
D846,664	S	*	4/2019	Martinez D21/662
10,272,288	B2	*	4/2019	Brown A63B 21/015
10,292,884	B2	*	5/2019	Silverstein A61G 7/053
10,307,635	B1	*	6/2019	Khalil A63B 21/4035
10,413,772	B2	*	9/2019	Zachariadis A63B 21/0605
D866,685	S	*	11/2019	Laurence D21/681
D868,911	S	*	12/2019	Rogers D21/691
D878,496	S	*	3/2020	Hoppe D21/680
D886,921	S	*	6/2020	Cedro D21/686
D890,269	S	*	7/2020	Grant D21/679
D891,539	S	*	7/2020	Sun D21/662
2003/0004042	A1	*	1/2003	Burrell A63B 21/00047
				482/121
2003/0104909	A1	*	6/2003	Teran A63B 21/00047
				482/141
2003/0199375	A1	*	10/2003	Edwards A63B 23/12
				482/148
2005/0101461	A1	*	5/2005	Johnson A63B 21/4025
				482/141

Figures 11.1a and 11.1b Continued

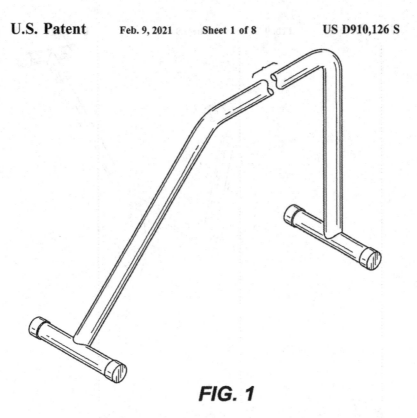

FIG. 1

Figures 11.2a and 11.2b **Examples of technical drawings related to Patent No.: US D910,126 S**. Well-crafted, accurate, and detailed illustrations are crucial in a patent application since they can help anyone skilled in the art to reproduce the invention. While drawings are required for full disclosure in patent applications, they can also be the object of trade secrets when a determination is made that disclosure will put an idea at risk.

Source: (DiMarco, 2021)

We should admire the brilliance behind the patent idea: to protect your invention, you must disclose it! The description of the invention in a patent application must be very detailed, to the point that anybody skilled in the art could independently reproduce the invention. Full disclosure facilitates the identification of infringement attempts and, at the same time, is a mechanism that promotes innovation by sharing knowledge on which future inventors can build.

11.3.2 *Copyright and copyleft*

Copyrights protect a different category of inventions of the mind, such as creative works, including literary, artistic, musical, and dramatic creations. Examples include novels, music, photos, website content, and computer code. This content must be original and created independently. Copyrights give creators exclusive rights to reproduce, distribute, display,

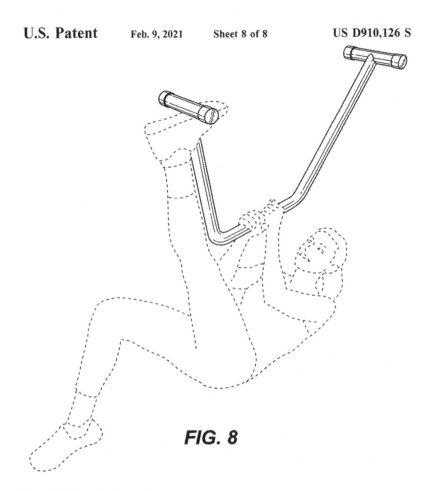

FIG. 8

Figures 11.2a and 11.2b Continued

perform, and modify their works. As with other forms of IP, copyright expires. In the United States and many other countries, the duration is 70 years after the death of the author.

It is essential to specify that the protection granted by copyright concerns how the idea is expressed and not the idea itself. Thus, if you have written a novel about a knight saving a princess, you can protect the actual text of the story. Still, you do not have exclusive rights over the story's theme (knights saving princesses).

Copyright protection is automatic upon creation and lasts for a specific duration, allowing entrepreneurs to control the use of their creative works. This means that simply because you have written or composed something, this something is yours, and you have a natural copyright on this creation. However, the USPTO specifies that this is true as long as the work is original and "fixed in a tangible medium of expression." You cannot copyright content that has not been recorded in some form (e.g., a musical recording or a published book) or lacks originality. You cannot appropriate content in the public domain (that is, you cannot copyright public-domain content) or copyright content that is obvious, commonly used, and not original, such as common shapes or words (e.g., you cannot appropriate common shapes such as squares and triangles).

However, in the United States and many other countries, you must register your copyright with the government IP authority to enforce copyright and sue unauthorized imitators.

For instance, publishers register a book's copyright by depositing a copy of the original work in the country's IP authority. The registration can be done for a modest fee and, unlike a patent, without specialized legal counseling. The process is much faster than with patents. Depositing copyright, however, does not guarantee that you have not infringed on anyone else's copyright.

You need to pay attention to the possibility of releasing your copyright to a third party. This is what typically happens when you work with a publisher. The publisher will ask you to sign a contract to transfer the copyright to the publisher in exchange for compensation, which could be a combination of a fixed amount of money and royalties based on actual sales. Once you transfer the copyright to a publisher, the publisher becomes the owner and can do what it wants with the content unless any restriction has been mentioned in the contract. This applies not only to books but to any medium in which a publisher or producer is involved, including film, photographs, songs, visual art, or a video game. So, if you are a movie director, photographer, songwriter, artist, or video game designer (among others), be sure to read all the fine print and be aware of any restriction or clause limiting your ability to monetize from this transaction. Sometimes, publishers may only want to pay a lump sum instead of royalties based on actual sales, or they promise royalties only for a limited amount of time, e.g., one year, and only on specific formats (e.g., printed books only, not e-books).

With the rise of the internet and the increasing amount of online content people want to share or access for free, nontraditional forms of IP have been created to facilitate content diffusion. "Copyleft" licenses turn the copyright logic on its head. Creators of digital content and software may be more interested in favoring the distribution of their creations than in preventing others from using these digital assets. However, these generous creators also want to prevent others from appropriating their free ideas. Copyleft and open-source licenses make the content available to everybody but introduce the constraint that no one accessing or building on it can appropriate. In this way, the open-source property propagates across users. As an example, open-source licenses help software developers access a massive body of knowledge for free and rely on free help from expert peers, but in exchange, developers are required to give up the code.

The family of Creative Commons (CC) licenses is an example of a copyleft. CC work is released for free. However, authors can and should add some restrictions for reuse. The most frequent include share-alike (SA), in which content can be modified and shared for free, but any modified version should be shared for free as well; attribution (BY), credit must be given to the original author when sharing; noncommercial (NC), which is free to share as long as the content is used for noncommercial application; and nonderivative (ND), in which derivative works are not allowed.

11.3.3 Trademarks

Trademarks protect brands, logos, symbols, and names used to identify goods or services. They distinguish one business from another and enable consumers to associate specific qualities with a particular brand or source. Trademarks protect both the companies owning the trademark and consumers, who need to be sure about the identity of who is providing goods or services to which consumers attribute certain qualities such as reputation or reliability.

A trademark can be a word, a logo, a drawing, a website domain, or a social media handle. Packaging, sounds, fragrances, graphic patterns, or color shades equally qualify if the identifier is unique and can be uniquely associated with the source. For instance, the luxury brand Burberry has trademarked its brown, white, red, and black plaid pattern.

By simply using a trademark on your products, you establish legal rights. However, registering the trademark is a better option. Registering a trademark gives entrepreneurs exclusive rights to use it and prevents others from using similar marks that may cause confusion. Trademarks are IP assets that can be sold or leased. They expire after ten years but can be renewed. When registering a trademark, you must tie it to specific goods or services. Apple is a registered trademark for computers and electronic gadgets, so it can't be used for a different category of goods, such as apparel or toys.

Creating and registering a trademark is something most people can do on their own. USPTO will reject trademarks that are confusing for the customers, are mere descriptions of goods or services, or are too similar to existing ones.

As with other forms of IP, the first thing to do is to perform a search to make sure something similar does not already exist (the whole point of a trademark is that it must be distinctive and unique). Then, you need some marketing wisdom, best obtained through the help of an experienced consultant, to make the trademark evocative of your value proposition.

Expressions such as "Just do it" and "The Ultimate Driving Machine" immediately evoke the brands they represent and what they stand for, action and energy for NIKE, and technology as a status symbol for BMW.[1]

Here is some advice for creating effective trademarks (Melman, 2023). A tagline must be evocative of your brand/product, witty, fancy, and easy to remember without being generic. Good trademarks include made-up words (Xerox, Kleenex), an allusive term (NyQuil), or an arbitrary association (e.g., Apple is not a fruit brand). The tagline should be associated with an equally evocative and distinctive graphic element, such as the Nike swoosh, suggesting movement, flow, and action.

11.3.4 *Trade secrets*

The dome of Santa Maria del Fiore in Florence is a Renaissance masterpiece and a testament to the genius of its architect, Filippo Brunelleschi. It was a titanic enterprise for the time (1420–1436), and it is still the world's largest masonry dome. Brunelleschi concocted many innovations in the design and construction techniques to build the dome using only stone and lime and without using any scaffolding, whose cost would have been prohibitive given the size of the building.

Brunelleschi was very wary about sharing his invention with others. That is understandable: at that time, there were few or no ways to enforce IP in a modern sense. When Brunelleschi presented his plans for the dome he intended to build in front of the committee charged with selecting the best project, he refused to tell the members how the dome would stay up during its construction without scaffolding. Brunelleschi proposed instead a challenge where the person capable of standing an egg upright on a table would earn the contract for constructing the dome. Despite his colleagues' unsuccessful attempts, Brunelleschi accomplished this task by gently pressing the egg's tip onto the table, causing it to stand upright. This practical solution angered his colleagues, who believed it lacked artistic merit and could have been easily conceived by anyone. However, Brunelleschi responded with a smile, stating that, in the same way, the dome's construction would be simple for anyone who witnessed his disclosure.

What Brunelleschi was using to protect his IP was a trade secret.

Trade secrets include confidential business information that gives a company a competitive advantage. This includes formulas, technical drawings, manufacturing processes, customer lists, and other valuable information, data, know-how, and marketing strategies. Negative know-how, i.e., knowing that specific methods or solutions do not work, is also typically covered by a trade secret.

Secrets may be the only way to protect your IP in all cases where disclosing IP, as in a patent application, would make anyone skilled enough to circumvent your IP or build quickly around it and create a better version. While other forms of IP, such as patents, are more celebrated and visible, a large part of a company's IP is considered top secret.

Unlike other forms of intellectual property, trade secrets are not registered but protected directly by the owner through strict confidentiality agreements and security measures. In practice, you must ensure everyone understands something is a secret and enforce and defend this secrecy. For instance, you must add "confidential" labels when sharing secret information. You need to secure information in a private, "fenced" space that is not accessible without trespassing or obtaining the necessary authorization and credentials. You must use passwords or encryption for the digital rendition of the information you protect. Suppose you left the information unattended or did not clarify that the information is confidential. In that case, you cannot sue those who appropriated it, even if they were not explicitly authorized.

11.4 How to find resources to develop and acquire IP

For startups, IP can be a critical asset in establishing a competitive edge and attracting investors. However, securing the necessary resources to develop and acquire IP can pose unique challenges for these early-stage ventures that need more capital and experience. This section focuses on practical strategies and tailored approaches to help startups find the resources to develop and acquire intellectual property effectively.

11.4.1 Leveraging internal resources

Identify and grow core competencies. Startups should assess their team's skills and expertise to identify areas where they can excel in IP development. Determine your team members' strengths and technical knowledge and align their efforts with the IP strategy. Encourage interdisciplinary collaboration and knowledge-sharing to foster innovative thinking. Hire or collaborate with people with the necessary technological skills and know-how.

11.4.2 Build an IP-focused culture

Foster a culture that values and encourages the creation and protection of intellectual property. Educate your team about the importance of IP and provide training on IP management and best practices. Implement processes to capture and document inventions and ensure employees know their roles in IP development. Do not consider IP as a secondary or premature objective for you.

11.4.3 External collaborations and partnerships

Join startup incubators, accelerators, and coworking spaces that provide access to resources, mentorship, and networking. These programs often focus on IP development and can help startups refine their ideas and navigate the IP landscape. Sometimes, funding is available to subsidize startups to access these spaces and obtain IP help. When entrepreneurial spaces work well, they provide affordable offices, business services, and learning opportunities for new entrepreneurs.

11.4.4 Universities and research institutions

Establish partnerships with universities and research institutions that have expertise in your industry. Collaborate on joint research projects to leverage their knowledge and access cutting-edge technologies. These collaborations can yield valuable IP and potentially attract funding opportunities. Try collaborating with academic researchers who may want to partner or are interested in seeing their research at work. If you are a student and are enrolled in an institution where research is carried out, try to engage with research groups that work in similar areas, and take advantage of the research resources available on campus, such as subscriptions to academic journals, workshops, conferences, reading groups, and research-based capstone classes.

Increasingly, most universities today offer various forms of support to academic entrepreneurs. Among these are access to technology, grants, training, accelerator programs, and competitions. Some of these initiatives are aimed at helping startups to secure IP. Find out if your school has an IP office. Sometimes, it is called the tech transfer office, liaison office, or office of grants and sponsored research. IP experts may be available at a university entrepreneurship center. Even if you have no interest in an academic career, acquiring basic research skills can give you the mindset of what doing research means and where to look for it when needed.

11.4.5 Industry networks and associations

Engage with industry networks and associations relevant to your startup's sector. Attend conferences, seminars, and networking events to connect with potential partners and investors interested in IP-driven startups. These platforms provide opportunities for knowledge exchange and collaboration and expose you to state-of-the-art technology and innovation in your field.

11.4.6 IP funding and grants

Research and apply for government grants and funding programs targeted to support startups in their IP development. Governments often have initiatives to encourage innovation and may offer financial support or tax incentives to protect and acquire IP. These incentives and initiatives can be available at any government level, so look for them everywhere, from city to state to federal.

11.4.7 Angel investors and venture capitalists

Seek funding from angel investors and venture capitalists who understand the value of IP and its potential impact on a startup's success. Craft a compelling business plan highlighting the IP's unique selling points and marketability. Many angel investors have industry experience and a relevant technical background. They can suggest what IP you need and how to acquire and enforce it. They can connect you with the talent you need to create IP in the first place.

11.4.8   Crowdfunding platforms

Utilize crowdfunding platforms to raise funds for your IP development initiatives. Present your IP concept compellingly and engagingly, offering attractive incentives to potential backers who believe in your idea.

11.5   Less heard but critical challenges and tips about IP

In this section, we provide additional practical tips that are often overlooked (Melman, 2023).

11.5.1   Sign nondisclosure agreements

Obtaining IP protection through one of these mechanisms for early-stage ideas can be challenging or unfeasible. Nevertheless, you may be in circumstances where you must disclose your ideas and information about your business to other stakeholders, such as potential investors. How can you ensure nobody will steal your IP during these presentations? You can ask them to sign a nondisclosure agreement (NDA) before you share any information, such as before you start projecting your slides and pitching. An NDA is a legal contract through which you can restrict an individual or party from releasing or sharing any confidential information. The NDA makes your counterparts aware of sensitive information that should be treated as confidential; its provisions can be enforced legally against anyone breaching the terms. Many free templates are available online, but running your NDA past a seasoned legal expert is strongly advisable. On the other hand, do not be overly cautious. If you are participating in a pitch competition, for instance, you will not typically be able to provide enough details about your idea to allow someone else to reproduce what you do. Remember that IP does not protect ideas per se, but their embodiment into a device or physical shape (patent) or their expression (copyright). Asking your listeners to sign an NDA in cases like this will make you look bad. Just be relaxed and savvy about what you show (and what you don't).

11.5.2   Mark your territory

Use the copyright symbol (©) on the materials whose copyright you own. You can use the sign even if the copyright is not registered. Use TM for your trademark (add ® if your trademark is registered). Add a "Patent pending" label if you have filed a patent application and are waiting for a determination.

11.5.3   Check your organization's IP policy

Many entrepreneurial ideas are developed by people who work for a company or by students enrolled in a university. These organizations may have an IP policy for employees and students that requires you to disclose your idea to the employer or the university. These policies also provide criteria to ascertain if the IP is the exclusive property of the individual or if the organization is entitled to some IP ownership. For instance, if you are a student or a researcher at a university and your idea stems from research funded by your school, the university may claim IP for the idea, exclusively or in part. If, instead, you worked on the idea in your own free time and did not use any organizational resources, you are typically the sole owner of the idea, but you still may be required to disclose it. Failing to observe these terms may put you at risk of legal action by your employer, former employer, or school. Therefore, ensure you know if such policies exist, become familiar with the terms, and yield to them. Again, do not be overly cautious. Universities, in particular, are all about their students getting patents because that is prestigious for the institution. The fact that these institutions want disclosure is just a legal check and should not be interpreted as universities wanting to "take" your IP.

11.5.4   Do your homework

Before pursuing intellectual property protection, entrepreneurs should conduct thorough research to ensure their ideas or creations are original and not already protected by existing rights. This involves searching patent databases, copyright registries, and trademark databases to identify potential conflicts.

11.5.5   Be careful with what you publish, especially online

If you use works created by others, ensure these works are copyright-free. This is true when the copyright is expired or when the creators release their copyright to the public, such as through a Creative Commons license (if that is the case, check the conditions). If none of these conditions are true, contact the creator and obtain written permission (make sure they are, in fact, the creators and have any right on those works—you'd be surprised how often the supposed creators think it's their IP but they do not actually own it).

Be particularly cautious when posting content online. People often infringe copyright online without being aware. However, the real owner of the content can come after you. The fact that some material is online does not imply it is up for grabs. An exception is the "fair use doctrine," which guarantees that copyrighted content can be freely used for education and other noncommercial uses. When in doubt, however, do not use the content.

Finally, be meticulous when contracting creatives to design copyrighted materials for you, such as logos or web design. The contracted designer owns the copyright unless the contract says differently. You want to work out this contract carefully to ensure you own or at least can reuse the material in the future without permission or paying; the same applies to you if you are the designer. If you commit to releasing the copyright to your buyer, you will lose it forever. Book publishers tend to ask for that, but you can negotiate conditions.

11.5.6   Talk with an IP lawyer before it's too late (and after)

Entrepreneurs face the risk of intellectual property infringement and counterfeiting, which can harm their businesses. Monitoring the market, conducting regular audits, and taking legal action against infringers are crucial to protecting intellectual property rights. In intellectual property disputes, entrepreneurs may need to engage in litigation to defend their rights. It is advisable to consult with intellectual property attorneys who specialize in litigation to navigate these complex legal processes effectively.

11.5.7 IP mining

Most people do not know they can register different versions of the same IP. This is undoubtedly true with trademarks. To some extent, and with more money, you can acquire multiple patents by adding nonobvious modifications to your original design. Why would you do that? Because in this way, you will prevent potential competitors from making a relatively simple addition to your patent and claiming a new patent that will allow them to sell a product that is very similar, perhaps better, than yours. You can think of this as a negative IP strategy: using legal ways to make your competitors' lives more difficult. Large companies do this frequently, and many patents are created more to form obstacles for the competition than for actual use.

11.5.8 When in Rome

Intellectual property laws and regulations may vary depending on the jurisdiction, and entrepreneurs must consult legal experts in their respective regions to ensure compliance with local laws. Intellectual property protection varies from country to country, so entrepreneurs expanding their businesses internationally must be aware of and comply with the intellectual property laws of each jurisdiction. Seeking expert advice and utilizing international treaties and agreements can help protect intellectual property assets globally. The Patent Cooperation Treaty (PCT) allows U.S. inventors to receive protection in other countries. You must file an international patent application to take advantage of the treaty. It is more expensive than a national application but will allow you concurrently to seek protection in the more than 150 current PCT member countries.

11.5.9 Beyond IP acquisition: monitoring and enforcement

Securing intellectual property rights is insufficient; entrepreneurs must actively monitor and enforce their rights. This involves tracking the market for potential infringement, taking appropriate legal action when necessary, and maintaining the validity of their registrations through renewal processes.

11.6 Conclusions

Understanding and protecting intellectual property is essential for entrepreneurs seeking to establish and grow successful businesses. By recognizing the different types of intellectual property, securing the necessary rights, leveraging their assets strategically, and addressing potential challenges, entrepreneurs can maximize the value of their innovations and creations.

Remember, this chapter serves as an introduction to intellectual property for entrepreneurs. We recommend that you seek legal advice from IP professionals for specific guidance tailored to individual circumstances.

Key takeaways for this chapter

Lesson learned	Implications for your project
Mind your and others' IP (sooner than later)	• Do not procrastinate on IP assessment and acquisition. IP is vital for entrepreneurs. It may be the only capital you have, and pursuing IP comes with an enormous amount of learning about how to design your product better and about your competition. • Consult with a lawyer and budget for IP acquisition costs. If you cannot afford to, a DIY approach is less safe but entirely possible in many cases. Flawless drawings are critical in patent applications, so here you may need external help. • Be savvy about what you disclose. If needed, get signatures on NDAs. Nevertheless, do not be overcautious about sharing your idea (remember that it's not the idea you protect, but the way you package it into an invention or copyrighted content). • Do not infringe on other people's IP. It's unethical and can cost you money. Besides, it gives the impression you have not done your homework.
Understand what IP you need	• Become familiar with and understand the various forms of IP, and how to apply for them, from patents to Creative Commons licenses. • Analyze your product and your business and identify any IP opportunity you have (follow Starbucks example in the beginning of this chapter and identify what makes your product unique).
Piggyback	• Take advantage of any available support to acquire IP. It could be available in your university office or through grants to small businesses and startups. • Learn the state of the art in your field. Get inspirations through researching existing patents and understanding how other inventors are dealing with the same user problem.

Note

1 Oddly, the Nike tagline was inspired by the words of a man who was about to be executed (see Wikipedia, 2023).

References

DiMarco, J. (2021). Body stretching bar (US D910,126 S). *US Patent and Trademark Office*. https://patents.google.com/patent/USD910126S1/en?oq=US+D910%2c126+S

DiMarco, J. (2023). The role of digital technologies in developing the Shape Stretch body stretching bar: A case study in product innovation and management resources. *Cases on Digital Entrepreneurship: How Digital Technologies Are Transforming the Entrepreneurial Process in Existing Businesses and Start-Ups*, p. 35.

Gates, B. (1991). *Challenges and strategy company memo*. https://wiki.endsoftwarepatents.org/wiki/Microsoft#cite_note-25

Insights. (2023). *Starbucks patents – Key insights and stats*, June 2023. https://insights.greyb.com/starbucks-patents/#:~:text=Starbucks%20has%20a%20total%20of%20941%20patents%20globally.,patents%2C%20557%20patents%20are%20active

Melman, D. (2023). *Intellectual property for innovators and entrepreneurs* (Guest presentation). St. John's University.

SBIR. (2023). *Timeline and costs for patent filing.* https://www.sbir.gov/sites/all/themes/sbir/dawn-breaker/img/documents/Course16-Tutorial2.pdf

USPTO. (2023). *IP Identifier: Learn to identify and protect your intellectual property.* https://ipidenti-fier.uspto.gov/#/identifier/welcome, last accessed June 2023.

Wikipedia. (2023). *Just do it.* https://en.wikipedia.org/wiki/Just_Do_It

Chapter 12

How to craft effective investor presentations

Rem tene, verba sequentur: *grasp the subject, and the words will follow. This, I believe, is the opposite of what happens with poetry, which is more a case of* verba tene, res sequentur: *grasp the words, and the subject will follow.*

Umberto Eco, Postscript to *The Name of the Rose* (1980)

12.1 Connect, expect, respect

In a thought-provoking review of the *Indiana Jones and the Dial of Destiny* movie, Frank Lehman, associate professor of music at Tufts University, explores the music score's critical importance in moviegoers' experience (Lehman, 2023). The movie score, authored by John Williams, one of the top film composers of all time, who wrote the soundtracks for epic movies such as *E.T.* and *Star Wars*, has a crucial role in augmenting the emotional tension of the story during the exciting scenes in which Jones, an archaeologist, risks and saves his and other characters' lives by escaping all kinds of bizarre threats in the most audacious and unlikely ways. Lehman observes that "some of the best, most complex, musical compositions are written for scenes where they can barely be heard." This is a fundamental requirement for a soundtrack: the score must be an auxiliary and nonintrusive communication channel. Yet, try to tune out the music from the rolling boulders scene in *Raiders of the Lost Ark*, and you will notice that a lot is missing—so much so that Lehman wonders if we have been watching movies the wrong way all these years and if we should watch by closing our eyes from time to time.

The review also questions the traditional purists' distinction that relegates music scores to an inferior expression of art compared to more "noble" musical formats and styles, such as symphonies. In contrast, Lehman provides many examples of Williams's virtuosic composition talent, such as in the rolling boulders scene in *Raiders of the Lost Ark*. He describes how Williams created loud and aggressive music by utilizing the London Symphony Orchestra trumpeters masterfully in "their most piercing register, or by describing the most virtuosic parts ever written for six piccolos in the mine cart sequence in *Indiana Jones and the Temple of Doom*."

But Lehman's review's main point is about something other than celebrating the genius behind these compositions and the sophisticated playing ability the scores required. It's instead the observation that Williams's work has been chiefly "a quest to find ever more innovative techniques for writing memorable music that will be barely heard."

Call this a paradox of human communication. Why would someone put so much effort into creating music that is hardly noticed? Because the score creates a fundamental emotional background that helps us understand scenes on a much deeper level.

DOI: 10.4324/9781003346463-13

This digression on the importance of film music helps highlight a few crucial characteristics of human communication that we can apply to design communication strategies and tools when we present our business ideas to potential investors and other stakeholders. Even the most sophisticated ability to create technically flawless digital presentations will do little if the design is not anchored to these principles:

- Multi-channeling: Human communication always happens simultaneously across multiple channels and senses: visuals, sounds, environment, digital, and physical; everything counts.
- Foreground and background: What is not the immediate focus of attention can be equally important, if not more, than the content in the foreground. Only a fraction of what we communicate is about "what" we speak; the rest is about "how," the complex mix of background signals we share when communicating with someone (body language, emotional clues, settings, formats, colors, etc.).
- Empathy and emotions: The primary objective of any communication act is not to transfer content but to connect, engage, and build trust. These require developing a deep understanding of the listeners' expectations and respecting their beliefs on an issue, even when we disagree. Connection, engagement, and trust have an emotional basis that cannot be built solely by leveraging our argument's rational side.
- Mastering techniques and tools: Professionally using communication media and devices, acquiring good technical skills, especially in the use of digital media, and understanding the strengths and limitations of different media are crucial abilities you need to develop and cultivate.

In the third part of this chapter, we will provide actionable ways to implement some of these principles. Before doing that, in the next section, we provide an overview of some key findings from cognitive science that help us understand why certain communication tricks and techniques work and how to avoid communication failure.

12.2   How people communicate: conversation and storytelling

An extensive review of the science of good communication would require too much time and is clearly out of the scope of this book. Thus, we will limit this section to describing some fundamental mechanisms in human cognition and communication, leading to actionable ideas and principles to help us design a compelling business presentation. Here is a non-exhaustive list of aspects that we must consider:

1. Working memory and attention limitations;
2. Nonverbal communication;
3. Storytelling;
4. (Visual) metaphors;
5. The medium is the message.

12.2.1   Working memory and attention limitations

Human attention span is brief, 15–30 seconds of uninterrupted focus. This time is shrinking even more because of the pervasiveness of digital interruptions and the multitasking attitude associated with using our digital devices and apps. This observation does not imply that people can't listen. What it indicates is that you are going to lose your listeners' attention frequently. The implication is that you must find ways to recapture the lost focus by reengaging with the listeners. Instead of considering your presentation a speech, picture it as a conversation. Can you imagine conversing with a friend who speaks to you for 10 minutes without interruptions?

Another significant cognitive limitation is the reduced size of our working memory. While the metaphor has many misleading sides, think of your brain as a computer. The working memory, similar to the random-access memory (RAM) in a computer, processes current and incoming information. Long-term memory is like a hard disk or cloud archive, where much more data is organized and stored for later retrieval. Our brain's working memory is relatively small and easily overloaded. When this happens, the transfer of information from short-term to long-term memory is compromised and very little will be remembered and understood. Subject to information overload, listeners will feel frustrated and anxious. This fact has important implications for regulating the amount of information and the pace at which the information is provided in a presentation. Less and slower is better!

12.2.2   *The importance of nonverbal communication*

We tend to overstate the importance of speech and written texts in our communication. Electoral debates are a clear example: post-debate surveys show that listeners remember little of what was said. Their memory goes instead to specific events and "micro-behavior," such as a blunder, a joke, a gesture, or the candidate's posture, and viewers always develop an opinion about who won that is influenced more by nonverbal clues than what the candidates said.

As an additional example, consider how often online written communication goes astray. People are more likely to get angrier and lose their cool when they have an "in-writing" conversation, such as an email chain or replying to social media posts, than face-to-face interaction. Why does this happen? Because when we speak in person with another human being, we exchange much more than words. A complex set of social signals and social intelligence guides and informs our verbal statements. These nonverbal signals clarify the tone, provide the context of the conversation, and communicate to the other person that we understand each other. Think of how a smile accompanying a statement can modify its meaning, how the emphasis on selected words imparted through the tone of our voice can help remark on their importance, or how nodding while the other person is speaking signals that we pay attention and understand.

Conversations are better than emails and PowerPoint presentations because they help us build common ground (Clark, 1996) and engage with our listeners. In a conversation, you are a presenter as much as a listener. By showing a listening attitude, you signal respect and interest in what people in your audience think and are better able to connect with them genuinely.

12.2.3   *Storytelling*

Jerome Bruner (1985) identifies two basic modes of thought: argumentation and storytelling. Argumentation is the scientist's thinking mode, which we should use to verify if a statement is true or false. Storytelling is the artist's mode, which we should use to illustrate that something is possible. We have referenced this duality in many parts of this book to model the contradictory nature of entrepreneurial creativity (see Chapter 2). Not surprisingly, the storytelling mode is more effective at persuading our listeners.

Stories work better than arguments for several reasons. They leverage the emotional side of our brains. When content is emotionally tainted, it is easier to remember because it triggers empathy and possibly our identification with parts of the story. Another reason is that narratives have well-known structures that are easier to recall, understand, and reproduce. Finally, a story presupposes agency, that is, individuals having intentions and purposes, devising plans, acting, and achieving (or failing) a specific outcome.

Humans are social animals, so our brain is particularly effective at recognizing other people's intentions, anticipating possible behavior, or making sense of what they do. Even when such narrative interpretations are not correct or are biased, we tend to buy into stories more than we do with sound arguments. In a series of studies on jurors, Pennington and Hastie (1991) showed that jury members were more inclined to be persuaded when incomplete evidence was presented in a way that made sense narratively compared to when complete evidence was delivered without a story.

12.2.4   Visual metaphors

A metaphor is a comparison between two different concepts that have something crucial in common. Quite often, a metaphor is visual. When we think of time as money, we picture the abstract notion of time as a valuable and finite resource. We "see" money as a fluid that flows, and this helps us highlight many aspects of time, such as the fact that it can be spent, bought, saved, poured, and wasted.

Our understanding and language are substantially built on metaphors (Lakoff & Johnson, 2008). Identifying the appropriate metaphor can significantly facilitate understanding by our audience and, more importantly, help us focus on the essential aspects of the message we want to share. Think of a metaphor as a magnifying lens, a curved mirror, or other deliberate distortion that adds the proper emphasis to the message you want to convey. Many brilliant and iconic advertising campaigns have been based on a metaphor, such as BMW's ultimate driving machine, comparing a car with a piece of advanced technology.

12.2.5   The medium is the message

As illustrated in the opening quote, we distinguish between content and form, the medium and the message in communication. Traditionally, these aspects are separated and imagined in a hierarchy. First, we must craft the content and make the message clear and compelling; then, we must find an appropriate medium to package and deliver the content. This distinction is incorrect. As Umberto Eco says in the quote, in the case of poetry and art, things go the other way around: first, artists play with the medium, then meaning emerges. If you think the artist's example is irrelevant because you will talk with businesspeople or customers who do not expect you to create a work of art, think again!

Isn't art a powerful medium to communicate profound concepts while engaging emotionally with its consumers? Aren't great ads based on creative metaphors and powerful storytelling? Aren't people, today more than ever, expecting beautifully crafted visual communication?

When we separate the medium from the message, we make two mistakes. First, we prevent ourselves from experimenting with different media. Is our message better delivered through a video, a slide deck, a pitch, a storyboard, or a simulation? Trying and failing can help us find the most appropriate medium for our content and uncover possibilities and meanings we had initially neglected. For instance, if you play with different color schemes in a presentation or other visual, is there a color combination that can suggest something subtle about our product or value proposition?

Second, by arbitrarily coupling a message with a medium, the latter can prevail and create unnecessary constraints and limitations. An example is how many, if not most, people use PowerPoint slides. Is a bulleted list the best way to communicate your ideas? Do people expect a list and many words on a slide, or do those slides just include notes to help you remember what to say? In the latter case, you are misguided: the point of using slides is not to help you remember but to make your content memorable for the listeners.

Sometimes, choosing an appropriate but nonobvious medium can be a distinctive factor that can help your presentation stand out from the crowd. How about using a video teaser created following a logic like movie trailers? It is also a good idea to use physical props to make your communication more tangible. And what about adopting original communication format and styles, such as retro video-game themes and graphics, to engage with an audience that is attracted to that format for whatever reasons, such as out of a nostalgic attachment to specific graphic patterns and storytelling?

12.3   How to craft great presentations

Now that we have explored fundamental mechanisms and dynamics in human communication, let's translate the theory into practical suggestions to create meaningful and compelling presentations. Before starting, here is an important caveat: never try manipulating your audience. We should never sacrifice truthful and honest communication. Besides, if you are genuine and authentic, you will sound natural and trustworthy, which will go a long way in connecting with your audience.

12.3.1   The basic structure

Given human working memory and attention span limitations, a critical rule of thumb is "less and slower is better." Too often, we assume that abundant information helps decision-making and understanding. Unfortunately, this is not true. The human mind is not a computer that linearly amasses data. Novel information can sometimes be problematic because our brain tries to examine it in light of what we already know. For instance, research shows that if you want to make an argument and you have a long list of reasons to support it, you are better off shortening the list; each additional piece you include dilutes the strength of the other points and exposes you to potential criticism (Grant, 2021).

Once you have reduced the information you want to deliver to the essential, you must repeat your critical statements. Finally, you need to organize the presentation to facilitate memorization and understanding. The basic structure of each presentation should be based on three parts (Koegel, 2007):

1. Tell them what you're going to tell them (opening);
2. Tell them (body);
3. Tell them what you just told them (wrap-up).

While too much repetition is annoying, do not be shy at aiming at some redundancy. This can create a few opportunities for the same message to resurface and finally reach the minds and, hopefully, the hearts of your listeners.

12.3.2   *Opening: grab attention, communicate relevance, and excite!*

The way you open a presentation is critical. Research shows that human judgment is disproportionately affected by first impressions. The objective of a good opening is to raise a relevant question and generate curiosity and a little suspense to keep people willing to know how it ends. Finally, the opening is also foundational: it sets the stage and creates the premise on which the rest of the presentation will rest.

To generate a positive first impression, carefully curate all the details. Punctuality, appropriate attire and posture, proper personal introduction, accurate choice of the first words you utter, and confident and relaxed tone are all determinant factors.

Some level of surprise or provocation can help create suspense and nurture curiosity. You can start with a provocative quote, a striking statistic, an emotional video, or an intriguing story. These approaches will work if they reveal some unexpected or surprising finding or problem. However, do not sacrifice the accuracy and veracity of the information for the sake of generating surprise.

Here is an example:

[Opening quote]:"The US energy transition to green energy is moving way faster than expected; by 2025, renewables will be the first energy source in the US energy mix, trumping coal and other fossil fuels"

[Reference]: add a reference if this is a slide or have it available if someone questions the opening quote (Gelles et al., 2023)

[Your statement]: Our company is part of this grand movement to build a sustainable future for our children. This presentation will show how we accomplish this result through these steps.

You can accompany the statement with a striking video in the background, followed by a concise outline of the rest of the presentation. The finding may sound surprising to many people; it may resonate with their environmental concerns, support your statements with some credibility borrowed from authoritative sources, and help introduce the presentation outline.

Of course, you must do your homework beforehand to ensure you understand your audience's expectations. If, for instance, your audience is not so worried about the environment, the story will not resonate with them. It can even be met with hostility by those who think the environmental emergency is exaggerated. In that case, you need to come up with a different story. The cited article mentions that climate-change skeptics appreciate renewables' convenience and savings (Gelles et al., 2023). The opening then could sound like:

"The cost of renewable energy has plummeted exponentially in the last few years. Switching to an electric car will save you $3,000 per year and many trips to the gas station."

Finding the right surprise to open your presentation is an excellent exercise for investigating and anticipating what your audience wants.

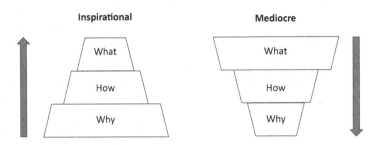

Figure 12.1 Inspirational (narrative) versus mediocre (descriptive) communication strategies. Starting from why we do something is proven to be a more impactful communication strategy than focusing on how great our product or idea is. The why–how–what approach talks to our emotional brain, and it facilitates the building of good stories.

12.3.3   Tell a story

Consultant and communication guru Simon Sinek (2009) says: "People do not buy what you do; they buy why you do it." Sinek's point is that what makes a product or an idea great is not its implementation, because many other entrepreneurs can build high-quality products. What makes the difference is the distinctive meaning your listeners will associate with the idea. Is a computer just a digital instrument or something that questions the status quo? Apple followed the second perspective in its Think Different campaign. In contrast, most computer companies try to convince us that their computers are the most capable, reliable, and technologically advanced machines on the market. However, a well-functioning piece of hardware is not a source of excitement. Apple's message, instead, was inspiring.

Why does this work? Because inspirational messages have a narrative structure. Sinek's idea is about building a convincing why–how–what narrative (Figure 12.1). Ordinary people and companies base their communication on the "what" and "how": we build great computers (what), they are beautifully designed and user friendly (how), but they forget the "why." With its Think Different campaign, Apple reversed this logic. According to Sinek, Apple's message was: We believe in innovation and challenging the status quo (why); we do so by building beautiful, user-friendly technology (how) that is made available to you through our great computers (what).

The inspirational strategy has a narrative structure based on intentions, while mediocre communication is based on a description. The inspirational strategy talks to our emotional brain and is faster and more memorable, while a descriptive strategy talks primarily to our rational brain, resulting in a slower and emotionally neutral message.

Intentions and why you do what you do are vital ingredients of any story. You can use a standard story model in your presentation (see Figure 12.2). Each story starts with the world or people in some predicament generated by a crisis that needs to be solved. Sometimes, there is a villain or a monster that the heroes need to defeat or keep at bay. If the issues are not dealt with, there will be dire consequences. Fortunately, the heroes (you and your team) have a plan and will undertake appropriate actions leading to the desirable outcomes.

Figure 12.2 illustrates just one possible story model. Many more are available, such as the hero's journey (think of the Odyssey) or the "from rags to riches" framework (think

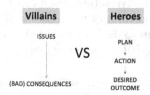

Figure 12.2 **A "saving the world" story model to create narrative presentations based on the villain versus hero storytelling**. The underlying structure of most stories always involves the same ingredients: an issue to be fixed, provoked by a villain, and a hero with a plan to save the world.

of Cinderella). Stories also come with a narrative arc, a mechanism to create and resolve emotional tension. Think of a movie, for instance; things start in a given condition (a peaceful summer on a beach island), from which they worsen (a shark is attacking and killing tourists) until a climax is achieved (the hero sets out to kill the monster by risking his life), followed by the resolution of the tension (the shark is killed and people go back enjoying the beaches).

Notice how story models essentially support the inspirational communication strategy depicted in Figure 12.1. Heroes have noble purposes (why) and, with their unique means and qualities (how), do the right thing (what).

Contrast the narrative approach with the more tedious approaches based on building arguments, outlining pros and cons, data, and numbers, and then picking the lesser evil. The emotional arousal and engagement levels produced by such an approach will be inferior. Of course, you can and should use numbers and rational arguments in a story as appropriate. Still, you should stitch this information into the overall narrative plot without sacrificing the emotional tension created by the events and the "drama" that is about to unfold and resolve.

12.3.4   Re-engage

Presentations should not be designed based on a monodirectional information flow from a speaker to a listener. This channel metaphor, created by information scientists to model information transfer over a digital or physical channel between machines, is hard to replace and is commonly adopted even though human communication does not work in this way. As Herbert Clark illustrates in his book (1996), language use is a joint action in which two or more people engage to understand each other. Note that this does not mean communication must generate consensus, but only that people aim to develop common ground based on some mutual understanding of what they are saying to each other.

The underlying structure of any communication is then a conversation. Conversations work because, through them, we can achieve mutual understanding. Conversations are based on a turn-taking structure in which two or more people take turns exchanging content and replying, along with a mix of verbal and nonverbal feedback. This feedback signals to the other person whether we understand what is being said (e.g., by nodding) or are confused or in disagreement (e.g., by showing uncertainty or frustration on our face or explicitly asking for clarification).

The construction of common ground requires continuous interaction and engagement by all parties to collect the necessary feedback as the conversation unfolds.

A presentation is not exactly a conversation, but it can be modeled using a conversational metaphor by creating many opportunities to engage with the listeners. Then we need to continuously re-engage with them to deal with the reduced attention span of our listeners. Here is a list of nonverbal and verbal ways to engage:

- Eye contact: Search for eye contact with individual participants, as you would if conversing only with that person. If the audience is large, lock onto one person, then onto another, then onto another, distributing your attention without fixating for too long on someone in particular.
- Do not gravitate to friendly faces only; gaining the trust of those who look distracted or even hostile is essential.
- Keep your shoulder squared: When talking with someone, rotate your body so that your shoulders face the person to signal you are ready and willing to engage, as you would in a conversation.
- Smile and assume a relaxed posture.
- Stand and move. Use your hands and body, but do not fidget or move too much, which will communicate anxiety.
- If appropriate, address your listeners by their first names. If possible, learn their names in advance or ask them, then try remembering them for future interactions.
- Use humor and fun.

To regain attention, you can create a mini break to reduce the listeners' fatigue from focusing too long on something.

- Ask a question, perhaps for their opinion on how they feel about something.
- Use anything that can briefly interrupt the presentation flow, such as a short story, a joke, a video, or a nice picture.
- Ensure the break does not create excessive space for digressions, side discussion, or disengagement.

Look for signs of engagement, such as:

- Nodding
- Sustained eye contact
- Leaning forward
- Smiling
- Actively taking notes
- Test what your audience is getting by asking comments and questions.

12.3.5   Understanding and mastering the medium

Presentations are increasingly delivered with the help of digital media and visual aids. The combination of speech and a digital medium creates a setting where our audience expects some form of digital entertainment. If we think of ourselves as performers on a stage in front of the public, we should ensure this performance is professionally curated in all aspects. Thus, you should invest time and resources in acquiring professional presentation skills and technology to master the digital media you plan to use.

Research shows that the quality of audio is more important than anything else. Whether it comes from a confident and warm voice, a loudspeaker, or a great room acoustic, we should do our best to guarantee our listeners an enjoyable auditory experience. Audiences expect more and more professionalism and elegant visuals in a presentation.

The number of available presentation tools and formats is constantly evolving. Luckily, you can find plenty of tutorials and examples online and offline. We suggest you pick the ones that best fit the story you want to tell while keeping an eye on what your audience expects and is used to. Here, we want to provide some principles and guidelines to appropriately use your medium of choice.

First, never delegate to the medium. Ample criticism has been directed towards Power-Point since the publication of Edward Tufte's pamphlet on the cognitive style of PowerPoint (Tufte, 2003). Tufte, one of the most well-known experts on data visualization, identifies a significant weakness in the tool's design in that it focuses on the speaker and imposes a rigid structure that hinders interaction between the presenter and the other participants. Whether the flaw is in the design of this tool or in how people use it, many presenters create slides more for themselves than to keep their audience engaged. A common mistake, for example, is to use too much text. Since people read much faster than you talk, if you have too much text on a slide, your listeners will rush to read it and get out of sync with you (Kogel, 2007). This time lag creates a disconnection with your audience. It's possible that if you pack too much text into your slides, you may be afraid of forgetting what you want to say. In this case, the slide is serving you and interfering with how you connect with your audience.

An interesting approach is to get rid of text almost entirely. This is the 20 × 20 PechaKucha, a storytelling format in which a presenter shows 20 text-free slides for 20 seconds each. Developed by Astrid Klein and Mark Dytham of Tokyo's Klein-Dytham Architecture, PechaKucha is inspired by the communication principle of "talk less, show more" (Pink, 2007). This format is perfect for a short presentation, such as a pitch. Even if your final format is not a PechaKucha, you can use this approach to design your presentation. By forcing us to convey a presentation mainly through images, this method helps us think visually and empathically and find creative connections and associations between ideas.

12.3.6 Practice

This section is short because the message is straightforward: practice! It is just an invitation to rehearse your presentation. Rehearsing can help you identify problematic parts of your speech where you or your audience may get stuck. Ideally, invite someone you trust to the rehearsal for honest feedback. If you rehearse enough, you may notice that you start to memorize your presentation. That is a great thing to do. In his account of how he prepared for a TED Talk, Tim Urban (2016) suggests we should stick with the "Happy Birthday" song rule. Virtually everyone knows the song from singing it at birthday parties, so we do not need to focus on the words or the singing; rather, we can relax and engage with the other guests to celebrate the birthday person. The same should happen in a presentation. Once the content flawlessly and automatically comes out of your mouth, your brain can attend to social intelligence tasks such as noticing the mood and the signs your listeners offer you, connecting with them, engaging, and re-engaging as and when needed.

12.4 Conclusions

In this chapter, we have provided some fundamental guidelines for designing and delivering your presentation. We based our suggestions on crucial human communication and cognition principles identified by research and studies in these fields. All these suggestions agree that good communication creates opportunities for dialogue, connection, engagement, and trust. This objective should be your compass, and you should not be distracted by technicalities or get enslaved by conventions and media constraints. We also made the point that even a presentation design is a creative task that should be based on the same principles we have adopted in this book for developing a product: empathy, experimentation and prototyping, feedback, and revisions.

Your presentation may need to include one more section when presenting to potential investors. Even if your idea is at an early stage of development, investors may want to have an initial sense of whether your proposal has business potential. This book focuses on the early stages of developing an entrepreneurial idea and specifically on transforming an initial idea into a testable prototype. At this stage, you are unlikely to have an in-depth market analysis, let alone a full-fledged business plan. In the following chapter, we help you to make preliminary economic assessments and considerations based on the work you have done so far and some smart and educated projections. The output of these analyses can be used to create one or two slides to report crucial financial information that investors may want to see at this stage. Typically, these include the following:

- An idea of your revenue and cost models via a profit and loss statement
- What comes next, how much funding you need in the following steps, and what is the expected timeline for the subsequent financing rounds

Key takeaways from this chapter

Lesson learned	Implications for your project
Presentations as conversations	• Presentations should not be designed to convey information but to connect and engage with your audience. • Think of a presentation as a conversation. Conversations work and are pleasant because they offer people an effective way to connect and build mutual understanding
Get your story straight	• Stories are effective because they talk to our emotions. Even business communication should keep this into account. Stories are better ways to persuade someone than logical arguments. Stories are more easily remembered and recalled. • Use prototypical story models and structures that people can recognize and create tension by building narrative arcs. • Stories are about intentions and motives. Use the why–how–what approach to inspire people. Tell them why you are there and how you are going to help them. What you do and how you do it are relevant only when your purpose is clear.
Understand the medium and craft the message; understand the message and craft the medium	• Get to know the medium you will use and what people expect to see and hear. • Do not be a slave to the medium—you are in control. Communication supports are effective only if you use them to augment your message, not as a prosthetic to cover communication deficiencies and insecurity. • Use technology wisely and competently. Delivering and packaging your message professionally will go a long way.

- How long the investors will have to wait before your company becomes profitable (time to first dollar, time to first profit)
- A glimpse of how big your market is and whether it will grow in the future
- Potential future company value and the return on investment investors can reasonably expect.

References

Bruner, J. (1985). Chapter VI: Narrative and paradigmatic modes of thought. *Teachers College Record*, 86(6), 97–115.

Clark, H. H. (1996). *Using language*. Cambridge University Press.

Gelles, D., Plumer, B., & Tankerlsey, J. (2023). The clean energy future is arriving faster than you think. *New York Times*. www.nytimes.com/interactive/2023/08/12/climate/clean-energy-us-fossil-fuels.html, last accessed August 2023.

Grant, A. (2021). *Think again: The power of knowing what you don't know*. Penguin.

Koegel, T. (2007). *The exceptional presenter*. Greenleaf Book Group.

Lakoff, G., & Johnson, M. (2008). *Metaphors we live by*. University of Chicago Press.

Lehman, F. (2023). How to write music for rolling boulders. *New York Times*. https://www.nytimes.com/interactive/2023/07/07/opinion/indiana-jones-movie-john-williams-music.html

Pennington, N., & Hastie, R. (1991). A cognitive theory of juror decision making: The story model. *Cardozo Law Review*, 13, 519.

Pink, D. (2007). *Pecha Kucha: Get to the PowerPoint in 20 slides then sit the hell down*. www.wired.com/2007/08/st-pechakucha/#, last accessed August 2023.

Sinek, S. (2009). How great leaders inspire action. *TED Talk*. www.ted.com/talks/simon_sinek_how_great_leaders_inspire_action?language=en, last accessed August 2023.

Tufte, E. R. (2003). *The cognitive style of PowerPoint: Pitching out corrupts within*. Graphics Pr.

Urban, T. (2016). *Doing a TED talk: The full story*. https://waitbutwhy.com/2016/03/doing-a-ted-talk-the-full-story.html, last accessed August 2023.

Chapter 13

Let's talk money

"Where's the money, Lebowski?!"
— Mark Pellegrino playing The Dude in the movie *The Big Lebowski* (1990)

13.1   Venturing out

In 2021, one of the authors (Kevin) ventured into creating his own business with his wife. They founded Ayewah Aesthetics, Inc., an aesthetic practice. There mission is to provide nonsurgical, surgical, and medical spa services to enhance the natural beauty of its clients. In 2023, Kevin and his wife/partner decided to expand their services and open a new office in New York City. The expansion of the business required significant investment, and funding at that scale was not available in the founders' bank account. In this case, it was then necessary to seek external financial assistance. The need for external funding is actually a very common situation and aspiring entrepreneurs should not be afraid about seeking financial help.

Funding, however, can be challenging to obtain. Entrepreneurs must be able to look holistically at their resources and recast their thinking about what they don't have toward what they could do with what they have. This chapter explores different ways entrepreneurs can find the resources they need to realize their ideas and concepts.

13.2   The challenges: what to fund and when

External capital can be necessary for several reasons, depending on where you are in the development of your business. Here are some typical moments when entrepreneurs might apply for external funding, and the reasons why.

- Product development: While much time can be spent transforming an idea into a prototype, significant additional time and energy will have to be spent bringing your prototype to the level of refinement required to demo the product to investors and customers.
- Incorporating: Once you have a high-fidelity prototype, you may need to seek capital to start a company. This capital will fund the acquisition of facilities, equipment, materials and other inputs. You will have to hire some people and have enough money to start and keep the production going until you start to make money through sales.
- Expanding the business: The company exists and is doing well. It is time to expand the business. This can be done in several ways, including expanding the production of current products, developing new products, accessing new markets, or acquiring another company.

DOI: 10.4324/9781003346463-14

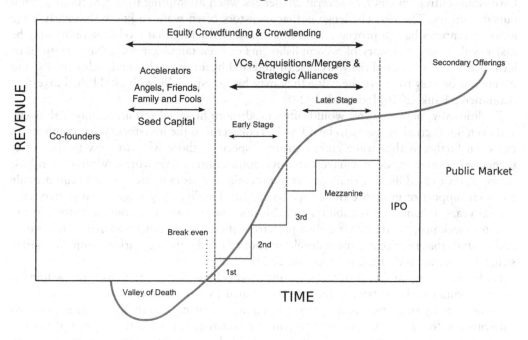

Startup Financing Cycle

Figure 13.1 **Startup financing cycle**. Amount and sources of funding vary along the life cycle of a startup. Initial capital infusions come from entrepreneurs, family and friends, and angel investors. Larger capital infusions, obtained through funding series, are typically provided by venture capitalists or large companies and usually occur in later stages.

Source: Kmuehmel, VC20 CC BY-SA 3.0, https://commons.wikimedia.org/w/index.php?curid=41190293

Figure 13.1 shows what type of funding is needed and when, during the company life cycle, from its first steps to when the company is sold or goes public (through an initial public offering, or IPO). In the very beginning of the business, new startups often seek funding from Angel Investors and even Friends and Family (Zwilling, 2013), often they provide critical seed funding. These investments often are critical to help support a business pushing forwarding within the Valley of Death, which is the time, where a startup may experience negative cash flow (Zwilling, 2013).

The investment life cycle shows that, ideally, revenues will grow as new capital is infused into the company. The sources of funding will change as the company grows. Initially, you will be able to count only on your money. As you progress, you can apply for seed capital from various sources, including angel investors, accelerators, and crowdfunding/crowdlending. Seed money is the capital that helps a company to come into existence and take off. After the initial phase, you must apply for more substantial investments from sources like venture capitalists and large companies. In this phase, there could be multiple financing rounds, also called series.

As the funding sources, motivation, and mechanisms change throughout the company life cycle, so do the challenges that the entrepreneur will face. Paradoxically, the magnitude of these challenges is highest at the beginning, when a company needs the least money in absolute terms.

13.3   Debt versus equity financing

Early-stage entrepreneurs face several challenges when attempting to secure funding from outside entities. The first challenge is that investors often want to know that early-stage ideas or ventures have a proven record of success. Attracting that level of support may be easier with a unique history of accomplishments or even tangible results. New ventures or ideas are often considered risky because of untested business models and technologies, and it may not be easy to prove the value they may bring, especially with established investors (Commerce Bank, 2020; Exitfund, 2023).

Traditionally, new ventures would often need more financial resources, physical assets, and even intellectual property to be offered as collateral to the investors. What complicates this even further is that some entrepreneurs, especially those who are new to the entrepreneurial ecosystem, do not have extensive connections or networks. Without a robust network, it can be difficult to gain access to potential investors or mentors who can provide financial support or guidance (Investopedia, 2022). Finally, early-stage ventures may take several years to achieve profitability, and this uncertainty can deter some investors. Many investors seek projects that offer a clear path to profitability within a reasonable timeframe, and startups that require extensive development or face significant market competition may struggle to attract funding (Investopedia, 2022).

High uncertainty and lack of track records and collateral make it almost impossible for entrepreneurs to rely on typical debt funding issued by banks. Since incurring debts is not an option, many startups typically resort to equity financing. Equity financing requires an entrepreneur to issue shares of the company in exchange for a certain amount of money. For instance, an angel investor can ask for 10% of the company in exchange for $50,000. This equates to or assumes the company's market value is $500,000.

Notice that this is not a loan. You are instead selling 10% of your company in exchange of the money. Funding without debts sounds like great news, and it certainly is. It means someone is betting that you are going to be successful. However, there is a price to pay.

First, your future wealth will depend not only on how much the company grows but also on how big your share will be. By accepting external equity funding, you are lessening your share. Second, investors may also ask for some level of control of the company in exchange of the money and want to have a say in the company decision-making. Whether the equity funding turns out to be a good idea will depend on the quality of the partnership and on crafting well-designed and clear legal terms with the help of skilled attorneys and accountants.

13.4   Looking for funding with a designer mindset

Throughout this book, we talked a great deal about the practice of design thinking within the product development process. The product development process is centered on empathy, understanding what our customers are looking for, and applying what they need to the final product you developed. The design thinking mindset can also be applied to obtaining funding for developing your product or business.

Individuals, companies, banks, and even angel investors have different motivations and interests in giving funding to a product developer. Some entities are motivated by the potential of financial return; an example would be banks and other financial institutions that often provide loans with the expectation of the return of their loans with interest (Exitfund,

2023). Individual investors and venture capitalists have a more long-term perspective. They want to see the company's value grow so they can maximize the value of their shares. Other entities, like foundations and government agencies, may care less about financial returns and more about social and technological impact.

We must truly understand our value proposition to communicate with these different entities. One way to do this is to rely on the why–how–what communication approach illustrated in Chapters 3 and 12 to differentiate your product or service from others (Sinek, 2009). While most businesses can explain WHAT they do (like selling products) and HOW they do it (identifying what makes their products unique), very few organizations can explain WHY they do it (identifying what their purpose is and why they exist). When seeking funding for innovative and early-stage ventures, having a clear and compelling message is critical for attracting the attention of investors. The why–how–what approach offers a way to portray a company's value proposition by accomplishing the following:

1. *Connecting to investors on a deeper level:* Investors tend to be motivated by more than just financial returns. When we map the WHY we exist to our prototype, we engage investors with a project that connects to their values.
2. *Differentiation*: Prototyping projects can involve technical details and features that might not immediately attract investors. By emphasizing your unique approach ("how") and the underlying purpose ("why") behind your prototype, you differentiate your project from others. This can make your venture more memorable and attractive in a competitive funding landscape.
3. *Storytelling*: Sharing your unique story and your successes and failures (as discussed in Chapter 9) can captivate investors. Stories stick with people more effectively than statistics or technical details, making it easier for potential investors to remember and champion your cause.
4. *Long-term vision*: Prototyping is often just the initial step in a larger vision. Sharing the bigger picture ("why") behind your prototype demonstrates that you have a long-term vision and strategy. Investors are more likely to support ventures with clear direction and growth potential.

13.5 Bootstrapping

As previously stated, when designing a product and preparing to invest in building a prototype, one challenge that many product developers often face is to secure funding. In many cases, entrepreneurs consider investing their resources in developing both low-fidelity and high-fidelity prototypes. This process is known as "bootstrapping." Bootstrapping uses personal savings, available technology, and even one's own space (remember, Microsoft started in a garage!) to develop a product or business (Shopify, 2022). The concept dates from the late 19th century, and figuratively refers to using only your own tools and abilities to achieve upward mobility (Harvey, 2022). For entrepreneurs, bootstrapping can be a challenge often limited by personal funding and the realistic amount of time that could be invested to support product development. In our opinion, bootstrapping is an essential step in the product development process. Investing your resources into building a prototype signals that you are financially and emotionally connected to the product (Harvey, 2022). Building this connection can motivate you to see your product succeed; a recent expression describes this as "having skin in the game."

To illustrate this, we share our experience with bootstrapping. Luca interviewed Kevin about Ayewah Aesthetics, Inc., (refer back to section 13.1) and discussed how bootstrapping affected the business. Here are some significant passages:

Kevin: "When we started the expansion of Ayewah Aesthetics, Martha and I sat down to really understand what it would take to open the first office in New York City, and the first thing we did was to review our personal finances to see if we could afford to fund the business ourselves. In this case I think this is really what we would consider to be bootstrapping—we used our own personal resources and time and invested in ourselves."

Luca: What happens emotionally when you start to use your own funding in a business?

Kevin: You become personally connected with your product or business, almost like it's like your baby. Your business/prototype can become a potential liability. It led to a lot of stress because we didn't want to lose our investment. In addition, with designing our brand and product we needed to spend more time on developing a marketing plan. I was working a full-time job while doing this at night. Martha was working another job while launching Ayewah Aesthetics.

Luca: Do you think bootstrapping has its limitations?

Kevin: I think the limits to bootstrapping are the limits you must establish with yourself. I think when you're bootstrapping you often must ask yourself, What is your threshold? How much time can you invest in this? How much money can you invest in this? What are your limitations? With bootstrapping you need to draw some line, because you can easily blur the lines between your personal and professional needs. I think when we started, we were so invested that the lines often get blurred, and we invested quite a bit more than expected. Eventually, we reached a point where it wouldn't have made sense to continue to invest our own dollars, so we decided to reach out and ask for additional funding and support from local financial institutions.

The story of Ayewah Aesthetics reflects a few critical points. When you personally invest your own resources, you are expected to be dedicated to the success of your prototype. If personal resources are scarce, it can lead to additional amounts of financial and physical stress. For any venture to be successful, product developers must have a sense of confidence, a tolerance for risk, self-discipline and determination. Finally, bootstrapping has its limitations; in many cases, there is simply not enough cash flow,[1] and it may become necessary to seek additional financial resources.

13.6   Traditional sources of funding: banks and credit cards

Traditionally, many entrepreneurs and business owners approach banks seeking funding to support their businesses. However, as mentioned earlier in this chapter, banks may not be the best place to seek funding for early-stage entrepreneurs. If you are developing a product for the first time, you may not have a traditional business associated with your idea. Banks provide personal or business loans to individuals. However, the qualifications to be approved may vary. For business loans, there is typically an expectation that the business has existed for at least five years, and have some capital (assets) to offer as collateral (Commerce Bank, 2020). In simpler terms, it can be difficult to get a business loan for a business that doesn't exist yet. Therefore, for a new entrepreneur, a personal loan may be the way to go.

One alternative that entrepreneurs may consider is using credit cards to fund the building of a prototype. We present this option with a caveat: don't take on a credit card without understanding how it works. Credit cards can be used as a resource to extend the buying power of an individual; you may use them sparingly, and it is relatively easy to apply for one. Ayewah Aesthetics, when seeking additional financial support, considered credit cards as an option.

Interestingly, when we were applying for additional lines of credit for our business, the process took less than five minutes online and less than ten minutes to receive the approval after the application submission. The best part about the credit card we applied for was that it had an introductory rate of 0% interest for 12 months. It was basically like having a no-interest loan for one year. These promotions are easy to find, but you need a good credit score. Be mindful that very high interest rates usually kick in after the promotion has expired, and there may be a transaction fee.

Credit cards, when managed well, can be a resource. Reviewing all the terms and conditions to understand the differences between introductory and regular interest rates is essential. Credit cards also have a minimum amount that must be paid each month. One strategy that many individuals take advantage of is to get a credit card, buy what they need at an introductory rate, and pay back the card before the introductory rate is over (Commerce Bank, 2020).

13.7   Crowdfunding

Crowdfunding is the use of a small amount of capital from many people to finance a new venture (Smith, 2022). Crowdfunding has become quite popular, and with the expansion of the internet, it can be relatively easy to accumulate large amounts of funds within a short period of time. Typically, crowdfunding occurs through popular web platforms like Kickstarter and GoFundMe (Smith, 2022). Table 13.1 lists the key elements of a crowdfunding campaign.

Unlike working with banks and investment firms, crowdfunding is typically done on a public platform—a website. Individuals who invest in these projects often must be convinced that the project is worth it, sometimes emotionally, because the funders must believe

Table 13.1 Crowdfunding campaign elements

Campaign videos and animation	A video or animation that shows what your product does
A realistic prototype	Depending on the phase you may be at, you may want to showcase a prototype that has some functionality to the general public.
A write-up/story	A write-up explains your product. However, don't limit it to that. Create a narrative to sell the product, and consider how you can emotionally connect to potential investors.
Rewards for their investments	Detail rewards that would be given to individuals who invest in your product.
	Example: The first 100 people who provide us with a donation will be able to purchase product X for only $5.

in the cause. When working on a crowdfunding campaign, it is crucial to understand what your target audience wants. We recommend reviewing the business model canvas to understand your value propositions and apply that thinking to the campaign elements before attempting to build your campaign (Smith, 2022).

Crowdfunding can come with several benefits.

First, it provides entrepreneurs an additional funding channel (Exitfund, 2023). A crowdfunding campaign may also validate product hypotheses by gauging interest in a particular idea. In most crowdfunding initiatives, crowd funders contribute by purchasing the product or by donating. These sales and donations provide significant evidence of a market. This was the case for Remarkable, the company that designed the digital notebook mentioned in chapter 8. Since it is impossible to acquire company shares via crowdfunding, this funding approach only requires entrepreneurs to give away their valuable equity.

Third, it provides a new platform for engaging a community. With the implementation of a campaign, developers can attract a community of early adopters and create a co-creation approach through which a company can obtain users' feedback and suggestions on how to improve the product.

On the other hand, crowdfunding can also come with several disadvantages (Exitfund, 2023). One disadvantage is that barriers to entry are very low. Almost anyone can post an idea on these platforms, and crowdfunding websites like Kickstarter and GoFundMe are often highly competitive. Thus, many young entrepreneurs and product developers begin campaigns but don't reach their funding targets.

If a product developer fails to build and execute their prototype, they may also risk hurting their reputation, especially as crowdfunding campaigns are easily visible to the public. In addition, many crowdfunding sites also charge a fee per transaction, which may reduce the overall amount of funds raised and the funds accessible to the product developer.

13.8 Angel investors

The exact opposite of crowdfunding would be seeking the support of an angel investor (aka business angels). An angel investor is an individual or a group of small investors that provides the initial seed money for a startup or prototype (Indeed, 2023). Typically, an angel investor seeks some form of ownership or equity in exchange for their investment. What makes angel investors unique is that they are open to investing in risky ventures and are often more willing to offer not just funding but also mentorship and industry expertise that may be helpful for product developers. There are different types of angel investors.

1. Family and friends: Sometimes the easiest place to seek funding is from individuals who know you personally. Friends and family may be more willing to fund people they know, even if the business/product may be risky.
2. Wealthy individuals: Examples include business executives, professionals, or people who have inherited wealth. Many of these individuals become angel investors to seek new opportunities to diversify their portfolios and earn higher returns from their funds.
3. Groups: Some angel investors pool their resources into investment groups that fund different types of businesses or product developers. This is a way angels diversify their investment across many businesses to manage risks.

There are several advantages to having an angel investor versus other forms of financing. First, there's less risk than in debt funding, since angels do not loan money but seek equity. In this way, angels have a genuine interest to see the company grow and thrive. The second is that angel investors often have quite a bit of experience and therefore may provide mentorship as well as funds. Finally, they can help build reputation and credibility for a young entrepreneur.

13.9 Coworking spaces

Coworking spaces can significantly improve funding opportunities for early-stage entrepreneurs in various ways. These spaces provide more than just a physical workspace; they offer a supportive ecosystem that can increase visibility, networking, collaboration, and access to resources—all of which can contribute to a product developer's success in securing funding. In the past few decades, there has been a significant rise in new companies investing in creating coworking spaces, which can become hubs of innovation in large cities. Utilizing a coworking space can provide numerous advantages beyond the physical workspace. Leveraging these spaces' networking, mentorship, and learning opportunities can significantly improve your funding prospects as a product developer.

A team of students in one of our classes collaborated on designing and launching a new coworking space, Greater Nexus, in New York City. The space opened its door to local businesses and entrepreneurs in September 2022 and now functions as a community innovation hub, providing affordable space, training, and funding to local small businesses, young entrepreneurs, and minority-owned small companies.

13.10 Common mistakes

Entrepreneurs may make several mistakes when seeking funding for building their prototypes. Some can occur during the design process but may manifest themselves or be exposed when seeking funding. Some of the common mistakes we have identified throughout various processes are:

1. **Lack of a clear vision**: As we mentioned in chapter 4, the articulation of your value proposition for your prototype is critical. Many entrepreneurs fail to really showcase why their prototype is the ideal solution for the problem that has been identified. When we are unable to communicate the vision of the products we want, many investors/banks will fail to jump on the bandwagon. Recall Simon Sinek's advice: we need to be able to communicate the WHY behind the products we build (Sinek, 2009).
2. **Ignoring market research**: Throughout the design thinking process, we are often challenged to understand the needs of the customer. A part of the process is to conduct market research to validate the demand and need of the product. Entrepreneurs ignore this at their own peril.
3. **Underestimating costs**: A common problem that occurs with prototyping is underestimating the financial resources needed to build a prototype. The worst thing that could happen is running out of funding before completing a prototype.
4. **Weak pitch**: Sometimes the pitch used to ask for funding may not outline the problem, solution, target market, or even a potential business model.

5. **Overdependence on a single source of funding**: There is a saying to never put all your eggs in one basket. This is also true for securing funding; some entrepreneurs fail to diversify their funding resources. This may be a problem, if that single funding source decide to back out of their commitment.

Seeking funding for prototypes is a critical stage for entrepreneurs, but it's rife with potential pitfalls that can harm chances of success. Paradoxically, many of these mistakes can often stem from the design process itself but become evident during the funding-seeking phase. To avoid these mistakes, entrepreneurs/product developers should focus on thoroughly understanding their market, developing a strong prototype, preparing a compelling pitch, and being realistic about their funding needs. It's also crucial to approach the fundraising process as a partnership, seeking investors who bring financial support, expertise, and guidance.

13.11 Numbers that investors want to hear

Writing a full business plan with financial projections is out of the scope of this book. However, even if it's too early to make reasonably accurate financial estimates, remember that your investors still want to know whether your idea has market potential. *Potential* is the key term here: an angel puts money in your high-risk enterprise that she hopes to multiply 10 or 100 times the value of the equity she gets in exchange. In Chapter 10, we used the business canvas to estimate the market demand, revenues, and costs. Once you have these estimates, you can build a profit and loss statement. Sharing or knowing these numbers is very important when you speak with your investors.

Other relatively easy financial metrics to estimate include break even and payback time. The break-even point is achieved when your sales grow to the point of compensating for all the costs. Estimating the break-even equates to calculating the minimum volume you need to sell to match your costs using the following formula:

Breakeven sales = Initial investment + fixed costs + variable costs

This can be shown as:

$Unit\ Price \times Quantity_{BE} = Initial\ investment + fixed\ costs + unit\_cost \times Quantity_{BE}$, hence

$$Quantity_{BE} = \frac{Initial\ investment + fixed\ costs}{Unit\_Price - Unit\_cost}$$

This formula shows how the break-even volume will be larger the higher the initial investment and fixed costs are and the smaller the margin, that is, the difference between the unit price and cost.

Knowing your daily output, you can estimate how long your company will take to achieve the break-even volume. If this time is shorter because you must sell a lot before recovering your initial investment, investors will perceive your company as risky. The Better Place case study presented in Chapter 10 provides an example of a startup that required such a large volume because of the high initial investment and fixed costs. That large volume was also impossible to achieve at a time when electric vehicles represented a tiny fraction of the car market.

Finally, an often-overlooked financial prospect is the cash flow analysis. Cash, more than sales and funding, is the driving force of any company. You do not risk bankruptcy if you have cash when you need it. Performing a cash flow analysis means estimating how much cash enters and leaves the company weekly. You must map all the sources and causes of cash inflows (e.g., sales, money from investors) and outflows (e.g., rent, utilities, wages, supplies, loan interest due, insurance). This great exercise can help you understand where potential financial bottlenecks could arise and estimate when you need the next capital infusion to allow the business to run every day.

13.12   Conclusions

This chapter delved into the complex world of funding early-stage ventures. We explored various strategies product developers can employ to secure the resources they need to bring their innovative ideas to life. The journey from modeling a concept to building a prototype has several challenges, particularly in financing, and demands a unique and multifaceted approach.

Early-stage ventures face formidable obstacles when seeking funding. Traditional funding channels' demands for a proven history of success can present a significant roadblock for startups with untested business models and prototypes. Moreover, a lack of capital and connections can further impede access to crucial financial support and mentorship.

The principles of design thinking (discussed throughout this book) prioritize understanding customer needs and value propositions and extend seamlessly to the quest to find resources. The why–how–what model, advocated by Simon Sinek, offers a framework to convey the purpose behind a product, thereby connecting with potential investors on a deeper level. Entrepreneurs can craft compelling narratives that resonate with investors by

Key takeaways for this chapter

Lesson learned	Implications for your entrepreneurial project
Consider funding challenges and strategies	• Early-stage ventures face significant funding challenges due to their lack of assets, track record, and established connections. • Explore alternative funding strategies, including bootstrapping, crowdfunding, angel investors, and coworking spaces. Some strategies offer different levels of risk and of support. Carefully review your options before committing to receiving funding.
Understand pros and cons of each funding source	• Understand the difference between debt and equity financing. • Craft communication strategies aligned with the type of investors you are talking to and use a designer mindset to identify their needs and the information they value the most.
Avoid common funding mistakes	• Be aware of common mistakes that can hinder funding efforts. These include lacking a clear vision, ignoring market research, underestimating costs, delivering a weak pitch, and relying too heavily on a single funding source. • To succeed in securing funding, thoroughly understand your target market, develop a strong and realistic prototype, and prepare a persuasive pitch. • Approach the funding process as a partnership, seeking investors who offer financial support, expertise, and guidance. • Be prepared to provide investors with some basic financial estimates and educated guesses.

emphasizing differentiation, storytelling, and a long-term vision. The journey from concept to prototype demands a strategic and holistic approach to securing resources and funding. Entrepreneurs who read this book must leverage their understanding of design thinking principles, compelling storytelling, and effective networking to capture investor attention and build a solid foundation for sustainable growth. In a landscape marked by challenges and opportunities, those who navigate this skillfully have the potential to transform their visions into reality.

Note

1 Cash flow is the amount of financial liquidity available to the company at a given moment.

References

Commerce Bank. (2020). *Do banks ever lend to startup companies.* www.commercebank.com/business/trends-and-insights/2020/do-banks-ever-lend-to-startup-companies#:~:text=So%20yes%2C%20banks%20do%20make,home%20or%20other%20significant%20asset

Exitfund. (2023). *The ultimate crowdfunding blueprint: A step-by-step guide.* www.linkedin.com/pulse/ultimate-crowdfunding-blueprint-step-by-step-guide-exitfund/

Harvey, I. (2022). Companies that succeeded with bootstrapping. *Investopedia.* https://www.investopedia.com/articles/investing/082814/companies-succeeded-bootstrapping.asp#:~:text=The%20Origin%20of%20Bootstrapping,-The%20origin%20of&text=%22Pull%20oneself%20over%20a%20fence,by%20tugging%20at%20ankle%20straps

Indeed. (2023). *Angel investors: Definition, advantages and disadvantages* www.indeed.com/career-advice/career-development/angel-investors

Investopedia. (2022). *Companies that succeeded with bootstrapping.* www.investopedia.com/articles/investing/082814/companies-succeeded-bootstrapping.asp

Shopify. (2022). *What is bootstrapping? It's* [sic] *definition and uses.* www.shopify.com/blog/what-is-bootstrapping

Sinek, S. (2009). How great leaders inspire action. *TED Conference*, September. www.ted.com/talks/simon_sinek_how_great_leaders_inspire_action

Smith, Tim. (2022). *Crowdfunding: What it is, how it works, popular websites.* www.investopedia.com/terms/c/crowdfunding.asp

Zwilling, M. (2013). 10 ways for startups to survive the valley of death. https://www.forbes.com/sites/martinzwilling/2013/02/18/10-ways-for-startups-to-survive-the-valley-of-death/?sh=e105dbc69eff

Chapter 14

Where do we go from here?

14.1 Concluding our journey and starting another

We have arrived at a pivotal moment in this journey, an inflection moment when your ideas, efforts, and creativity have led you to create something. Was it a product, a service, or something else? We encourage you to reflect on how valuable the journey has been. What have you learned, and what insights have you gained throughout the product development process about yourself? Did you succeed or have a few failures along the way? Is there more to learn in this process? More than just a final installment, this chapter serves as a bridge to your future, an exploration of what comes next as you transition from creating your products to embedding the spirit of creativity and innovation into your everyday life and your future career. Our exploration will start by reflecting on what you learned from this book. We will explore the importance of developing a creative mindset and the tools that can transcend just developing a product and be embedded in everyday life. Finally, we explore the different pathways one can take with the skills gained from this book, including how AI will affect the future of creativity and innovation in various industries.

14.2 Why creativity matters

This book serves as a comprehensive guide that explores entrepreneurship through the lens of creativity, innovation, and design thinking. It presents a unique road map for individuals to embark on this journey of product-centered development. At the same time, we acknowledge that entrepreneurship is more than just the concept of building a product. We look at the mental processes that help us to craft solutions that resonate with users and address the root causes of their problems. Our book's foundation lies in cultivating the design-driven mindset, transforming abstract ideas into viable prototypes and offering practical insights and guidance that reveal the creative process behind product development. Highlights include the following.

- The profound impact of observing and gathering insights to decipher customer behavior, Chapter 3;
- The imperative of empathizing with customers to grasp their emotions and needs, Chapter 3;
- The paradigm shift from concentrating solely on solutions to understanding and addressing underlying problems, Chapter 6;

DOI: 10.4324/9781003346463-15

- The art of conveying the "why" behind a venture through effective pitching, Chapters 12 and 13;
- The strategic significance of prototyping at varying stages, Chapters 5, 6, and 13; The art of managing complexity and striving for elegance in design, while acknowledging the value of an appropriate level of complexity, Chapters 6 and 8.

Creativity can be the spark that ignites innovation, often drives progress, and can transform the ordinary into the extraordinary (Deliorman, 2023). Throughout this book and especially in Chapters 2 and 3, we present a framework for why creativity is the key to entrepreneurship and explore how we can reimagine creativity. Although creativity is sometimes thought to be an individual pursuit or trait, we learned in Chapter 2 that it can be a collective process, influenced by external input—people like coworkers, users, customers, and bystanders. Online communities and professional memberships are ways to tap into this collective information pool. As well, simple human interaction like conversations plays a crucial role in generating new insights. The process involves help-seeking, help-giving, and reframing, creating a collective dance that fosters creativity (Hargadon & Bechky, 2006).

Companies today are seeking individuals who can collaborate on teams to solve various complex problems (Leavy, 2012). Team dynamics often play a critical role, especially when problems require a multifaced approach (Hargadon & Bechky, 2006). Design thinking, for example, often yields more benefits when embraced collaboratively within a group setting (Leavy, 2012). At the same time, dysfunctions in the help-seeking, help-giving, or reframing steps can hinder creativity. Factors like hubris, lack of trust, internal competition, and absence of diverse perspectives can impede the creative process. Effective teamwork is essential, as teams have the potential to generate creative insights but can also become obstacles to creativity. Simply put, the best way to be creative is to be creative together.

The creative process of product development often leads to the building of prototypes; this is where creative entrepreneurs transform into scientists. Entrepreneurs are encouraged to embrace a scientist's mentality, wherein they view failures as stepping-stones for progress. The concept of "intelligent failure," introduced in Chapter 9, suggests that systematic learning from setbacks is instrumental in driving innovation. From artists to scientists, the journey of the entrepreneur also parallels the hero's journey, as described by anthropologist Joseph Campbell. This shared metaphor also allows us to understand that the design-driven process is about navigating transformative journeys laden with challenges and failures. Embracing failures becomes a catalyst for growth and transformation, akin to the evolution of heroes in mythical quests. The tools we discuss in this book can guide individuals on their journey.

14.2.1   The implications of artificial intelligence in product development

One thing that has also dynamically shifted the way we approach creativity within different industries is artificial intelligence (AI). AI is "the social and cognitive phenomena that enable a machine to socially integrate with a society to perform competitive tasks requiring cognitive processes and communicate with other entities in society by exchanging messages with high information content and shorter representations" (Abbass, 2021, p. 2). AI—for example, the platform ChatGPT—has been seen as a tool to support individuals. AI can significantly affect design-driven thinking by enhancing creativity, providing data-driven insights, and expediting the design process. AI tools can generate design options, identify patterns in user behavior, and suggest innovative solutions. They can analyze vast amounts of data to inform design decisions, leading to a more user-focused design process. Additionally, AI can automate repetitive tasks, allowing designers to concentrate on higher-level strategic thinking and problem solving (Abbass, 2021). It's important for designers to strike a balance between human intuition and AI assistance to maintain human touch and empathy in the design process.

14.3   Choose your next adventure

The foundational principles we explored in this book can often be applied to various instances of product development. They are, however, not limited to just product development. Imagine now where you can choose to apply the principles and skills to go down several paths. The first path is more traditional: starting a venture. We encourage you to seek support in building businesses if you so choose. The second path is the path of the freelancer. The frameworks provided (design thinking, design-driven mindset) in this book provide a fundamental structure for becoming a freelancer and building solutions for others. The final path we discuss is the career-oriented individual; skills in this book can help individuals build a dynamic portfolio and seek jobs in various companies. No matter the path you choose, we hope this book opens your eyes to rethinking how we approach the various dynamic problems in the world.

14.3.1   Path 1: Start a Venture

After reading this book you may aspire to start your own venture. We emphasized the importance of product-centered entrepreneurship, and our book instills the significance of building solutions that resonate with a target audience.

If you choose to follow this path, you can benefit from the insights on design thinking and the designer mindset (Chapters 1 and 2). These concepts will serve as powerful tools to create prototypes and testable artifacts, and they provide guidance on how to conduct effective observation, stress customer empathy, and even how to properly identify problems.

Furthermore, the book outlines fundamental essential skills in crafting compelling pitches and presentations. These skills are invaluable when seeking funding, partnerships, or customers for a new venture. The chapters on complexity, elegance, and prototyping help entrepreneurs develop well-rounded products that strike a balance between simplicity and the necessary complexity to address users' challenges. The book also addresses the emotional roller-coaster of entrepreneurship, offering strategies to navigate failure and transform setbacks into growth opportunities. With the foundation laid in this book, individuals following the venture path are well equipped to embark on their entrepreneurial journey with creativity, innovation, and resilience.

14.3.2   Path 2: Become a Freelancer

For those leaning towards being a freelancer, the book's teachings remain highly relevant. Freelancers often need to create innovative solutions that align with clients' needs and challenges. The design-driven approach advocated in the book can be applied to freelancing projects, allowing freelancers to offer unique and valuable solutions.

The chapters that focus on observation, empathy, and problem-solving remain essential and provide us with tools in understanding clients' requirements deeply. The insights on complexity are valuable in delivering prototypes or solutions that meet clients' expectations while showcasing creativity and expertise. Additionally, the principles of effective communication, as emphasized in Chapter 11, on presentations, empower freelancers to effectively convey their ideas, gain client buy-in, and ultimately secure projects. The understanding of intellectual property and its protection can also be vital for freelancers seeking to safeguard their creative outputs.

14.3.3   Path 3: Build a Portfolio and Seek a Job

For the career-oriented individual who wants to build a strong portfolio and seek employment, the skills discussed in the book are a valuable road map. Our focus on design thinking, empathy, and problem-solving provide the foundation for creating impressive projects that showcase an individual's creativity and innovation. Individuals seeking careers often highlight their abilities for potential employers, so our chapters on presentations and effective communication are particularly relevant. Crafting a strong portfolio and presenting it in a compelling manner aligns with the principles outlined in the book.

A portfolio should reflect an understanding of complexity, prototyping, and elegance. This can help job seekers stand out from the competition by demonstrating their ability to design creative and effective solutions. This knowledge can be invaluable in interviews, allowing candidates to discuss their creative processes and problem-solving skills in depth.

14.4   Conclusion

Our book's foundation is focused on cultivating a design-driven mindset and translating abstract concepts into practical prototypes. Throughout this book, we've unearthed the profound impacts of observing customer behavior, the importance of customer empathy, and mastering the art of effective communication. Our journey underscores that the power of collaboration is critical to fostering creativity. At this juncture, it is now up to you to choose your next path (start a venture, be a freelancer, or seek employment). As you set forth, these principles should act as a compass that to guide your next decisions, the canvas upon which you paint your aspirations, and the armor that fortifies your resolve in the face of challenges. Your creativity and product development journey are just starting, and endless possibilities await. Let the creative spark from this book light your way to new horizons of achievement and fulfillment.

References

Abbass. (2021). Editorial: What is artificial intelligence? *IEEE Transactions on Artificial Intelligence*, 2(2), 94–95. https://doi.org/10.1109/TAI.2021.3096243

Deliorman, I. M. (2023). How learning, knowledge, and experience ignite the creative spark … Linkedin. https://www.linkedin.com/pulse/how-learning-knowledge-experience-ignite-creative-spark-deliorman/

Hargadon, A. B., & Bechky, B. A. (2006). When collections of creatives become creative collectives: A field study of problem solving at work. *Organization Science*, 17(4), 484–500. www.linkedin.com/pulse/dynamic-associations-fuel-creativity-işık-deliorman/

Leavy, B. (2012). Collaborative innovation as the new imperative – design thinking, value co-creation and the power of "pull." *Strategy & Leadership*, 40(2), 25–34. https://doi.org/10.1108/10878571211209323

Index

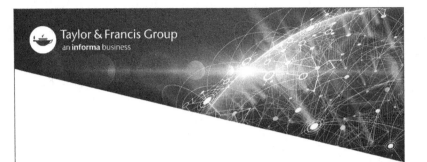

Printed in the United States
by Baker & Taylor Publisher Services